World History I

Robert Taggart

D1114341

WALCH PUBLISHING

POWER BASICS ®

Senior Author	Robert Taggart
Editorial Director	Susan Blair
Project Manager/Senior Production Editor	Maggie Jones
Project Editor	Erica Varney
Director of Marketing	Jeff Taplin
Interior Design	Mark Sayer
Cover Design	Roman Laszok
Typesetting	Sheila Russell
	Mark Sayer
	Ian Weidner
Editorial Staff	Elizabeth Lynch
	Richard Lynch
	Holly Moirs
	Kate O'Halloran
	Mary Rich
	Kathy Sammis

3   4   5   6   7   8   9   10

ISBN 0-8251-5679-3

Copyright © 1998, 2005

J. Weston Walch, Publisher

P. O. Box 658 • Portland, Maine 04104-0658

walch.com

Printed in the United States of America

WALCH PUBLISHING

Table of Contents

Table of Contents, *continued*

To the Student

Welcome to *Power Basics® World History I.* This book will teach you about the key people, places, and events in the history of the world from the beginning of human life to about 1500. You will also learn how these elements of history continue to affect societies around the world today.

In **Unit 1, The Earliest People,** you will learn about the first people and first communities on Earth. You will also learn about how these groups developed into the world's first civilizations.

In **Unit 2, The Ancient Greeks,** you will learn about Greek civilization and its lasting effects on today's world, including the development of democracy.

In **Unit 3, Ancient India and China,** you will learn about the development of these two great civilizations, which remain the basis of many Asian societies.

In **Unit 4, The Ancient Romans,** you will learn about Roman civilization and the wide spread of Roman culture throughout the far-flung lands of the Roman Empire.

In **Unit 5, Europe in the Middle Ages,** you will learn about the gradual development of European societies and the beginnings of today's nation-states.

In **Unit 6, The Middle East and the Rise of Islam,** you will learn about the rise of the world religion of Islam and the spread of Islamic culture throughout the vast Islamic Empire.

In **Unit 7, South and East Asia,** you will learn about developments in China, the Mongol Empire, India, and early Japan from the 300s to the 1600s.

In **Unit 8, Africa and the Americas,** you will learn about early societies in Africa and the Americas, and about the great kingdoms of West Africa.

Each lesson is made up of short sections that explain important elements of that time and place in history. Each of these sections is followed by a practice quiz to help you review what you have learned.

To the Student, *continued*

Each unit ends with a Unit Review and then an Application Activity. This activity lets you extend and apply what you have learned in the unit.

Power Basics® World History I has many special features that make learning easier. "Tips" give you hints on ways to master the ideas and facts in the text. "In Real Life" sections show you how what you are learning applies to the world outside the classroom. "Think About It" questions ask you to look at history in new ways. The "Words to Know" section at the start of most lessons includes important new terms introduced in the lesson. The first time the word is used, it is defined for you. This first use appears in **bold type.** All the terms in the "Words to Know" section are also defined in the Glossary at the end of the book. If you cannot remember what a term means, you can look it up in the Glossary. Finally, the "Dates to Know," "Names to Know," and "Places to Know" lists at the back of the book are handy reminders and reviews of these elements of the world history about which you are learning.

As you move through *Power Basics® World History I*, you will become more informed about world history, and you will understand its effects on the world we live in today. We hope that you enjoy this material as you learn.

A Note About Dates

You will see some abbreviations in this book that are commonly used when talking about history. Many historians use a timescale based on the birth of Jesus Christ. This scale uses the birth of Jesus Christ as its center point.

B.C.E.—This abbreviation for *"before the common era"* is used to refer to earlier times. It comes after the year. So 200 B.C.E. refers to a time that is 200 years before year 0 of the common era, which is considered the year of the birth of Jesus. (Some history books use the abbreviation B.C., which means *"before Christ."*)

C.E.—This abbreviation for *"common era"* is used to refer to more recent dates. So 200 C.E. refers to a date that is 200 years *after* the beginning of the common era. (Some history books use the abbreviation A.D. This stands for *anno Domini*, which is Latin for "in the year of the Lord.")

c.—When a date is not exact, the letter *c* is placed in front of it, as in c. 200 B.C.E. This letter is an abbreviation for the Latin word *circa*, which means "around." (Some historians use the abbreviation *ca.* instead.)

Here is a time line to show you the difference between B.C.E. and C.E.:

Two Tips for Keeping Your Dates Straight:

■ **B.C.E. and C.E.**—It is not too difficult to figure out how many years ago 500 C.E. was—just subtract 500 from the present year. But when you come across the date 500 B.C.E. remember to *add* 500 to the present year to find out how long ago the year occurred.

■ **Centuries**—It is easy to get confused about centuries and think, for example, that the eighteenth century covers the years 1800 to 1899. But, in fact, the eighteenth century refers to the 1700s. (If you start with the year 0 and go to the end of the 1700s, you have covered eighteen centuries.) Remember: The century name is *higher* than the period of years it covers.

UNIT 1

The Earliest People

LESSON 1: The First Communities

GOAL: To understand the characteristics of the earliest human communities; to understand the role agriculture played in early human development

WORDS TO KNOW

agriculture	domesticate	New Stone Age
civilization	glaciers	nomads
cultivate	goods	Old Stone Age
culture	Ice Age	

Earth and the First People

Planet Earth probably began as a hot, glowing ball. It took millions of years to cool and form into giant landmasses surrounded by oceans. Life probably began in the water. As living things grew and changed, life spread onto the land.

Humanlike creatures appeared perhaps 1 to 2 million years ago. They stood on two legs but looked more like apes than human beings. These early humans used simple tools that they made from stone. This was the beginning of the Old Stone Age—and the beginning of human history. The Old Stone Age lasted until about 10,000 years ago (c. 8000 B.C.E.).

The first modern humans, who looked much like we do today, appeared some 100,000 years ago. They lived in a world that was often quite cold. Huge sheets of ice, called glaciers, covered most of the land. So, this era is also called the Ice Age. From time to time, Earth would get warmer. The glaciers would melt at the edges, making the oceans rise. But then it would become cold again, and the glaciers would regrow.

The first humanlike beings emerged in Africa. From there, they fanned out widely to other continents. As they moved, the modern humans were able to use their mental powers to figure out ways to adapt to each environment they found.

■ PRACTICE 1: Earth and the First People

Circle the letter(s) of the correct answer(s) to each of the following questions. (*Hint*: There is more than one correct answer to each question.)

1. What happened during the Old Stone Age?
   a. Earth was a hot, glowing ball.
   b. Humans used simple tools.
   c. Humanlike creatures first appeared.
   d. Life began in the water.

2. What happened during the Ice Age?
   a. Glaciers covered most of the land.
   b. The oceans rose and fell.
   c. Life on land was fairly easy.
   d. Modern humans appeared.

Living as Hunters and Gatherers

Put yourself in the Old Stone Age. It is very cold, and you must wear animal skins to keep warm. There are no towns or houses. You and your family are nomads. This means you are always on the move, looking for caves in which to stay.

If you are a man, you go hunting with the other men. You hunt in small groups for animals that you can kill and eat. You might hunt deer, bison, or perhaps the giant, elephantlike animals called woolly mammoths. You and your family must follow these animals as they move from place to place. This is why you are nomads. Your only weapons are knives and spears. They may have sharp stone tips, or they may be carved out of animal bone.

If you are a woman or a child, you gather food, such as berries, nuts, and fruit. You use sticks to dig up roots. You know which plants are good to eat, and you have learned which plants can make you sick or even kill you.

Since your family keeps moving, your homes are very simple. They may be caves or tents made of animal hides (skins) or huts made of branches. But some caves have something special—paintings on their walls. If you are an Old Stone Age artist, you make paints out of things you find, such as berries and clay. Your paintings show the animals that you hunt. These amazing pictures will help people of the future imagine what your life was like.

■ PRACTICE 2: Living as Hunters and Gatherers

Match each description with a term from below. Write the letter of the correct term on the line before each description.

> **a.** knives and spears
>
> **b.** paintings of animals
>
> **c.** berries, nuts, fruits, and roots

_____ **1.** These were tools the hunters used.

_____ **2.** These were foods that were gathered.

_____ **3.** These made the cave walls special.

The New Stone Age

About 10,000 years ago (c. 8000 B.C.E.), the Ice Age came to an end. Earth grew warmer, and the glaciers shrank in size. At this point, human life changed in a very significant way. Historians refer to this time as the beginning of the New Stone Age and the end of the Old Stone Age.

The new, warmer climate was better for plants. People discovered that they could grow plants on their own. They began to clear the land, plant seeds, and take care of the growing plants. In other words, they began to cultivate crops. The crops they grew included wheat, barley, rice, and beans.

They also discovered that certain wild animals could be tamed. People began to domesticate these animals, or getting them used to living with humans. Animals such as sheep, cows, and goats were domesticated and used as sources of milk, meat, and hides. The people of the New Stone Age had stopped being hunters and gatherers and had become farmers.

■ PRACTICE 3: The New Stone Age

Circle the letter(s) of the correct answer(s) to each of the following questions.

1. When did the New Stone Age begin?
    a. about 10,000 years ago
    b. about 100,000 years ago
    c. about 20,000 years ago
    d. about 200,000 years ago

2. What new things happened during the New Stone Age? (*Hint*: There is more than one correct answer.)
    a. The Ice Age began.
    b. People began to plant and grow crops.
    c. People became hunters and gatherers.
    d. People raised their own animals for food and hides.

Village Life

Because they were planting and growing crops, families had to stay in one place. They could no longer be nomads, following animal herds. As more and more families settled down, they began to live together in small agricultural villages. (*Agriculture* is another word for "farming.") Instead of using caves or making temporary shelters, people built more permanent homes. If there were trees, they made wooden houses. If there were no trees, people built huts out of earth and clay. They also built pens to house their animals. Now there was plenty of food to eat, so people did not have to hunt and gather their food. They could learn new skills. Some became potters or weavers, making storage pots from clay and baskets out of straw. Toolmakers invented better tools, using metals like copper and iron. People from one village traded the goods they made and extra food with people from nearby villages. Many villages sprang up in river valleys. People learned to fish. Boatbuilding became an important craft. Communities began to grow.

You have just read that many villages were formed in river valleys. Why would a river valley be a good place to set up a village? How could the villagers use the river? Write your answers on a separate sheet of paper.

■ PRACTICE 4: Village Life

Decide if each statement below is true (**T**) or false (**F**). Write the correct letter on the line before each statement.

_____ **1.** People in villages had to be nomads.

_____ **2.** People in villages kept domesticated animals.

_____ **3.** People in villages had to spend all day looking for food.

_____ **4.** People in villages had time to learn new skills.

_____ **5.** People in villages traded goods with people in other villages.

The Earliest Cities

As villages continued to grow, they became towns. Some towns grew large enough to be called cities. Two of the earliest cities were Jericho and Çatal Hüyük.

The town of Jericho was built around 7500 B.C.E. in the Jordan River valley. Today, this area is in the country of Jordan, which is in the Middle East. Jericho covered four acres of land and was surrounded by a wall that was over twelve feet high. The wall was put up to protect the people of the city from outsiders. You can still see the ruins of this magnificent city.

In the 1950s, scientists discovered the ruins of another ancient city in Turkey. It was named Çatal Hüyük, and it contained what is now the world's oldest pottery and wool clothing. This early city was built a bit later than Jericho, in a region that used to be called Asia Minor. Çatal

Hüyük was at least eight times as big as Jericho. It contained many large brick and stone buildings packed tightly together with no streets or alleys between them. Apparently, to get from one house to another, a person had to travel across roofs and go down stairways or ladders.

Jericho and Çatal Hüyük

As time went on, more cities sprang up. These set the stage for the next major development in human history—the birth of civilizations.

■ PRACTICE 5: The Earliest Cities

Decide if each statement below is true (**T**) or false (**F**). Write the correct letter on the line before each statement.

_____ **1.** In the 1950s, the ruins of Jericho were found in Turkey.

_____ **2.** In Çatal Hüyük, there were no streets or alleys between buildings.

Cultures and Civilizations

Villagers of the New Stone Age shared a **culture.** They lived, worked, and ate together. They shared language, ideas, and habits. As more and more people settled in villages, the culture grew, with more beliefs, more jobs, and more to learn. Soon, the villages needed a way to be organized so life could run smoothly. The villages grew into a civilization. A **civilization** is a highly organized society that usually has

- a **government** to keep things in order. The government may be a group of people or just a single ruler.

- a **system of record keeping** to keep track of crops and items of trade, for example. (As you will see, a record-keeping system may grow into an actual written language.)

■ a **class system.** People in the highest class, such as kings, have power and riches. People in the lowest class, like poor farmers, have to work hard just to make a living.

Historians and scientists believe that they know where the first civilization in the world arose. It was in a region where two rivers—the Tigris and the Euphrates—came together. This civilization will be explored in the next lesson.

THINK ABOUT IT

Think about your own culture. What are the shared customs, beliefs, stories, and songs of this culture? How is your culture different from those of other people you know? Write your answers on a separate sheet of paper.

■ PRACTICE 6: Cultures and Civilizations

Circle the letter of the correct answer to each of the following questions.

1. Which term describes a shared set of language, ideas, and habits?
    a. civilization
    b. culture
    c. government
    d. class

2. Which of the following is part of a civilization?
    a. a government
    b. a system of record keeping
    c. a class system
    d. all of the above

LESSON 2: Mesopotamia, the First Civilization

GOAL: To discover the history and characteristics of the world's first civilization

WORDS TO KNOW

city-state	cuneiform	scribe
classes	empire	ziggurat
Code of Hammurabi	irrigated	
commoners	noble class	

NAMES TO KNOW

Akkadians	Hammurabi	Sumerians
Babylonians	Sargon the Great	

PLACES TO KNOW

Akkad	Mesopotamia	Tigris and Euphrates rivers
Babylon	Sumer	
Fertile Crescent		Ur

The First Four Civilizations

When people speak of the beginning of civilization, they are usually referring to four distinct civilizations. These four civilizations developed at different times and in different places. The map below shows where they were.

Early Civilizations

The chart below tells you something about these four civilizations. In this lesson, you will learn more about the oldest of the early civilizations: **Mesopotamia.** In Lesson 3, you will learn about ancient Egypt. You will learn about the last two early civilizations, ancient India and China, in the third unit of this book.

The Earliest Civilizations

Name of Civilization	River Valley Location	Location in the Modern World	When It Began
Mesopotamia	Valley of the Tigris and Euphrates Rivers	in the Middle East, in Iraq	c. 3500 B.C.E.
Egypt	Valley of the Upper and Lower Nile Rivers	in northeastern Africa, in what is still called Egypt	c. 3100 B.C.E.
Indus River Valley	Valley of the Indus River	in Asia, in northwestern India and Pakistan	c. 3000 B.C.E.– 2500 B.C.E.
China	Valley of the Huang Ho (Yellow) River	in Asia, near the Yellow Sea, in northeastern China	c. 2700 B.C.E.– 1800 B.C.E.

■ **TIP**

A chart provides a lot of information in a small amount of space. In the chart above, the top of each row tells you what kind of information each column contains. When you read across the other rows, you learn information about a single civilization. When you read down the columns, you can compare the four civilizations. The chart shows how they are alike (all began in river valleys) and how they are different (they rose up in different places and at different times).

■ PRACTICE 7: The First Four Civilizations

Circle the letter(s) of the correct answer(s) to each of the following questions. Use the map on page 10 to help find the answers.

1. Which two civilizations are closest to each other?
   a. Mesopotamia and the Indus River Valley
   b. Mesopotamia and Egypt
   c. Mesopotamia and China

2. Which civilizations are on the continent of Asia? (*Hint*: There are three correct answers.)
   a. Mesopotamia
   b. the Indus River Valley
   c. Egypt
   d. China

Circle the correct answer to each of the following questions. Use the chart on page 11 to help find the answers.

3. How are the four earliest civilizations alike?
   a. They all began in river valleys.
   b. They are all seaports.
   c. They are all on the continent of Asia.
   d. They are all on the continent of Africa.

4. What is the name of the oldest civilization?
   a. China
   b. Egypt
   c. the Indus River Valley
   d. Mesopotamia

The Fertile Crescent

The world's first true civilization began in southern Mesopotamia. The word *mesopotamia* comes from a Greek word that means "the land between the rivers," specifically, the Tigris and Euphrates rivers. Mesopotamia was part of an area called the Fertile Crescent. A crescent is a curved shape that looks like a quarter moon. The word *fertile* means "good for plants to grow in." The Fertile Crescent was rich farmland that reached from the eastern shore of the Mediterranean Sea north to the Syrian Desert and south to the Persian Gulf. Look at the map on the right. The Fertile Crescent is the dotted area.

☐ The Fertile Crescent

Sometime around 5000 B.C.E., people called Sumerians settled in southern Mesopotamia. This region of Mesopotamia came to be known as Sumer. The Sumerians built cities out of mud and clay. By 3500 B.C.E., the Sumerian cities of Ur, Nippur, and Eridu had thousands of people living in them.

■ PRACTICE 8: The Fertile Crescent

Match each term with a description from below. Write the letter of the correct description on the line before each term.

a. site of the earliest civilization

b. rivers in Mesopotamia

c. cities in Sumer

d. rich farmland on the Mediterranean Sea

e. settlers in southern Mesopotamia

_____ **1.** Fertile Crescent

_____ **2.** Mesopotamia

_____ **3.** Sumerians

_____ **4.** Ur and Eridu

_____ **5.** Tigris and Euphrates

Sumerian Achievements

A civilization is a society that has developed complex systems for such things as trade, communications, and government. When we refer to the earliest Mesopotamian civilization, we are actually referring to the Sumerian civilization. This is because the Sumerians were probably the first to develop aspects of a civilization. As you have read, the Sumerians lived in the southern region of Mesopotamia, in an area called Sumer.

The Sumerians were very inventive. Their civilization added three great achievements to early human history.

- **The Wheel** Before there were wheels, people had to move objects by hand or put the items on logs and roll them along. But animals pulling carts behind them could move much heavier loads. The first Sumerian wheels were made by attaching wooden planks together in a circle. The wheels were then attached to carts.

- **Irrigation and Flood Control** The Sumerians needed a way to keep their crops watered, or irrigated, during their dry summers. They also needed protection from river floods. Sumerians dug canals and built dams to water crops and to control flooding.

- **Written Language** The earliest writing used pictures to stand for words. But picture writing is not an effective way of expressing thoughts, since many words cannot be pictured. Over time, Sumerian writing changed into wedge-shaped marks. Each wedge-shaped mark stood for a group of sounds in words. Such marks are called cuneiform. The Sumerians did not have pencils or paper on which to write. So the writer, or scribe, used a sharp stick and pressed it into a tablet of wet clay to make his marks. The tablet was then left in the sun to dry.

The Sumerians invented other things, as well. They developed a number system based on 60, which is the basis for our modern way of telling time (1 hour divided into 60 minutes). They developed a lunar calendar—a calendar based on the phases of the moon. They also invented the sail and the plow.

■ PRACTICE 9: Sumerian Achievements

Decide if each statement below is true (**T**) or false (**F**). Write the correct letter on the line before each statement.

_____ **1.** The Sumerians invented the calendar.

_____ **2.** The Sumerians invented the wheel.

■ IN REAL LIFE

Imagine how different our lives would be today without Sumerian contributions. What kind of transportation would we have without the wheel? How could we grow enough food without irrigation systems? Without writing, how would we make notes, send messages, or write books? Write your answers on a separate sheet of paper.

Sumerian City-States

There were about 12 cities in Sumer, each with its own government that ran the city, the land around it, and any nearby villages. Such a city is referred to as a **city-state.**

Sumerian city-states often grew quite large. The city of Ur, for example, was a major trading city. By 2500 B.C.E., it had about 20,000 inhabitants. Five hundred years later—in 2000 B.C.E.—as many as 200,000 people lived there.

At first, each city-state was run by a group of city leaders. But, the city leaders did not always agree on what to do. So, the Sumerian city-states decided to change their form of government. Each city-state chose a king. The king ruled the city-state in times of peace. He also led its armies in times of war. City-states often went to war with one another, fighting to get more land or more power.

The most important building in each city-state was the **ziggurat.** The ziggurat, the center of city life, was also a holy site. The Sumerians worshiped many gods, but each city-state had its own special god. This god protected the city as long as the city dwellers paid him proper respect.

The Sumerians of each city-state believed that when their god came down to visit them, he would stay in the ziggurat.

■ PRACTICE 10: Sumerian City-States

Decide if each statement below is true (**T**) or false (**F**). Write the correct letter on the line before each statement.

_____ **1.** Sumerian city-states were not very large.

_____ **2.** City-states often went to war with other city-states.

_____ **3.** A city-state included the land around the city and any nearby villages.

Life in Sumer

Many civilizations are divided into different groups, or **classes.** In Sumer, the highest class was the noble class. The **noble class** was made up of the king, the king's family, priests, and priestesses (women priests).

Most Sumerians were **commoners.** This class included merchants (sellers of goods), scribes (writers), farmers, and skilled workers. Below commoners were laborers, a class of people who worked for the nobles.

The family was important in all classes of society, and men had most of the power. The father was the head of the family. Boys with rich parents were sent to school, while girls stayed home. Women in Sumerian society did have some power, though. Girls from rich families were usually taught to read and write at home. Women were allowed by law to own property, to start new businesses, or to take over their husbands' businesses. They could also hold important positions, such as priestesses.

For the boys who went to school, it was a long day, beginning at sunrise and ending at sunset. Students learned to read, write, and do math. They memorized important songs, stories, and prayers. School life in Sumer was not easy. Students were beaten if they were late, if they talked when they should not have, and even if their clothes were messy!

■ PRACTICE 11: Life in Sumer

Match each description with a term from below. Write the letter of the correct term on the line before each description.

a. boys   **c.** prayers   **e.** scribe

b. girls   **d.** priest   **f.** astronomy

_____ **1.** a member of the noble class in Sumerian society

_____ **2.** a commoner in Sumerian society

_____ **3.** children who went to school in Sumerian society

_____ **4.** one of the subjects taught in Sumerian schools

The City of Akkad and the First Empire

The city-states of Sumer sometimes warred with one another. In addition, cities outside of Sumer often tried to gain power. Akkad was a city to the north of Sumer. Its people, the Akkadians, first came to Mesopotamia from the deserts at the edge of the Fertile Crescent. They learned Sumerian writing, and they followed the Sumerian religion and the Sumerian laws.

Akkad had a famous king named Sargon the Great. King Sargon imagined having power far beyond what any previous king had ever had. His dream was to rule *all* the cities and *all* the people of the Fertile Crescent.

By 2350 B.C.E., Sargon ruled all of the Akkadian cities. He then went on to control all the cities of Sumer. By achieving this goal, he set up the world's first empire. An empire is made up of many different people and places under the power of one ruler. After Sargon died, other Akkadian kings ruled the land and kept his empire together. All in all, the empire that Sargon had set up lasted for about 200 years.

■ PRACTICE 12: The City of Akkad and the First Empire

Circle the letter of the correct answer to each of the following questions.

1. What was Akkad?
   - **a.** a city-state in Sumer
   - **b.** a group of people who came from the desert
   - **c.** a god worshiped by the Sumerians
   - **d.** a city ruled by King Sargon

2. Which statement about King Sargon is false?
   - **a.** He ruled over everyone in Akkad.
   - **b.** He was a Sumerian.
   - **c.** He set up the world's first empire.
   - **d.** His empire lasted 200 years.

The City of Babylon: A New Empire

Around 2000 B.C.E., Mesopotamia was invaded by a tribe of people called the Amorites. They built a village beside the Euphrates River that grew into a mighty city. It was named **Babylon.**

The greatest ruler of Babylon was **Hammurabi.** Like Sargon the Great, he dreamed of ruling an empire and made his dream into a reality. By 1790 B.C.E., he had conquered other city-states in Mesopotamia and formed the Babylonian Empire. Hammurabi and the **Babylonians** followed Sumerian ways, just as Sargon and the Akkadians had done. But, in some ways, Hammurabi was not like anyone else who had come before him.

Up until then, every group of people—whether a village or a city-state or a mighty civilization like Sumer—had its own laws. However, Hammurabi's empire included many different city-states and, therefore, many different sets of laws. His great contribution to human history was to combine these laws to create a single set, or code, of laws for every person in his empire. In this way, he felt, he could keep his empire in order.

This set of laws is known as the **Code of Hammurabi.** It contains over 280 laws. We know the laws that made up this code because Hammurabi had them carved on a *stele* (a large, black stone column). This stele was dug up in 1901, in three pieces. Its 3,500 lines of cuneiform writing spell out Hammurabi's code.

■ PRACTICE 13: The City of Babylon: A New Empire

Decide if each statement below is true (**T**) or false (**F**). Write the correct letter on the line before each statement.

_____ **1.** Hammurabi was the greatest ruler of Babylon.

_____ **2.** Hammurabi's chief contribution to history was a set of laws.

_____ **3.** Hammurabi's laws were found on a set of clay tablets.

_____ **4.** Babylon conquered the Egyptian Empire.

The Code of Hammurabi

Hammurabi's code helped the people of his empire to live under law and order by giving them the same rules to obey. Some rules told the Babylonians how to care for the sick, the poor, and the helpless. But many of the other laws sound harsh to us today because they are based on the ancient law of "an eye for an eye." This means that offenses against one person was met with an equal punishment against the offender. For example, if one person breaks the leg of another, that person must have one of his or her legs broken—or suffer some other, similar punishment. In his code, Hammurabi set exact prices that people had to pay if they hurt another person.

However, not everyone had to pay the same price. Nobles had more rights than commoners and slaves. Hurting a poorer person did not cost as much as injuring a member of the higher classes.

Here are some provisions of Hammurabi's code.

■ If a man breaks into a house, he shall be killed next to where he broke in and be buried there.

- If a woman wants to leave her husband, and she has done nothing wrong toward him, she may return to her father's house. But if the woman is at fault in any way, she shall be thrown into the river.

- If a son hits his father, his hands shall be cut off.

- If a man irrigates his crops and carelessly floods his neighbor's field, then he shall pay his neighbor for the lost crops.

The Babylonian kings who ruled after Hammurabi could not keep his empire together. It fell into ruin. But the ideas behind the Code of Hammurabi live on: People are responsible for what they do, and society must believe in justice for its people.

THINK ABOUT IT

What do you think of the "eye for an eye" law? Can you think of an example when this law would be unfair? Write your answer on a separate sheet of paper.

■ PRACTICE 14: The Code of Hammurabi

Decide if each statement below is true (**T**) or false (**F**). Write the correct letter on the line before each statement.

_____ **1.** Hammurabi created a code of laws because he wanted all of his people to obey the same rules.

_____ **2.** "An eye for an eye" means that the punishment for a crime depends on who commits the crime.

_____ **3.** Under Hammurabi's code, everyone was equal.

_____ **4.** Women had no rights under Hammurabi's code.

LESSON 3: The Civilization of the Nile

GOAL: To understand the characteristics and early history of ancient Egypt, and to learn about the civilization of Nubia

WORDS TO KNOW

archaeologist	exports	papyrus
Assyrians	hieroglyphics	pharaohs
candake	imports	pyramid
dynasties	mummy	scroll

NAMES TO KNOW

Hatshepsut	King Piye	Rosetta Stone
Howard Carter	Menes	Tutankhamen

PLACES TO KNOW

Kerma	Nile
Meroë	Nubia

A Civilization in the Desert

The Mesopotamian civilization is widely accepted as the first civilization. However, a second civilization sprang up in Egypt only a few hundred years later. In fact, the Mesopotamians traded goods and ideas with their Egyptian neighbors. What was ancient Egypt like? How have we managed to learn so much about these people?

Ancient Egypt

Egypt is in the northeast corner of Africa. Most of it is dry, windswept desert. But there is a narrow band of rich land on either side of a great river, the Nile. The Nile is the longest river in the world. It flows north to the

Mediterranean for more than 4,000 miles. Thousands of years ago, nomads moved into the Nile Valley. By 5000 B.C.E., these nomads had become farmers. Farming villages began to spring up along the Nile. These villages grew into city-states. The city-states eventually grouped together to form two kingdoms—Upper Egypt in the south and Lower Egypt in the north. This may seem upside-down, but remember that the Nile flows up, to the north. So, the lower part of the Nile is in the north.

■ PRACTICE 15: A Civilization in the Desert

Circle the letter of the correct answer to each of the following questions.

1. What river flowed through ancient Egypt?
   a. the Nile
   b. the Euphrates
   c. the Tigris
   d. the Indus

2. What two kingdoms made up ancient Egypt?
   a. Memphis and Cairo
   b. Lower Egypt and Upper Egypt
   c. the Nile Valley and the Sahara Desert
   d. Mesopotamia and Sumer

Egyptian Dynasties and Class Systems

The history of Egypt really begins with **Menes.** Menes was king of Lower Egypt until around 3100 B.C.E. Menes eventually gained control of Upper Egypt and united both Lower Egypt and Upper Egypt into one kingdom. Menes thus became the first king of Egypt. He chose Memphis as the capital city.

Today, when we speak of Egyptian ruling families and rulers, we speak of **dynasties** and **pharaohs.** A dynasty begins with a ruler who then passes control to a son or daughter, down through the generations. When a new family takes control, a new dynasty begins. Menes is thought to have begun the first Egyptian dynasty. The term *pharaoh* means "great house" in Egyptian, that is, the royal palace. Later in Egypt's history, it came to be used as a synonym for "king." By the twenty-second dynasty (c. 945–730 B.C.E.), "pharaoh" had become the proper title for Egyptian kings. A pharaoh had complete control over Egypt. The pharaoh headed the government and the army, set laws, and oversaw religious practices. The Egyptians believed that when their pharaoh was sitting on the throne holding the symbols of power, he or she became a god on Earth.

Like other ancient civilizations, Egypt had a class system. The ruling class was at the top, starting with the pharaoh. It included all the powerful and rich people, such as nobles and priests, who helped the pharaoh run the country. Below the ruling class was the middle class. This class was made up of professional people, such as merchants, scribes, doctors, skilled workers, and soldiers. Below this class was a third class, which was made up of poor farmers and slaves. The people in the third class basically worked for the ruling class. The farmers gave much of what they grew to the pharaoh, and slaves worked for their wealthy owners. Most Egyptians were in this third class.

■ PRACTICE 16: Egyptian Dynasties and Class Systems

Decide if each statement below is true (**T**) or false (**F**). Write the correct letter on the line before each statement.

_____ **1.** Menes united Lower Egypt and Upper Egypt into one kingdom.

_____ **2.** The term *dynasty* means "great house" in Egyptian.

_____ **3.** The third class in Egypt was made up of poor farmers and slaves.

_____ **4.** The term *pharaoh* came to mean "king."

Egyptian Beliefs

Like other ancient civilizations, the Egyptians worshiped many gods. Their gods and goddesses were usually linked to animals and were often pictured as having the heads of animals. On the following page is a chart of some of the gods and goddesses who were important to the Egyptians.

Name	Description	Animal Link
Ra (or Re)	god of the sun	hawk wearing a disk that stands for the sun
Hathor	goddess of love	cow
Thoth	god of wisdom	ibis (a long-billed wading bird)
Anubis	judge of the dead	jackal (a wild dog)
Horus	god of the sky	falcon (a hawklike bird)

The Egyptians believed that every person had a soul. They also believed that when a person died, part of this soul lived on. The Egyptians called it the *ka*. The *ka* liked to eat, drink, and do the same things that the living person had done. The longer a body was kept intact, the better chance the *ka* had for happiness after death. Thus, the Egyptians developed the art of preserving a dead body. First, the insides of the body were stored in special jars. The body was then rubbed with salt and left to dry in the hot Egyptian sun. Next, it was packed with cloth and spices to form a lifelike shape. Finally, it was wrapped in bandages that had been soaked in a special mixture. It was now a **mummy**.

Only the highest-ranking people were made into mummies, placed in coffins, and buried in large tombs. The most important people ended up in the largest tombs.

■ PRACTICE 17: Egyptian Beliefs

Decide if each statement below is true (**T**) or false (**F**). Write the correct letter on the line before each statement.

_____ **1.** The Egyptians believed that when a person died, part of his or her soul lived on.

_____ **2.** All Egyptians were made into mummies.

The Tombs of the Pharaohs

When powerful and rich Egyptians died, their bodies were mummified, put in carved stone coffins, and buried in tombs filled with treasure. As you have read, pharaohs were the most powerful Egyptians of all. When a pharaoh died, the Egyptians erected an enormous tomb, called a pyramid, with a hidden chamber for the coffin. The earliest pyramids were built in steps and are known as "step pyramids." Later pyramids had smooth sides. The largest pyramid was built for the pharaoh Khufu, whom the Greeks called Cheops. This pyramid, located in Giza (see map on page 21), is the largest single building ever built. It took between 20 and 30 years to complete.

Perhaps the best known tomb in the world, though, is the one found by the British archaeologist Howard Carter in 1922. (An archaeologist studies the remains of the past to learn what ancient people were like.) Carter uncovered the tomb of the pharaoh Tutankhamen. King Tut, as he is known, came to power in the twelfth century B.C.E. and was only a teenager when he died. What made Carter's discovery so special were the amazing treasures he found in the boy-king's tomb: a golden throne, a golden chariot, a bed, statues of servants, baskets of fruit, jewelry, and a toy box.

THINK ABOUT IT

Think about the Egyptians' religious beliefs. Why do you think the young pharaoh's tomb would be filled with these treasures? Write your answer on a separate sheet of paper.

■ PRACTICE 18: The Tombs of the Pharaohs

Circle the letter of the correct answer to each of the following questions.

1. What are the tombs of the pharaohs called?
   a. temples
   b. sphinxes
   c. barrows
   d. pyramids

2. Which pharaoh had the largest tomb?
   a. Cheops
   b. Tutankhamen
   c. Hatshepsut
   d. Akhenaton

Egyptian Writing

Egyptian writing began around 3100 B.C.E. It may have evolved from Sumerian writing, which began as picture writing.

The Egyptians invented a system that we call **hieroglyphics.** In hieroglyphics, pictures and symbols stand for whole words, syllables, or single sounds. For example, a picture of a woman stood for the word *woman.* But a picture of a lion stood just for the letter *l.* The Egyptians had about 600 hieroglyphs that their scribes had to learn. (As in Sumer, formal writing was usually done by scribes.) To make things more difficult, hieroglyphs could be written from left to right, from right to left, or from top to bottom.

Sumerian scribes wrote on wet clay tablets that were later dried in the sun. Egyptians sometimes carved words in stone, but they also wrote on material that was much like paper. It was made from **papyrus,** a reed that grew in the swamps along the Nile. If you think the English word *paper* is similar to *papyrus,* you are correct. To make their writing material, the Egyptians peeled the papyrus reeds into long strips and laid the strips close together. Then, they laid another layer, crosswise, on top and pressed the layers together to form a mat. The mats were glued together to form a long sheet called a **scroll.** Many ancient Egyptian scrolls survive today.

■ PRACTICE 19: Egyptian Writing

Decide if each of the following statements is true (**T**) or false (**F**). Write the correct letter on the line before each statement.

_____ 1. Egyptian writing was called hieroglyphics.

_____ 2. Egyptian writing used wedge-shaped symbols.

_____ **3.** Sumerian writing was written on clay tablets.

_____ **4.** Nearly everyone in Egypt knew how to write.

_____ **5.** The Egyptians invented the first paperlike material.

The Mystery of Hieroglyphs—Solved!

Modern-day Egyptians speak and write Arabic, a very different language from that of their Egyptian ancestors. In fact, ancient Egyptian hieroglyphs might still be a mystery to us were it not for the **Rosetta Stone.**

In 1799, the French army was in the middle of an invasion of Egypt. Along with the soldiers came 167 scholars and scientists who wished to study Egypt. One day, a French officer came across a large, black stone near the Egyptian city of Rosetta. It was about 4 feet high and 2 1/2 feet wide. It was covered with ancient writing. The rock was given to the scholars. They figured out that the writing was in three different languages: Egyptian hieroglyphs, a simpler Egyptian language, and ancient Greek. The scholars knew ancient Greek and could figure out that part of the writing. It told about a pharaoh named Ptolemy who had been a Greek general. But the Egyptian writings remained a mystery.

Over the next few years, scholars came to realize that the writings were three different versions of the same message. A French history teacher named Champollion was one of the people working on the Rosetta Stone writings. In 1821, he did what no one else had been able to do: He successfully matched up these languages and figured out the Egyptian alphabet.

IN REAL LIFE

Champollion "broke the code" of the Rosetta Stone. To do so, he used some of the same decoding strategies that we all did when we first learned to read and write. Starting with a word he knew (the name Ptolemy), Champollion figured out which hieroglyphs stood for which sounds. Then he looked for those same hieroglyphs in other words. In English, for example, once you know the word *top*, you can figure out the word *pot*.

■ PRACTICE 20: The Mystery of Hieroglyphs—Solved!

Decide if each statement below is true (**T**) or false (**F**). Write the correct answer on the line before each statement.

_____ **1.** The Rosetta Stone is a rock covered with ancient writing.

_____ **2.** There are three different versions of the same message on the Rosetta Stone.

Three Thousand Years of History

The civilization of ancient Egypt lasted almost 3,000 years. Historians have divided this huge span of time into three major periods: the Old Kingdom, the Middle Kingdom, and the New Kingdom. During these periods, powerful kings ruled the land. In between these periods, Egypt was at war or under the rule of outsiders. The chart below and on the next page shows some key people and events in ancient Egypt's history.

TIP

Look the chart over quickly for now. Get a general sense of the information it contains. In other words, skim the chart. Then, read the questions in Practice 21. What information do you need to answer them? Scan the chart, looking for specific information. Use chart headings to figure out where in the chart the information is likely to be. If a question mentions a specific person, place, or period, scan the chart to find that name.

The History of Ancient Egypt

Time Period	Some Important Events	Some Important People
Old Kingdom c. 2700–2200 B.C.E.	■ All the pyramids are built. ■ The Great Sphinx is created.	■ Imhotep, the designer of the first pyramid ■ Pharaoh Khufu, whose tomb is the largest pyramid

Middle Kingdom c. 2050–1850 B.C.E.	■ Strong pharaohs reunite the land and restore law and order. ■ The middle class arises. ■ The capital is moved to Thebes. ■ Egypt conquers Nubia, a kingdom to the south. ■ Egypt is conquered by the Hyksos.	■ Senusret III, a warrior king who led his army against Nubia ■ the Hyksos, nomads from the Fertile Crescent who invaded Egypt
New Kingdom c. 1570–1090 B.C.E.	■ The term *pharaoh* comes into use. ■ The Egyptian Empire grows, and trade expands. ■ The temple of Karnak is built, with the world's largest hall of columns. ■ The Obelisk of Hatshepsut (a giant stone column) is built. ■ Pharaoh Amenhotep renames himself Akhenaton (son of Aton) and tries to get Egypt to worship one god, Aton.	■ Hatshepsut, one of the only female rulers; the only female pharaoh of the New Kingdom ■ Pharaoh Akhenaton and his queen, Nefertiti ■ Pharaoh Tutankhamen, whose tomb is opened in 1922 by British archaeologist Howard Carter

■ PRACTICE 21: Three Thousand Years of History

Decide if each statement below is true (**T**) or False (**F**). Write the correct letter on the line before each statement.

_____ **1.** Ancient Egyptian history is divided into three time periods: the Old Kingdom, the Middle Kingdom, and the New Kingdom.

_____ **2.** Between 2050 and 1850 B.C.E., the capital of Egypt was moved to Cairo.

_____ **3.** Imhotep was the designer of the first pyramid.

_____ **4.** Hatshepsut was the god of the dead.

The Other Great Nile Civilization

Because of archaeologists such as Howard Carter and scholars such as Champollion, people all over the world know about ancient Egypt. Fewer people, however, know about the other great Nile civilization, **Nubia.** (It is sometimes called the Kingdom of Kush, its Egyptian name.)

Like early Egypt, early Nubia was divided into Lower Nubia in the north and Upper Nubia in the south. (Remember, the Nile flows "up" to the Mediterranean.) The first Nubians moved into the region about 10,000 years ago. Their cave paintings and carvings can still be seen today. Like other early peoples, the Nubians developed from hunters and gatherers into farmers. About 6,000 years ago, they began settling in small farming villages on the Nile.

The Kingdom of Nubia

Around 3100 B.C.E., Upper Nubia and Lower Nubia were united into one kingdom. (This is about the same time that Upper Egypt and Lower Egypt were uniting.) The Nubians traded with their Egyptian neighbors. Nubian exports, the goods sent to Egypt, included animal skins, ivory from elephants, and pottery (the Nubians were skilled potters). Nubian imports, the Egyptian goods they traded for, included oil, honey, and linen cloth.

However, problems arose between Nubia and Egypt. They began to fight over who controlled the best trade routes. By 2800 B.C.E., Nubia and Egypt were at war. When the Egyptians won, some Nubians were taken as slaves. The rest fled to the south. The southern city of Kerma became the center of the Nubian kingdom.

New trade partners were found, and new trade routes were set up with other peoples inside Africa. Nubian craftspeople developed more and more skills. They carved stone statues, designed gold and silver jewelry, created painted tiles, and made tools and weapons out of copper.

But, by 1600 B.C.E., the Nubians and Egyptians were at war again. This time, the powerful Egyptian army captured the city of Kerma and put an Egyptian ruler in charge. Under Egyptian rule, Nubians came to know and practice Egyptian ways. They built pyramids in which their rulers were buried. They worshipped Egyptian gods, and wrote with Egyptian hieroglyphics.

By 800 B.C.E., the Egyptian government was falling apart. There was no law or order in Nubia or Egypt. In the middle of the eighth century B.C.E., a Nubian king named King Piye invaded Egypt, took over the government, and became pharaoh. He saw his rule as restoring Egypt's former glory. King Piye's dynasty lasted for about 100 years, until about 660 B.C.E. Then a warlike people called the Assyrians conquered Egypt and drove out the Nubians.

Separate from Egypt once again, the Nubians made the city of Napata their new capital. The kings of Napata ruled Nubia until the third century B.C.E. Around 270 B.C.E., the capital was moved yet again—from Napata to the city of Meroë.

■ PRACTICE 22: The Other Great Nile Civilization

Match each description with a term from below. Write the letter of the correct term on the line before each description.

a. Nubia   **b.** Kush   **c.** Kerma   **d.** Piye   **e.** Napata

_____ **1.** the center of Nubia around 2800 B.C.E.

_____ **2.** the Egyptian name for Nubia

_____ **3.** the Nubian king who became pharaoh

_____ **4.** the capital of Nubia after 660 B.C.E.

_____ **5.** the civilization that developed around the Nile, south of ancient Egypt

The Glorious Kingdom of Meroë

Meroë became the center of a rich and powerful Nubian nation. The city itself was surrounded by beds of iron ore. The Nubians, who knew about iron making, used the iron to craft tools and weapons. The Meroites were skilled traders. Egypt was their most important trade partner. They also traded with other Mediterranean cultures and with India. They developed a written language with a 23-letter alphabet. (Scholars have not yet decoded the Nubian language.) Among Meroë's great buildings were a temple to the Egyptian god Amon and temples to Nubian gods.

Unlike women in most early civilizations, Meroite women had an important place in their culture. A female ruler was called a candake. The most famous candake was Amanirenas. She was able to keep the powerful Roman army out of her kingdom. She also worked out an agreement with the Romans to keep them from taxing her people.

Meroë reached its peak in the first century C.E. By the fourth century C.E., the trade routes of Meroë were in the hands of African people known as Axumites.

■ PRACTICE 23: The Glorious Kingdom of Meroë

Circle the letter of the correct answer to each of the following questions.

1. What natural resource was plentiful in Nubia?
   a. coal
   b. bronze
   c. iron ore
   d. salt

2. What nation was Meroë's most important trading partner?
   a. India
   b. Syria
   c. Sumer
   d. Egypt

3. Who was Amanirenas?
   a. a powerful, Nubian female ruler of Meroë
   b. a powerful priestess of Meroë
   c. an Egyptian female ruler of Meroë
   d. a wealthy female trader of Meroë

4. Which people had taken control of Meroë by the fourth century c.e.?
   a. Egyptians
   b. Axumites
   c. Nubians
   d. Hittites

■ TIP

Studying with a partner is a good test-taking strategy. Try finding a "study buddy." Quiz each other on the terms, people, places, and events at the beginning of each lesson. Take turns asking each other questions to prepare for the Unit Reviews.

LESSON 4: Other Cultures of the Fertile Crescent

 GOAL: To understand the characteristics and history of other significant ancient cultures in and around the Fertile Crescent

WORDS TO KNOW

bronze	conquerors	provinces
cavalry	famine	
colonies	monotheism	

NAMES TO KNOW

Abraham	Hebrews	Phoenicians
Assyrians	Hittites	Saul
Chaldeans	Moses	Sea People
Cyrus	Nebuchadnezzar	Solomon
Darius I	Persians	
David	Philistines	

PLACES TO KNOW

Carthage	Nineveh
Hanging Gardens of Babylon	

The Hebrews

Mesopotamia and Egypt were the oldest civilizations in the region of the Fertile Crescent. But other important cultures also emerged in this region. In this lesson, you will learn about some of these other important ancient civilizations.

Canaan is the ancient name of the land at the western end of the Fertile Crescent. (This land is now Israel, Lebanon, and parts of Syria and Jordan.)

Canaan was a rich and prosperous land. It had huge forests of cedar trees, its soil was good for farming, and it was in a strategic location for trade with Africa and Asia.

Around 2000 B.C.E., a man named **Abraham** left the Mesopotamian city of Ur with his family. They lived as nomads, wandering across the Fertile Crescent with their sheep and goats. Finally, they settled in Canaan. According to the Bible, Abraham made a special agreement, or covenant, with the god Yahweh (also known as Jehovah). The agreement was that Abraham and his followers, the **Hebrews,** would be Yahweh's chosen people, and Canaan would be their land. In return, the Hebrews would worship only Yahweh. The Hebrews were the first to practice **monotheism.** That is, they believed in only one god. This single god has come to be called God.

■ PRACTICE 24: The Hebrews

Decide if each statement below is true (**T**) or false (**F**). Write the correct letter on the line before each statement.

_____ **1.** Canaan is the ancient name of the land now known as Israel, Lebanon, and parts of Syria and Jordan.

_____ **2.** Monotheism is the belief in many gods.

■ IN REAL LIFE

Ancient peoples had many, many religions. Today, most religious people belong to one of several major "world" religions. Three of these world religions—Islam, Christianity, and Judaism—grew out of the monotheism of the Hebrews.

Egypt and the Hebrews

The Hebrews continued to live in Canaan for many, many years until a **famine** came over the land around 1700 B.C.E. This meant that little or no food was growing and that there was not enough to eat. People were starving. The Hebrews fled to Egypt in search of food. Once they were there, the Egyptians put them to work, forcing them to be slaves for the pharaohs. Around 1280 B.C.E., a man named Moses led the Hebrews out of Egypt and back to Canaan.

These stories of the early Israelites, of Abraham, and of Moses, come from the Torah, a collection of writings set down hundreds of years after the time when Moses is said to have led the Hebrews back to Canaan. The collection in the Torah is also the beginning (the first five books) of the book known as the Bible.

While the Hebrews were in Egypt, another culture known as the Sea People settled around the Mediterranean Sea. We know very little about these people except that they were mighty warriors and fierce in battle. One group of Sea People, called the Philistines, were living in Canaan. When they returned from Egypt, the Hebrews found themselves sharing their "promised land" with the warlike Philistines. Not surprisingly, these two groups found it difficult to live together in peace.

■ PRACTICE 25: Egypt and the Hebrews

Decide if each statement below is true (**T**) or false (**F**). Write the correct letter on the line before each statement.

_____ **1.** The Egyptians made slaves of the Hebrews.

_____ **2.** The Hebrews and the Philistines shared their land peacefully.

_____ **3.** The Hebrews fled from Egypt into Canaan.

The Great Kings of Israel

Around the end of the eleventh century B.C.E., the Hebrews were at war with the Philistines. The Hebrews needed someone to lead them, so they chose Saul as their king. Saul proved to be a brave and wise leader. In one battle, a boy named David killed a giant Philistine warrior called Goliath. This battle ended the war, and the Hebrews came to control Canaan. From then on, the land of Canaan was known as Israel.

When Saul died, the Hebrews chose David as their king. David united all the tribes of Israel and made the city of Jerusalem the capital of the nation. When he died, his son Solomon became the king. Solomon helped Israel to become a rich and strong kingdom. Israel traded with Egypt and with other kingdoms in Africa.

When Solomon died (c. 920 B.C.E.), the kingdom of Israel split in two. The northern part kept the name Israel. The southern part called itself Judah, and the people living there came to be known as Jews. These two new kingdoms were weaker than the single kingdom of Israel had been. Eventually, Israel was taken over by the Assyrians. Judah was conquered by the Chaldeans.

■ PRACTICE 26: The Great Kings of Israel

Decide if each statement below is true (**T**) or false (**F**). Write the correct letter on the line before each statement.

_____ **1.** David united Hebrew tribes and made Jerusalem the capital of Israel.

_____ **2.** Solomon led the Hebrews in their war with the Philistines.

_____ **3.** Under Saul, the Hebrews won control of Canaan.

■ IN REAL LIFE

When Israel split into two parts, two of the twelve tribes of Israel were in Judah, the southern part. The other ten tribes were in the northern kingdom, now called Israel. As you just read, the Assyrians conquered the northern kingdom in 721 B.C.E. The history of those ten tribes ends at that date. From then on, the history of the Jews is the history of the two tribes in Judah. (The word *Jew* comes from the word *Judah*.) What happened to the ten "lost" tribes of Israel remains one of history's greatest mysteries.

The Hittites—Innovations in Warfare

Between 1400 B.C.E. and 1200 B.C.E., a civilization known as the Hittites ruled most of the Fertile Crescent. They were mighty in battle. Two factors helped make them so successful in war.

- **Iron weapons** For at least 1,000 years before the Hittites, soldiers had been using bronze weapons. Bronze is made from copper and tin but is harder than either of these soft metals. Iron is harder still. The Hittites knew the secret to making weapons from iron. They kept that secret to themselves for a long time.

- **Horses in battle** The people of Mesopotamia had been using horses for about 1,000 years. But these horses were quite small and were only used to pull loads. The Hittites were able to raise horses that were larger and stronger. The Hittites used these horses to pull chariots during battle.

The empire of the Hittites fell apart around 1200 B.C.E. In part, this was because too many of their neighbors were also great fighters. Of these great fighters, the greatest of them all were the Assyrians.

THINK ABOUT IT

Why would a soldier using a horse-drawn chariot have an advantage over a soldier on foot? Write your answer on a separate sheet of paper.

■ PRACTICE 27: The Hittites—Innovations in Warfare

Circle the letter of the correct answer to each of the following questions.

1. What kind of weapons did the Hittites use?
    a. steel
    b. bronze
    c. copper
    d. iron

2. How did the Hittites use horses in battle?
   a. The soldiers rode the horses.
   b. The horses pulled chariots.
   c. The horses carried weapons and supplies.
   d. The officers used the horses for sport.

The Assyrians

The Assyrians had always been fighters, ever since they first lived in the hills around the Tigris River. Until about 2000 B.C.E., they were ruled by the kings of Sumer or Akkad. In the ninth century B.C.E., Assyria marched on its neighbors. The Assyrian army was cruel, either killing the people who were conquered or making them into slaves. Soon, the fierce Assyrians ruled all of the Fertile Crescent. Their rule lasted some 300 years.

The Assyrian army was a mighty force, especially once it had learned to make its weapons out of iron. Foot soldiers in the Assyrian army carried iron shields and spears. Some soldiers trained to become archers, using bows to shoot arrows. The Assyrians had the finest archers in the ancient world. Their army also had a cavalry and used war chariots, small horse-drawn carriages that were open at the back and top.

Assyrian cities served as centers of government, the army, trade, and religion. They contained many temples because the Assyrians worshiped many gods. These temples were often quite beautiful. Along with palaces and temples, the capital city of Nineveh even had a zoo. Located in a huge park, the zoo had plants and animals from all over the empire and beyond.

But even such a great army could not be victorious forever. Around 605 B.C.E., the Assyrian Empire was gone. The Chaldeans were now in charge.

■ PRACTICE 28: The Assyrians
Circle the letter of the correct answer to each of the following questions.

1. Which word best describes the Assyrians?
   a. peaceful
   b. beautiful
   c. warlike
   d. monotheistic

2. What was Nineveh?
   a. the king of Assyria
   b. the capital of Assyria
   c. a park with a zoo
   d. a country in the Fertile Crescent

The Chaldeans

Around 900 B.C.E., a people known as the Chaldeans settled in Sumer. They fought against the Assyrians, who controlled Sumer at the time. In the end, the Chaldean army won and went on to take over the empire.

The most famous Chaldean king was **Nebuchadnezzar,** who ruled from 605 B.C.E. to 562 B.C.E. When he and his army conquered Judah, they destroyed King Solomon's temple. Nebuchadnezzar had its contents brought back to Babylon, the city that the Chaldeans chose as their capital.

At this time, Babylon was the greatest city in the Fertile Crescent. A city of more than 1,000 temples, Babylon was a center of trade and learning. But it was—and still is—most famous for one thing. As part of his palace, Nebuchadnezzar had called for a garden to be built on terraces that rose more than 400 feet into the air. Plants from all over the ancient world were planted there. It was called the **Hanging Gardens of Babylon,** and it came to be known as one of the Seven Wonders of the Ancient World.

After Nebuchadnezzar's death, the empire grew weaker. In 539 B.C.E., a Persian king named Cyrus conquered Babylon and let the Hebrews return to their homeland.

■ PRACTICE 29: The Chaldeans

Circle the letter of the correct answer to each of the following questions.

1. What happened to King Solomon's temple?
   a. It was filled with plants from all over the ancient world.
   b. It was destroyed by the Chaldeans.
   c. Its contents were left in Judah.
   d. It became a center of trade and learning.

2. What was named the Hanging Gardens of Babylon?
   a. the greatest city in the Fertile Crescent
   b. a city of more than 1,000 temples
   c. the palace of the king
   d. a set of terraces that were part of the royal palace

The Persians

The earliest **Persians** were nomads from Central Asia. They settled in the Fertile Crescent around 1300 B.C.E., in a region that is now the country of Iran. **Cyrus** became king of Persia in 549 B.C.E. He set out to build an empire. By 539 B.C.E., King Cyrus had taken over the Chaldean Empire. Many inhabitants of this empire welcomed the Persians. In part, this was because Cyrus was known to be a fair king. He respected local customs and religions. But he was not king of his empire for long. Ten years later, he was killed in battle.

A weak king ruled for the next eight years. Then **Darius I** became the king. He is considered Persia's greatest leader. To control his huge empire, Darius divided it into 20 **provinces.** Each province was run by a governor, a Persian noble whom Darius had appointed. Darius regularly sent inspectors called "the Eyes and Ears of the King" to check on the governors.

The Persians were the first to come up with a mail service. Their system depended on a huge highway that stretched across the empire. Along the highway, over 100 stations were set up, each with horses and riders. A rider on horseback with bags of mail would set out for the first station. There, another horse and rider would take over and ride on to the next station, and so on. At each station, mail was picked up and delivered.

The highway system helped to unite the far-flung Persian Empire. So did the use of metal coins with a standard value, an idea promoted by Darius. This created strong trading links across the empire.

When Darius I died in 486 B.C.E., his son Xerxes became king. He was not a strong ruler, and the empire weakened. Finally, a great conqueror named Alexander the Great took over the empire. To learn more about Alexander the Great, read "The Ancient Greeks," the second unit in this book.

■ PRACTICE 30: The Persians

Circle the letter of the correct answer to each of the following questions.

1. Who conquered the Persian Empire?
   a. Darius I
   b. Cyrus
   c. Alexander
   d. Xerxes

2. How was the huge Persian Empire controlled?
   a. The army was very strong.
   b. It was divided into provinces.
   c. The people worshiped its rulers as gods.
   d. The emperor executed all the local kings.

The Phoenicians

The Phoenicians were not warriors, conquerors, or empire builders. Yet they managed to spread their civilization throughout the ancient world. They did this by being great sailors, explorers, and traders.

At first, the Phoenicians were farmers living on a strip of land between the Mediterranean Sea and the Lebanon Mountains. The population grew, and there was not enough farmland to go around. So, people turned to the sea. They sailed around the Mediterranean and beyond, into the Atlantic Ocean. Wherever these sea traders went, they set up colonies of settlers. The settlers established city-states that became trading partners with other Phoenician city-states. Their most famous trading city was Carthage.

The most important achievement of the Phoenicians was their system of writing. Sumerian and Egyptian writing had used symbols to stand for groups of sounds or for single syllables. Around 1500 B.C.E., the Phoenicians invented an alphabet—a series of letters. Each letter was based on a single sound. As the Phoenicians traveled around, they spread their alphabet system. English is one of many modern languages that uses an alphabet based on that of the Phoenicians. Our alphabet has 26 letters, mostly consonants with a few vowels. The Phoenician alphabet had 22 letters, all consonants!

■ PRACTICE 31: The Phoenicians

Decide if each statement below is true (**T**) or false (**F**). Write the correct letter on the line before each statement.

_____ **1.** The Phoenicians were great warriors, explorers, and traders.

_____ **2.** Carthage was the most famous Phoenician city-state.

_____ **3.** The major invention of the Phoenicians was their system of writing, which used an alphabet.

UNIT 1 REVIEW

Circle the letter of the correct answer to each of the following questions.

1. When did modern humans first appear on Earth?
   a. during the New Stone Age
   b. when Earth was a hot, glowing ball
   c. about 100,000 years ago
   d. about 1 to 2 million years ago

2. Which of the following best describes a civilization?
   a. a large city built in a river valley
   b. a group of people sharing a way of life, a set of beliefs and customs, and a language
   c. a large society that is highly organized
   d. many families living together as nomads in caves

3. What do all four early civilizations have in common?
   a. They started about the same time.
   b. They began in the Fertile Crescent.
   c. They were located in river valleys.
   d. They had the same written language.

4. What is a city-state?
    a. a large city in an empire
    b. a group of different people and places under a single ruler
    c. a city with its own ruler, army, and laws
    d. a city that changes its government

5. What was the Code of Hammurabi?
    a. a set of laws that was used for the whole empire of Hammurabi
    b. a set of laws based on the ancient "eye for an eye" law
    c. laws written on a stone column that was dug up in 1901
    d. all of the above

6. Which of the following statements describes the ancient Egyptian class system?
    a. It had three classes: the ruling class, the middle class, and a class of poor farmers and slaves.
    b. It had an upper and a lower class.
    c. Most Egyptians were in the middle class.
    d. It had four classes: the pharaoh, the ruling class, the professional class, and the working class.

7. Why were the Egyptian pyramids built?
    a. to honor the pharaoh Khufu
    b. to store great treasures
    c. to serve as the tombs of pharaohs
    d. to be temples for Egyptian gods and goddesses

8. What made Meroë different from most early civilizations?
    a. Women could be rulers.
    b. The Meroites had a written language.
    c. Meroë had temples.
    d. The Meroites exported goods to other countries.

9. How was the Hebrew religion different from other religions in the Fertile Crescent?
   a. The Hebrews were monotheists.
   b. The Hebrews were nomads.
   c. The Hebrews only had one religion.
   d. The Hebrews brought their religion with them when they fled to Egypt.

10. What was the Phoenicians' major contribution to human development?
    a. They set up colonies throughout the Fertile Crescent.
    b. They were the greatest archers of the ancient world.
    c. They were the first to have a cavalry.
    d. They invented the alphabet.

UNIT 1 APPLICATION ACTIVITY
The Seven Wonders of the Ancient World

What does this title mean? It refers to a famous list of ancient structures from long ago. The list, printed below, includes two structures that you read about in Unit 1. Do you remember which ones they are?

- The Colossus of Rhodes

- The Hanging Gardens of Babylon

- The Mausoleum of Halicarnassus

- The Pharos at Alexandria

- The Egyptian Pyramids

- The Statue of Zeus at Olympia (Zeus is his Greek name. His Latin name is Jupiter. The statue is known by both names.)

- The Temple of Artemis at Ephesus (Artemis is her Greek name. Her Latin name is Diana. The temple is known by both names.)

Choose one of the seven wonders to research. Look in encyclopedias, almanacs, and on the Internet to find information. Take notes below. Then use the notes to write a report on another sheet of paper.

Name of ancient wonder: _____

Location (including country): _____

_____

Description: _____

_____

_____

_____

_____

_____

_____

Resource(s) I used: _____

_____

_____

_____

_____

_____

_____

UNIT 2

The Ancient Greeks

LESSON 5: Early Greek Civilizations

GOAL: To learn how the geography of Greece influenced its early history; to learn about two early Greek civilizations—the Minoan and the Mycenaean

WORDS TO KNOW

artifacts	isthmus	peninsula
dark age	legends	Trojan War

NAMES TO KNOW

Dorians	Minoans	Minotaur
Homer	Minos	Mycenaeans

PLACES TO KNOW

Aegean Sea	Crete	Peloponnesus
Asia Minor	Knossos	

The Greek Peninsula

The geography of Greece had a lot to do with how its early civilizations developed. In this lesson, you will learn about Greek geography and about two early Greek civilizations.

Greece is in the southern part of what is called the Balkan Peninsula. A **peninsula,** which literally means "almost an island," is land that is almost completely surrounded by water. (The state of Florida is an American peninsula.)

The Greek Peninsula reaches far out into the Mediterranean Sea. The southern half of Greece, called the

Greece

Peloponnesus, almost looks like a large island. It is attached to the northern mainland by a thin strip of land called an isthmus.

To the east of Greece is a part of the Asian continent often called Asia Minor. (Today, this area is known as Turkey.) Between Greece and Asia Minor is the Aegean Sea.

■ PRACTICE 32: The Greek Peninsula

Match each description with a term from below. Write the letter of the correct term on the line before each description.

     a. Asia Minor   **b.** peninsula   **c.** the Peloponnesus

_____ **1.** the southern part of Greece

_____ **2.** land that is almost completely surrounded by water

_____ **3.** the land that faces Greece across the Aegean Sea

Greek Geography and Greek Culture

Early civilizations usually rose up in valleys beside great rivers. The Mesopotamian culture developed in the valley between the Tigris and Euphrates rivers. The Egyptian city-states rose up beside the Nile. The Indus Valley people lived by the Indus River. And the earliest Chinese civilization grew up beside the Huang He River. These valleys had areas of rich farmland that were watered by their mighty rivers.

But what about Greece? Its rivers are short and not very deep. There are no large areas of rich farmland. Most of the country is covered by high mountains. What effect did this have on early Greek peoples? For one thing, early civilizations rose up along the coast and on the islands of the Mediterranean, rather than along rivers. For another, the high mountains made travel very hard in ancient times. As a result, people lived in small settlements, each with its own government and ruler. Small farms sprang up wherever there was a patch of earth that could be farmed. Greek farmers raised crops of olives, grapes, and some grain. They raised animals such as sheep, goats, cattle, and pigs.

Why would the coast of a sea be a better site for a city than beside a short, shallow river? Most early civilizations rose up beside great rivers. What advantages does a large river have over the ocean? Write your answers on a separate sheet of paper.

■ PRACTICE 33: Greek Geography and Greek Culture

Decide if each statement below is true (**T**) or false (**F**). Write the correct letter on the line before each statement.

_____ **1.** The earliest civilizations always rose up beside the sea.

_____ **2.** It was hard for people to travel in ancient Greece.

A Legendary Civilization Proves to Be Real

The earliest people in Greece lived along the coast of the Aegean Sea beginning somewhere between 13,000 B.C.E. and 11,000 B.C.E. Between 7000 B.C.E. and 6000 B.C.E., these Aegean people began to farm.

By about 3000 B.C.E., certain groups of Aegean people were making tools from bronze. (Historians call this time the Bronze Age.) They lived on the southern mainland of Greece, on the islands called the Cyclades, and on the island of **Crete.**

Greek legends tell of a mighty civilization that rose up on Crete. These legends speak of a great king named **Minos** who had glorious palaces and a giant maze called the Labyrinth. In the middle of the Labyrinth, the king placed a monster that was half man and half bull. It was known as the **Minotaur.** Minos, it is said, sent young men and young women into the Labyrinth, and they never returned. The Minotaur destroyed them.

Legends are stories passed from generation to generation. Many people believe that they are true. But how much—if any—truth the stories contain is hard to tell. In this case, we do know that part of the legend is true. In the early 1900s, archaeologists discovered a city called **Knossos**

on the island of Crete. In it was a magnificent palace. Other sites were uncovered on Crete. It was clear that a mighty civilization had lived there, beginning as early as 2000 B.C.E. The people of this civilization are sometimes referred to as the Cretans, but they are often called the **Minoans,** after their legendary king, Minos.

TIP

Historians and readers of history must be careful to separate fact from fiction. When you read, be on the lookout for words, such as perhaps, maybe, it is said, some people believe, and legendary. These words are signals from the writer that there is some doubt about the information given. For a date, it means that historians are not exactly sure of that date. For people and events, it means that historians are not sure if these people and events were real.

■ PRACTICE 34: A Legendary Civilization Proves to Be Real

Decide if each statement below is true (**T**) or false (**F**). Write the correct letter on the line before each statement.

_____ **1.** Early Aegean people knew how to make bronze tools.

_____ **2.** The people known as the Minoans were part of a mighty civilization on the island of Crete.

The Minoans

Between 1900 and 1905, archaeologists dug up an enormous palace in the ancient city of Knossos. The palace was five stories high in places and contained close to 1,300 rooms. It had a plumbing system with flush toilets. As the dig continued, other ancient sites were uncovered in Crete.

The buildings and **artifacts** (objects made by people) that were found in Crete can tell us about Minoan life. Some Minoans were farmers.

And some were craftspeople and artists. Some were sea traders who traded Minoan olive oil, pottery, and cloth for goods from Africa and the Middle East.

The walls of many buildings were covered with paintings. In several, one or more young men are shown leaping over the back of a bull. So, we might guess that "bull leaping" was a sport that the Minoans enjoyed watching. Or perhaps it was a religious practice. There is no way to be sure.

The Minoan civilization flourished until about 1500 B.C.E. Then disaster struck. On the nearby island of Thera (now called Santorini), a volcano erupted. Around the same time, several earthquakes struck the area. The Minoans appear to have survived these events, but evidence shows that many of their cities were burned soon after. The civilization never fully recovered. Was Crete invaded and taken over by the Mycenaeans from the Greek mainland? Perhaps. We do know that from about 1450 B.C.E. on, there was a blending of Minoan and Mycenaean cultures.

■ PRACTICE 35: The Minoans

Decide if each statement below is true (**T**) or false (**F**). Write the correct letter on the line before each statement.

_____ **1.** The Minoans traded with people in Africa and the Middle East.

_____ **2.** The Minoans covered many of their walls with paintings.

_____ **3.** The Minoan civilization was destroyed by a volcanic eruption in 1450 B.C.E.

The Mycenaeans

Mycenaean is the name given to a civilization that flourished in south and central Greece between 1600 B.C.E. and 1100 B.C.E. The name comes from the city of Mycenae, where the remains of this civilization were first found in 1876 C.E.

The Mycenaeans began trading with the Minoans around the end of the fifteenth century B.C.E. They soon adopted some of the Minoans' ways. The Minoan writing system became the basis for the Mycenaean writing system, although the two cultures spoke different languages. The Mycenaeans began to do wall paintings in the Minoan style. They also seem to have borrowed the Minoan religion. For the Minoans, a goddess had always been their most important religious figure. She appeared on Crete in many forms—as a snake goddess, as a goddess of the sea, and as a goddess of caves. Around the end of the fifteenth century B.C.E., she began to show up in Mycenaean art. A wall painting from this period shows a parade of people bringing gifts to a goddess.

■ PRACTICE 36: The Mycenaeans

Decide if each statement below is true (**T**) or false (**F**). Write the correct letter on the line before each statement.

_____ **1.** Mycenaean civilization flourished between 1600 B.C.E. and 1100 B.C.E.

_____ **2.** The Mycenaeans and the Minoans did not trade with one another.

The Trojan War

Around 1200 B.C.E., some Mycenaeans are believed to have attacked Troy, a city on the west coast of Asia Minor. The people who lived there were known as Trojans. What we know about the **Trojan War** comes from two epic poems, the *Iliad* and the *Odyssey*, which were written about 500 years after the war. Many scholars believe that these epics were both written by the Greek poet **Homer.**

Homer's poems tell how a Trojan prince named Paris carried off Helen, the beautiful wife of the Greek king Menelaus. Paris brought Helen to Troy. Menelaus called on other Greek kings and their armies to help him get Helen back and to punish Troy. For ten years, the Greeks tried to break through the walls of Troy. Then a clever Greek named Odysseus made a plan to get inside the city. He had a huge, hollow wooden horse built.

Several warriors hid inside. The horse was left as a "gift" at the city gates of Troy. The rest of the Greek army withdrew, as if they were giving up. The Trojans took the horse inside Troy. That night, the Greek warriors climbed out of the horse and opened the gates. The hidden Greek army swept in and destroyed Troy. Helen was taken back to Greece.

For the Greeks who came after Homer, the Trojan War was not merely a legend—it was part of their history. And, in fact, archaeologists in the nineteenth and twentieth centuries dug up the ruins of the ancient city of Troy. They found evidence of a war with the Mycenaeans. Is the rest of the legend true? That we do not know.

IN REAL LIFE

The *Iliad* and the *Odyssey* are an important part of Western literary tradition. Books, plays, and movies have been based on the tales they tell. They have also become part of our language. We use the term *Trojan horse* to describe a hidden trick. We talk about someone's weak spot as his *Achilles' heel.* And we call a journey of discovery an *odyssey,* a word taken from the long journey Odysseus made to return home after the Trojan War.

■ PRACTICE 37: The Trojan War

Circle the letter of the correct answer to each of the following questions.

1. What two Greek epics tell about the war between the Trojans and the Mycenaeans?
   a. *Helen* and *Paris*
   b. *Menelaus* and *Iliad*
   c. *Iliad* and *Odyssey*
   d. *Odyssey* and *Troy*

2. How did the Greeks defeat the Trojans?
   a. They burned the city walls.
   b. They lured the Trojans outside the city walls.
   c. They climbed over the city walls.
   d. They used a trick to get inside the city walls.

A Dark Age?

Around 1100 B.C.E., the Mycenaeans were conquered by a group of people from the north called the Dorians. Greek historians of later centuries tell us that Greece then entered a dark age. (A **dark age** is a time when learning and discovery are not valued and knowledge is kept hidden.) According to these historians, overseas trade stopped. Much of the previous knowledge and art of people such as the Minoans and Mycenaeans were lost. This dark age lasted 200 or 300 years. Then, around 800 B.C.E., the city-states of Greece first appeared. Civilization flowered again.

Some modern historians do not believe this version of Greek history. They point out that these later Greeks greatly disliked the Dorians. They would have considered a Greece under Doric rule "uncivilized." And, in fact, archaeologists have uncovered evidence that trading continued throughout this dark age. They have also discovered that the great city-states did not suddenly spring up in 800 B.C.E. Some had begun much earlier, during the so-called Dark Age.

We know almost nothing about this period. We are not even sure that it was a true dark age. Not until after 800 B.C.E. does the historical record of ancient Greece come alive again. It was then that the great city-states ruled over ancient Greece and led to the famous Golden Age of Greece.

 THINK ABOUT IT

Greek and other historians may have rewritten part of the past. What does this mean for you, a reader of history? Write your answer on a separate sheet of paper.

■ PRACTICE 38: A Dark Age?

Decide if each statement below is true (**T**) or false (**F**). Write the correct letter on the line before each statement.

_____ **1.** A dark age is a time when learning and discovery are not valued.

_____ **2.** Homer's epic poems tell us that Greece entered a dark age around 1100 B.C.E.

_____ **3.** The Dorians may have ruled Greece during its dark age.

LESSON 6: The Rise of the City-States

GOAL: To understand the organization of early Greek city-states, especially Athens and Sparta; to trace the history of these city-states from the Archaic through the Classical Greek periods

WORDS TO KNOW

acropolis	debt	Greek-Persian Wars
agora	democracy	Olympic Games
ally	expansionism	polis
assembly	First and Second	
clan	Peloponnesian Wars	

NAMES TO KNOW

Darius II	Themistocles
Solon	Xerxes

PLACES TO KNOW

Athens	Plataea	Sparta
Marathon	Salamis	Thermopylae

The Archaic Greek Period

Do you know where the word *politics* comes from? It comes from the Greek word *polis,* which meant the kind of city-states that came to power in Archaic Greece. What were these city-states like?

As you may recall, we know very little about what happened in Greece between roughly 1100 B.C.E. and 800 B.C.E. This period is sometimes called Greece's Dark Age.

But beginning around 800 B.C.E., Greek history comes alive for us again. Historians usually call the next three centuries (c. 800–500 B.C.E.) the Archaic Greek period. The word *archaic* means "very old" or "so old that it is no longer in use." The Archaic period refers to the time between the end of the Dark Age and the beginning of the Classical Greek period. The Classical period occurred during the fifth century B.C.E. The word *classical* can be used to describe something that has been around for a long time, is admired and imitated, and continues to be in use.

During the Archaic Greek period, the Greek alphabet flowered. This writing system was based on the Phoenician alphabet. In fact, the word *alphabet* comes from the first two Greek letters, *alpha* and *beta*.

A	α	Alpha	N	ν	Nu
B	β	Beta	Ξ	ξ	Xi
Γ	γ	Gamma	O	o	Omicron
Δ	δ	Delta	Π	π	Pi
E	ε	Epsilon	P	ρ	Rho
Z	ζ	Zeta	Σ	σ	Sigma
H	η	Eta	T	τ	Tau
Θ	θ	Theta	Υ	υ	Upsilon
I	ι	Iota	Φ	φ	Phi
K	κ	Kappa	X	χ	Chi
Λ	λ	Lambda	Ψ	ψ	Psi
M	μ	Mu	Ω	ω	Omega

■ PRACTICE 39: The Archaic Greek Period

Decide if each statement below is true (**T**) or false (**F**). Write the correct letter on the line before each statement.

_____ **1.** The word *archaic* means the kind of city-states that came to power in Greece.

_____ **2.** During the Classical Greek period, the Greek alphabet flowered.

Organizing into City-States

As you have read, the geography of Greece includes high mountains and small areas of farmland. Such geography encouraged the growth of small, independent farming communities. The farmers depended on one another for protection against invaders and bandits. The center of a community was often a walled fortress, where people could go to protect themselves. This fortress was often built on a high hill. The Greek name for it is **acropolis,** which literally means "high city-state." In fact, it was around these fortresses that the city-states developed.

What we know of these city-states dates after 800 B.C.E., although many had begun to form before then. Each city-state was the trading center for the countryside that surrounded it. It was filled with shops and buildings that were built around a central, large open-air market called an **agora.** People went to the agora not just to buy and sell goods. They also came to talk about the news of the day and to exchange ideas.

■ PRACTICE 40: Organizing into City-States

Decide if each statement below is true (**T**) or false (**F**). Write the correct letter on the line before each statement.

_____ **1.** The acropolis was a large open-air market.

_____ **2.** People went to the agora to trade goods and to exchange ideas.

The Growth of City-States

Around the eighth century B.C.E., several large city-states began to mark out their borders, taking over any villages within those borders. In other words, they began to act as separate states. Each state was ruled by one or more wealthy clans. (A **clan** is a large number of people who are related, either by blood or by marriage.) These city-states included Corinth, Megara, Thebes, **Sparta,** and **Athens.**

As these city-states grew in power and population, they began to trade with other countries. They also sent people to other lands, since city-states had limited farmland and resources. These people set up colonies. The colonies were a source of needed goods, such as grain and iron ore. The colonies were also a source of wealth and new ideas. Colonies were set up in Asia Minor and on various Mediterranean islands, as well as in areas that today are part of Italy, France, Spain, and the former Soviet Union.

City-states competed with one another for trade and power. Sometimes, this meant that two city-states went to war. At other times, however, city-states would engage in "symbolic" wars. In these symbolic wars, one city-state competed against another in sports contests. The best known of these contests happened every four years in the city-state of Olympia. The Olympic Games began in 776 B.C.E., as far as historians can tell. This ancient tradition continues today.

IN REAL LIFE

The Olympic Games of today are divided into the Summer and Winter Olympics. Each one occurs every four years on a different site and in a different country. The contestants come from all over the world. Because these games began in Greece, the first nation to march in the Parade of Nations that begins each Olympics is always Greece.

■ PRACTICE 41: The Growth of City-States

Decide if each statement below is true (**T**) or false (**F**). Write the correct letter on the line before each statement.

_____ **1.** Poor farmers ran the early city-states of Greece.

_____ **2.** Powerful city-states set up colonies as a source of needed goods and resources.

_____ **3.** The city-states engaged in "symbolic wars" every two years.

_____ **4.** The Olympic Games began in 776 B.C.E.

The Rise of Sparta

At the beginning of the eighth century B.C.E., Sparta was like most city-states. It was governed by a three-part system: a king, a council of elders, and an assembly (a lawmaking body made up of the male citizens). All three helped make state decisions. But something happened that forced Sparta to change.

In the second half of the eighth century B.C.E., Sparta took over the larger city-state of Messenia and made its people slaves. They called these slaves "helots." There were seven helots for every Spartan, and the helots tried to revolt more than once. To keep the helots "in their place," Sparta became a total military state, unlike any other Greek city-state. Spartan boys were taken from their homes at the age of seven and trained in state military schools. These schools were quite strict, and discipline was very harsh. Men stayed in the military until they were 30 years old. Then they were expected to marry and have strong children. Any children who were born sickly or deformed were killed.

TIP

Today, we use the word *spartan* to describe someone who is very self-disciplined or something that is very simple, with no extras or frills.

■ PRACTICE 42: The Rise of Sparta

Decide if each statement below is true (**T**) or false (**F**). Write the correct letter on the line before each statement.

_____ **1.** Sparta was the only city-state governed by a king, a council of elders, and an assembly.

_____ **2.** In Sparta, sick or deformed babies were killed.

_____ **3.** All city-states were total military states.

_____ **4.** Male citizens between the ages of 7 and 30 in Sparta often volunteered for the military.

The Rise of Athens

The other great city-state of Greece, and the most famous, was Athens. It ruled over the region called Attica. Athens had a splendid acropolis (fortress) with its own water supply. It was protected on all sides by four rocky mountain ranges. It had rich sources of silver (for coins and other metalwork) and of marble (a hard rock used in buildings and sculptures). However, it had poor farmland and not much forest land. Taking advantage of its long coastline, Athens became a trading power, bringing in needed goods, such as grain and wood, by boat.

Today, we think of Athens as the birthplace of **democracy.** But there was a time when Athenian law was less than admirable. The first law code was created around 621 B.C.E. by a lawmaker named Draco. Some of his laws were so harsh that Draco's name has come to stand for legal cruelty. "Draconian" laws are laws that are very harsh and punishing.

In general, Athenian government at that time was run by wealthy Athenian men. Women could not vote. Foreigners, basically, could not vote. The rich had more power than the poor. Farmers often lost their land and went into **debt** to rich landowners. In all, less than half the population could vote and be part of the assembly that helped run Athens.

Around 594 B.C.E., the half of Athens that was out of power was about to rise up against the half that was in power. In other words, Athens was on the brink of a civil war. To prevent this, an Athenian named **Solon** created a new set of laws.

■ PRACTICE 43: The Rise of Athens

Decide if each statement below is true (**T**) or false (**F**). Write the correct letter on the line before each statement.

_____ **1.** The city-state of Athens is considered the birthplace of democracy.

_____ **2.** Around 594 B.C.E., an Athenian named Solon set up the first law code in Athens.

Solon's Reforms

Solon is often called the father of Athenian democracy. He was given the task of reforming Athens's laws to prevent a civil war. His laws, passed in 594 B.C.E., did their job. A civil war was avoided. Below are some important features of Solon's laws.

- All debt was canceled. People who had been made slaves or sent into exile for debt were freed. A rich man could no longer enslave a poor person because he was owed money.

- An appeal process was added to court cases. This gave people more choices when coming into court. It was an early form of trial by jury, but it was not really a true jury system. That would come to Greece about 150 years later.

- The lowest class in Athens could be admitted to the assembly, one of the three governing bodies. No longer would the assembly be made up of only the rich and powerful.

- To be able to run for public office, a man needed a certain amount of money, but he no longer had to come from the upper class of society.

Solon's laws were designed to make the family (and the social class a person was born into) less important than the city-state, or polis. He gave the common man (though not the women or slaves) more power and voice in his government. Still, only wealthy landowners could serve in many government positions. And many free men were not allowed to be citizens of Athens.

THINK ABOUT IT

How do Solon's laws seem truly democratic? How do they seem undemocratic? Write your answers on a separate sheet of paper.

■ PRACTICE 44: Solon's Reforms

Decide if each statement below is true (**T**) or false (**F**). Write the correct letter on the line before each statement.

_____ **1.** By canceling all debt, Solon freed those who had been made slaves or sent into exile because of debt.

_____ **2.** Solon's laws made family less important and the state more important.

The Classical Greek Period

The fifth century B.C.E. in ancient Greece is referred to as the Classical period. Many of the ideas and achievements from the latter half of this time have helped shape the Western world we know today. Many great thinkers and writers of ancient Greece are still studied. Classical Greece is still an important part of our culture.

One great contribution of the Classical period was in architecture. Greek architects created three styles that they used in the making of Greek columns. Columns were an important feature of Greek architecture. The plainest style was called the Doric column. The Ionic column had scrolls (resembling a ram's horns) at the top. The fanciest, the Corinthian column, had leaves carved into the top. These three styles are still used today in Greek Revival architecture.

Doric

Ionic

The Classical period began with war. At the turn of the fifth century B.C.E., there were several Greek colonies in Asia Minor. This region was under the rule of Darius II, king of Persia. In 500 B.C.E., the Greek colonies revolted against Persian rule and asked the Greek city-states to help them. Athens responded by sending 20 ships to the aid of the colonists. Sparta chose to stay out of the conflict.

Corinthian

Darius and his army stopped the revolt. But the Persian king was angered by Athens's support of the colonists. He wanted revenge.

This began a period of tension and warfare between Greece and Persia that lasted for more than a century. The first great battle of the Greek-Persian Wars took place in 490 B.C.E. It occurred near Athens, on a plain called Marathon.

■ PRACTICE 45: The Classical Greek Period

Decide if each statement below is true (**T**) or false (**F**). Write the correct letter on the line before each statement.

_____ **1.** In Classical architecture, Greek architects created three different column styles.

_____ **2.** During the revolt, Sparta supported Darius II.

_____ **3.** Conflict between Greece and Persia lasted for more than 100 years.

The Battle of Marathon

When the Persians set out to take revenge on Athens, the Athenians called on their ally, the Greek city-state of Plataea. (Allies are people who come together for a common cause.) In 490 B.C.E., the Greek and Persian armies met on the plain of Marathon. It was a glorious victory for Greece and a terrible loss for Persia. By the end of the battle, 6,400 Persians lay dead. Only 192 Greek soldiers had lost their lives.

The Battle of Marathon has become legendary. One legend tells of an Athenian general who wanted to get news of the victory back to Athens as quickly as possible. He sent his fastest runner, a man named Phidippides. It is said that Phidippides ran the entire distance—just over 26 miles—without stopping. With his last breath, he gasped out the good news to the Athenians. Then he died.

Does the name *Marathon* sound familiar to you? Long races, known as marathons, are run all over the world today. The marathon is also an event in the Summer Olympics. If you have ever wondered why this race is always 26.2 miles long, now you know. Its length is the distance that the ancient Greek runner supposedly ran to tell his city about a glorious victory on the plain of Marathon.

After their loss at Marathon, the Persians retreated. Soon after, in 486 B.C.E., Darius II died. The new Persian king was his son **Xerxes.** He had plans, but not just for Athens. He wanted to rule all of Greece.

■ PRACTICE 46: The Battle of Marathon

Decide if each statement below is true (**T**) or false (**F**). Write the correct letter on the line before each statement.

_____ **1.** Darius II and the Persian army invaded Greece in 192 B.C.E.

_____ **2.** Athens and Plataea fought together against the Persian invasion of Greece.

_____ **3.** The battle was on the plain of Marathon.

_____ **4.** The Persians won the Battle of Marathon.

Other Major Battles in the War

To carry out his conquest of Greece, Xerxes put together a huge army and a giant fleet of ships. In response, the Greek city-states united in 481 B.C.E. to fight against Persia. Xerxes' fleet had to struggle against storms, losing some ships and men, as it crossed the Aegean Sea from Asia Minor to Greece. But the remaining Persian fleet was still three times the size of the fleet that the Greeks had put together. This giant Persian force slowly pushed back the Greek forces. An army from the city-states of the

Peloponnese, led by the Spartan king Leonidas, tried to make a stand in 480 B.C.E. They stopped the Persians at the mountain pass of **Thermopylae**, but only for a time. When the battle was over, Leonidas and his 300 Spartans, along with many other Peloponnesian soldiers, lay dead. The Persians pressed on into Athens and destroyed the great city.

The Persian fleet now entered the narrow waterway on the northeast coast of **Salamis.** But the Greek commander **Themistocles** and his troops were waiting for them. The Greeks had fewer ships. Their ships were also heavy and hard to manage. Yet the Greeks won at Salamis. Because the battle took place in a narrow waterway, having more ships did not really matter. Nor did it matter which ships could move better. The narrow waterway was so jammed with ships, none of them could move. The fighting was hand to hand.

After the Persian loss at Salamis, Xerxes returned home. His general Mardonius stayed behind with some troops. They fought the Greeks once more—at Plataea in 479 B.C.E. The Greek army, made up largely of Spartans, was again the winner.

■ PRACTICE 47: Other Major Battles in the War

Decide if each statement below is true (**T**) or false (**F**). Write the correct letter on the line before each statement.

_____ **1.** Themistocles was a king of Persia who invaded Greece.

_____ **2.** The sea battle at Salamis was won by the Greeks.

_____ **3.** Thermopylae was the victorious commander of the Greek troops.

The Peloponnesian Wars

To protect themselves from further Persian attacks, Athens created an organization known as the Delian League in 478 B.C.E. The league was made up of various city-states in Attica and certain Aegean islands. (The league gets its name from one of these islands—Delos.) Sparta, on the other hand, belonged to an organization called the Peloponnesian League. The Olympic Games of 476 B.C.E. were the first after the Greek-Persian Wars. The hero Themistocles was there. So were athletes from all over Greece, including Athens and Sparta. There was a show of Greek unity, but cracks were beginning to form.

The problem was Athens's desire for power. It wanted to expand its control. In doing so, it clashed with the city-state of Corinth. This led to the First Peloponnesian War (460–446 B.C.E.), with Athens on one side and Corinth (getting help from Sparta) on the other. The war ended in an uneasy peace that did not last long. Athens once again began to test its power. Other city-states called on Sparta to stop Athenian expansionism (expanding a nation's wealth or size, thereby gaining more power). In 431 B.C.E., Sparta invaded Athens, setting off the Second Peloponnesian War. This war lasted until 404 B.C.E.

Twice, Sparta offered to make peace with Athens, and twice Athens refused. The Athenians clearly thought they could win. Then, in 408 B.C.E., an unlikely alliance was formed between Sparta and Persia. It was formed by Lysander, a Spartan military leader, and Cyrus, the young son of King Xerxes of Persia. Athens lost the war. Sparta now ruled. The Greek unity that had existed during the Greek-Persian Wars was completely gone. Various city-states warred against one another and against Spartan rule. Thebes came to power briefly. All this fighting weakened the city-states.

■ PRACTICE 48: The Peloponnesian Wars

Decide if each statement below is true (**T**) or false (**F**). Write the correct letter on the line before each statement.

_____ **1.** Athens formed the Delian League as a team for the Olympic Games.

_____ **2.** In the First Peloponnesian War, Athens fought against Corinth, which had help from Sparta.

LESSON 7: The Golden Age: The Gifts of Greece

 GOAL: To appreciate how the Classical Greek tradition has contributed to, and continues to influence, our culture

WORDS TO KNOW

amphitheaters	Golden Age	moderation
drama	historical narrative	mythology
fable	lyric poem	

NAMES TO KNOW

Aeschylus	Euripides	Sappho
Aesop	Herodotus	Socrates
Aristophanes	Hippocrates	Sophocles
Aristotle	Pericles	
Democritus	Plato	

PLACES TO KNOW

Mount Olympus	Parthenon

Greece in the Fifth Century B.C.E.

You may be surprised to learn that, in many ways, the ancient Greeks are still alive today. In this lesson, you will find out what gifts we have received from the Classical Greek period.

You have just read about the major historical events in Archaic and Classical Greece. But the Classical Greek period is not necessarily famous for its historical events. It is most famous for its Golden Age. This was a time of great achievements in areas such as architecture (building), drama (plays), literature, science, and philosophy.

Before we begin to explore the Golden Age of Greece, it is important to note that most of what we know about fifth-century Greek culture comes from the city-state of Athens. Other city-states had their great thinkers, artists, and writers. But very little has survived from these places, especially in the way of writings. So when we speak of the Golden Age of Greece, we are mainly talking about the achievements of Athens.

Many historians believe that democracy—the new political system that flourished in Athens and elsewhere in Classical Greece—set the stage for these achievements. Democracy encouraged people to test out new ideas.

■ PRACTICE 49: Greece in the Fifth Century B.C.E.

Decide if each statement below is true (**T**) or false (**F**). Write the correct letter on the line before each statement.

_____ **1.** Most of what we know about the fifth century B.C.E. comes from writings that have survived from Athens.

_____ **2.** The new political system of democracy discouraged the Greeks from testing out new ideas.

Pericles, Democracy, and Architecture

The leader of Athens during its Golden Age was named **Pericles.** He was a great believer in democracy. Under him, people began to be paid to serve as jurors or government officials. This meant that any citizen—rich or poor—could sit on a jury or hold office.

Pericles also supported excellence in art, science, and thought. He encouraged the exploration of ideas. He hired the best artists to work on the public buildings of Athens. And so it was that one of the greatest glories of ancient Greece was its architecture.

Perhaps the highest architectural achievement of the Greeks was the **Parthenon.** Pericles had it built atop the Acropolis to celebrate victory over the Persians. It has come to be a symbol of Athenian greatness. Inside was a gold and ivory statue of the goddess Athena, protector of Athens. The statue, which was 38 feet high, was created by the great sculptor Phidias.

The Parthenon, like many Greek buildings and sculptures, was made of marble. Many workers were needed to cut the heavy stone out of quarries and to bring it out in huge blocks.

The Parthenon

▓ IN REAL LIFE

"Greek Revival" is a style of architecture that was particularly popular in nineteenth-century Europe and America. Most of the government buildings in Washington, D.C., are built in the Greek Revival style. Buildings that have columns supporting a triangle-shaped roof reflect Greek Revival architecture. Look for some in your area.

■ PRACTICE 50: Pericles, Democracy, and Architecture

Circle the letter of the correct answer to each of the following questions.

1. Who was the leader of Athens during its Golden Age?
  a. Pericles
  b. Darius
  c. Athena
  d. Phidias

2. What building came to be a symbol of Athenian greatness?
  a. Acropolis
  b. Parthenon
  a. Olympic Stadium
  d. agora

Greek Mythology

The ancient Greeks believed in many gods. When the gods visited Earth, it was said, they lived on top of **Mount Olympus.** (This mountain is the highest point in Greece.) Thus, the gods and goddesses were also known as the Olympians (of Olympus).

The Greeks passed along stories called myths about their gods and what they did. These stories are known as Greek **mythology.** Below and on page 73 is a chart of the most important gods and goddesses in Greek mythology.

The Twelve Major Gods and Goddesses of Olympus

Name	Title	Symbols*	Comments
Zeus	king of gods	thunderbolt, eagle, oak tree	He was the greatest of all the gods and the husband of Hera.
Hera	queen of gods, protector of marriage	peacock, cow	Many myths tell of her jealousy over her husband, Zeus's, affairs with other women.
Poseidon	god of the sea	bull, trident (a spear with three points at one end)	The second most powerful god, he was Zeus's brother.
Hades	god of the underworld (world of the dead)	often associated with Dis, God of Wealth, because of the riches (such as gold and silver ore) buried underground	He was the brother of Zeus and Poseidon.
Hestia	goddess of the hearth (home)	eternal flame	She was the sister of Zeus. The Greeks began and ended every meal with an offering to her.

*Items associated with or sacred to the god or goddess

(continued)

Ares	god of war	vulture, dog	The son of Hera and Zeus, he was an unpopular god.
Hermes	messenger of the gods, master thief	winged hat and sandals, caduceus (a staff with two snakes curled around it)	One of Zeus's sons, he was admired for his cleverness.
Athena	goddess of wisdom, goddess of household crafts	owl, olive tree	She was Zeus's favorite child. At birth, she leaped full-grown out of his head.
Aphrodite	goddess of love and beauty	myrtle tree, dove	She was Zeus's daughter, born out of the sea.
Apollo	god of Light, god of poetry and song	golden lyre (a small harp), laurel tree, dolphin, crow	He was the twin brother of Artemis and a son of Zeus.
Artemis	goddess of the moon, goddess of the hunt	silver bow and arrow; cypress tree; all wild animals, especially deer	She was the twin sister of Apollo and a daughter of Zeus.
Hephaestus	god of fire, god of metalcraft	ax	The son of Hera and perhaps Zeus, he walked with a limp.

According to mythology, the ancient Greek gods were involved in the lives of humans. They helped people and cities that they liked. Athena looked after the city of Athens, which was named for her. Hera's favorite city was Argos.

The gods also punished those who angered them. The Greeks offered prayers, gifts, and sacrifices to their gods to make them happy. These gods were beautiful and powerful, but they were not perfect. They did make mistakes.

The Greeks worshiped their gods at home, in public places, and in temples. Temples were built as homes for the gods to stay in when they came down to Earth to visit a particular Greek city. Inside each temple was the statue of the god who lived there.

■ PRACTICE 51: Greek Mythology

Match each description with the name of a god or goddess from below. Write the letter of the correct name on the line before each description. Use the chart on pages 72 and 73 to help find the answers.

a. Hermes   **b.** Zeus   **c.** Athena   **d.** Hera

_____ **1.** the king of the gods

_____ **2.** the queen of the gods

_____ **3.** the god who carried the caduceus, a staff that is now a symbol for medicine

_____ **4.** the goddess of wisdom

Greek Drama

The ancient Greeks did not group their writings into categories, such as comic and tragic drama, epic and lyric poetry, or fiction and nonfiction. People in later times created these categories. But ancient Greek writers did create literary masterpieces in all these forms.

A **drama** is a play performed for an audience in a theater. It may have a happy ending (comedy) or a sad one (tragedy). It is generally believed that drama, especially tragedy, was a Greek invention. Drama was a part of Greek religious festivals. The most important of these festivals was for the god Dionysus. Many of the greatest Greek plays were performed at this festival.

Every city in ancient Greece had a theater. In the warm Greek climate, it was possible for them to be in the open air. They were called **amphitheaters.** These large theaters curved around in a half circle with stone seats set into a hillside. So that they could be clearly seen by the audience, Greek actors wore thick-soled shoes that made them appear much taller. They wore masks with large features that expressed their characters' feelings. The mask of a tragic hero had a sorrowful expression painted on it. A comic character's mask had a silly grin.

The earliest Greek plays consisted of a chorus. This was a group of actors who spoke their lines in unison. Later plays, beginning with those of **Aeschylus,** had actors in individual roles. But they still had a chorus. The dramatist used the chorus to tell part of the story and to comment on the action of the play. It was a way to make sure that the audience understood what was happening and what it meant.

Along with Aeschylus, the most important Greek dramatists were **Euripides, Sophocles,** and **Aristophanes.** The first three wrote tragedies. Aristophanes wrote comedies, poking fun at people of his time. All four dramatists' plays are still performed today.

■ PRACTICE 52: Greek Drama

Decide if each statement below is true (**T**) or false (**F**). Write the correct letter on the line before each statement.

_____ **1.** Many of the greatest Greek dramas were performed during the religious festival for the god Aeschylus.

_____ **2.** An amphitheater is an open-air theater with stone seats in a half circle set into a hillside.

Other Greek Literature

The Greeks of the Golden Age enjoyed the writings of earlier Greeks. Athenians celebrated the epic poems that were said to be written by the poet Homer. These poems told of great heroes and great events. (The *Iliad* and the *Odyssey,* you may recall, were about the Trojan War.) The Greeks also appreciated the poetry of Sappho, a woman who is considered one of the greatest lyric poets. (A lyric poem expresses a poet's personal feelings. In ancient Greece, lyric poems were sung.)

The Classical Greeks also read fables that were supposedly put together by a slave named Aesop. A fable is a short tale that teaches a lesson, or moral. The characters in the fables are usually animals, such as foxes, crows, lions, dogs, and goats, who can talk. Have you ever heard the expression "look before you leap"? People use it as a warning to be careful. Below is a retelling of the fable by Aesop that gave us that expression.

The Fox and the Goat

A Fox fell into a well. It was not too deep, but the Fox could not get out. Soon a thirsty Goat came by.

The Goat thought that the Fox had jumped into the well to drink the water. He asked if the well water was good.

"It's wonderful!" cried the clever Fox. "Jump down and try some!"

The Goat jumped in without thinking and began to drink. Just as quickly, the Fox jumped up on the Goat's back and leaped out of the well.

The silly Goat realized that he had been tricked. He begged the Fox for help.

While running off, the Fox called back to the Goat.

"Next time, be more careful!" cried the Fox. "You should make sure there is a way out before you jump in!"

Moral: Look before you leap.

■ PRACTICE 53: Other Greek Literature

Decide if each statement below is true (**T**) or false (**F**). Write the correct letter on the line before each statement.

_____ **1.** Aesop was a woman who is considered one of the greatest of all lyric poets.

_____ **2.** A fable is a short tale with a moral.

_____ **3.** An epic poem tells of great heroes and great events.

Science and History

The Greeks of the Golden Age celebrated reason and logic. To them, a clear argument supported by strong ideas was a thing of beauty. They applied reason and logic to everything: to the natural world around them, to the events in their world, and to their own lives. This led Greek thinkers to take the first steps toward what we call modern science, history, and philosophy.

In ancient Greece, people began to study the natural world and how it worked. They made observations and tested their ideas. An Athenian named Democritus concluded that everything was made up of tiny particles called "atoms." Another scientist, Hippocrates studied the bodies of both sick and healthy people. He showed how illnesses result from natural causes.

Herodotus, a Greek of this period, is often called "the father of history" because of the way he wrote. He wanted to record what happened during the Greek-Persian Wars. He began by collecting information from people. Then he tried to report the events fairly and to explain why certain events happened. His study was the first historical narrative and a model for later historians.

Another Greek historian, Thucydides, is considered the greatest historian of ancient times. His history of the Peloponnesian Wars is still read and studied today.

Have you heard of the Hippocratic oath? Even today, doctors follow the ideals of Hippocrates by promising to do all in their power to help and heal their patients and to lead honorable lives.

■ PRACTICE 54: Science and History

Decide if each statement below is true (**T**) or false (**F**). Write the correct letter on the line before each statement.

_____ **1.** Thucydides and Herodotus were great historians from ancient Greece.

_____ **2.** The Greeks of the Golden Age still influence our culture today.

Philosophy

Many people feel that the greatest contribution the ancient Greeks made was in philosophy (the study of ideas). While Greek scientists and historians studied the nature of the world and of world events, Greek philosophers studied the nature of wisdom. The greatest Greek philosophers were **Socrates, Plato,** and **Aristotle.** All these men lived and worked in Athens.

Socrates used what we now call the Socratic method in his teaching. He did not lecture his students. Instead, he asked them questions to encourage them to think more deeply about their ideas. One question led to another. Plato was one of Socrates' students.

After studying with Socrates, Plato began to teach. He taught that the proper goal of all humans was to try to be as perfect as possible and to do good. He wanted all Athenians to have these four qualities: courage, wisdom, a sense of justice, and **moderation** in all things. Today, we still speak of Platonic ideals.

One of Plato's students was Aristotle. He is considered one of the most influential philosophers of all time. In turn, one of Aristotle's students has become even more famous than his teacher. His name was Alexander the Great.

■ PRACTICE 55: Philosophy

Decide if each statement below is true (**T**) or false (**F**). Write the correct letter on the line before each statement.

_____ **1.** Plato was a teacher of Alexander the Great.

_____ **2.** The Socratic method involves asking questions to encourage thinking.

Greeks Who Were Part of the Golden Age

Below and on the next page are brief descriptions to help you remember some of the ancient Greeks who played important parts in the Golden Age of Greece. Note that some of the birth and death dates are followed by question marks. These marks indicate that the historian is not sure if a date is accurate. The date given is a best guess, based on historical records.

Aeschylus (525–465 B.C.E.) One of the four great Greek dramatists. His tragedies were the first to include two actors in addition to the chorus. Of his ninety dramas, only seven survive today.

Aesop A sixth-century B.C.E. Greek slave. He is believed to be the author of a collection of short tales with morals that are known as fables.

Aristophanes (448?–388? B.C.E.) One of the four great Greek dramatists. He is considered the greatest ancient writer of comic drama.

Aristotle (384–322 B.C.E.) A student of Plato who taught in Athens. His philosophy was based on observation and logic. He was a teacher of Alexander the Great.

Democritus (460?–370? B.C.E.) A Greek scientist who believed that all matter is made up of tiny particles called "atoms."   *(continued)*

Euripides (480?–406 B.C.E.) One of the four great Greek dramatists. He wrote more than ninety tragedies, but only eighteen of them have survived.

Herodotus A fifth-century B.C.E. Greek historian who is known as the "father of History." He wrote about the Greek-Persian Wars.

Hippocrates (460?–377? B.C.E.) A Greek scientist who is known as the "father of medicine." He based his findings on his observations of both sick and healthy people.

Homer A Greek poet who lived during the ninth century B.C.E. He is believed to have written the *Iliad* and the *Odyssey,* great epics about the Trojan War.

Pericles An Athenian leader who died in 429 B.C.E. He is famous for his support of democracy in Athens and for bringing about the construction of the Parthenon.

Phidias A fifth-century B.C.E. Athenian sculptor who oversaw work on the Parthenon. His statue of Zeus at Olympia was one of the Seven Wonders of the Ancient World.

Plato (427?–347? B.C.E.) A Greek philosopher who studied with Socrates. He presented his ideas in *The Republic,* a work that is still widely studied today.

Sappho A seventh-century B.C.E. Greek lyric poet. She is considered one of the greatest poets of ancient times, although only scraps of her poetry have survived.

Socrates (470?–399 B.C.E.) A Greek philosopher who created the question-and-answer method of teaching. His most important student was Plato. Considered by some to be a dangerous thinker, he was forced to stand trial and was put to death.

Sophocles (496?–406 B.C.E.) One of the four great Greek dramatists. His most famous work is a set of three tragic plays: Oedipus the King, Antigone, and Oedipus at Colonus.

Thucydides (?–401 B.C.E.) A Greek historian whose history of the Peloponnesian Wars is still read and studied today.

■ PRACTICE 56: Greeks Who Were Part of the Golden Age

Decide if each statement below is true (**T**) or false (**F**). Write the correct letter on the line before each statement.

_____ **1.** Phidias was a sculptor.

_____ **2.** Aristophanes wrote comic dramas.

The Gifts of the Ancient Greeks

Perhaps the greatest gifts the ancient Greeks have given us are their ideas about how people should live. They believed in being curious about the world. They believed in the importance of reason and logic. They believed in the value of learning and of staying healthy. They felt it was important for people to take part in public life and to be responsible for their actions. The Greeks were certainly not the only ancient people to value such things. But their political system encouraged them to follow their pursuits. As a result, the Greeks were able to explore, discover, and record their findings. And we in the modern world are able to explore, discover, and respond to what they have left behind for us.

■ PRACTICE 57: The Gifts of the Ancient Greeks

Match each description with a name from below. Write the letter of the correct name on the line before each description.

a. Euripides	**c.** Sappho	**e.** Pericles
b. Democritus	**d.** Herodotus	**f.** Sophocles

_____ **1.** Greek leader during the Golden Age

_____ **2.** Greek dramatist

_____ **3.** Greek scientist

_____ **4.** Greek poet

_____ **5.** Greek historian

_____ **6.** Greek philosopher

LESSON 8: Alexander the Great and Hellenism

GOAL: To understand the impact of Macedonian rule on Greece; to appreciate Alexander's impact on and influence over the civilizations of the Mediterranean and Asia

WORDS TO KNOW

descent	Hellenistic
Gordian knot	propaganda

NAMES TO KNOW

Alexander the Great	Darius III
Antipater	Philip II

PLACES TO KNOW

Alexandria	Persepolis
Macedonia	Pharos

Philip of Macedonia

At the end of Lesson 6, you learned that after the Peloponnesian Wars, Sparta was the major power in Greece. But the city-states soon began to fight among themselves for power. Greeks fought against Greeks.

In 359 B.C.E., while all this fighting was going on, a strong ruler came to the throne in a region of northern Greece. The region was called Macedon in those days. We now call it Macedonia. The Macedonians, mostly farmers and shepherds, claimed to be of Greek descent. (This means that they claimed to have Greek ancestors.) But the other Greeks seemed to look on the Macedonians as foreigners. They considered them old-fashioned and "behind the times."

The new Macedonian king was named Philip II. He dreamed of ruling Greece. As the city-states warred with one another, Philip built up a powerful army. He then began to expand his kingdom. By 338 B.C.E., Philip was in control of all of Greece. Uniting the city-states under his rule, he made plans to go to war against the Persians. However, he did not live to carry out these plans. In 336 B.C.E., at his daughter's wedding, he was killed by one of his officers. The reason for his murder has never been learned.

■ PRACTICE 58: Philip of Macedonia

Decide if each statement below is true (**T**) or false (**F**). Write the correct letter on the line before each statement.

_____ **1.** Macedonia was ruled by Philip II in 359 B.C.E.

_____ **2.** Philip II did very little to expand his kingdom or to unite the city-states.

Alexander Takes Over

As a boy, **Alexander the Great** had been taught by the great philosopher Aristotle. Now, at 20 years of age, he found himself king of Macedonia and ruler of Greece. His father had just been murdered. There was unrest throughout Greece.

The young king showed that he could act quickly and coolly in a crisis. He immediately had the two main suspects in his father's murder put to death. He then turned his attention to the rest of Greece. It took him only one year to restore order to the country. Drawing on his military training, he used force when he felt he needed to.

In 334 B.C.E., with Greece under his control, Alexander was ready to carry out the plans his father had made. He set out to conquer Persia. He left behind his general **Antipater** as governor of Greece, along with 12,000 foot soldiers and 1,500 cavalry. He took with him an army of more than 40,000 foot soldiers and 6,000 cavalry. He put Philip's great general Parmenio in charge of the left wing of the cavalry. Alexander himself led the right wing. Supply wagons traveled with the army. Some carried the parts of giant stone-throwing machines that could quickly be put together to attack walled cities.

Alexander stopped at the city of Troy to visit the tombs of the great

Greek warriors Achilles and Ajax, who had died in the Trojan War. Soon after, he met Persian troops sent by Darius III, king of Persia. The armies fought at the Granica River. Alexander's victory at this battle was largely a result of his heroic leadership. He led his wing of the cavalry with a battle cry to Ares, god of war.

■ PRACTICE 59: Alexander Takes Over

Decide if each statement below is true (**T**) or false (**F**). Write the correct letter on the line before each statement.

_____ **1.** Alexander's teacher was the great Greek philosopher Aristotle.

_____ **2.** Alexander took little action when his father was killed.

_____ **3.** Alexander led his own army to victory over the Persians with a battle cry to Ares.

_____ **4.** The king of Persia in Alexander's time was Darius II.

Alexander Takes Egypt

After his first victory against the Persians, Alexander moved east. Heavy fighting followed. Alexander knew that his weary troops and the Greeks back home needed proof of his power. So he staged a piece of wartime propaganda at the town of Gordium in 333 B.C.E. (Propaganda is information that is spread to raise public support for an idea, an event, or a group.) An old legend stated that whoever could untie the tangled knot on an ancient Gordian chariot would rule Asia. Others before him had tried and failed to untangle the Gordian knot. Alexander simply sliced through it with his sword. He "solved" the problem not by figuring it out but by removing the problem. By cutting the Gordian knot, Alexander "proved" he was meant to conquer Asia.

Events soon supported the prediction. Alexander's army fought the much larger army of Darius at Issus later that year. When Alexander charged straight at Darius, the Persian king fled, and his army followed him.

We use the expression "cut the Gordian knot" to describe solving a complex problem in a simple, direct way. Life is full of "Gordian knots"—it is up to us to decide which ones need to be carefully untied and which ones should simply be cut.

Alexander now turned his sights on Egypt, which was part of the Persian Empire at the time. The Egyptians disliked Persian rule and did not fight against the Greek troops. In the spring of 331 B.C.E., Alexander joined together several Egyptian villages to form a city on the Nile that he named after himself—Alexandria. (Alexander would set up cities named after himself throughout his empire.) Once he was made pharaoh, he did not linger in Egypt. He still had the Persian army to conquer. After a few months, he set out after Darius.

■ PRACTICE 60: Alexander Takes Egypt

Decide if each statement below is true (**T**) or false (**F**). Write the correct letter on the line before each statement.

_____ **1.** Alexander cut the Gordian knot so that he could steal the ancient Gordian chariot.

_____ **2.** When Alexander took over Egypt, the Egyptians did not fight back.

Alexander Takes Persia and India

In the fall of 331 B.C.E., Alexander and his army met Darius's troops—for the third and last time—at Gaugamela. Alexander won the battle, but Darius managed to escape. To show his power over Persia to Greece and the rest of the world, Alexander had Darius's palace at Persepolis burned down in 330 B.C.E.

Alexander continued his conquest of Asia, taking over many other kingdoms. During this time, he quarreled with one of his senior officers.

In the end, Alexander killed the man with his bare hands (328 B.C.E.).

In 327 B.C.E., Alexander moved farther east and marched on India. In 326 B.C.E., he won his first major battle in India against a king named Porus and an army that included a force of elephants. His path then turned south, through the Indus River valley. During this march (still in 326 B.C.E.), Alexander was almost killed when an arrow pierced his lung.

By the end of 326 B.C.E., Alexander's empire had stretched from Europe's Danube River in the west to the Indus valley of India in the east. The map to the right shows his empire as it existed in 323 B.C.E.

The empire of Alexander the Great, 323 B.C.E.

■ PRACTICE 61: Alexander Takes Persia and India

Number the events below in the order in which they occurred. Put a **1** next to the event that occurred first, a **2** by the second event, and so on.

_____ **1.** Alexander defeats Darius's army.

_____ **2.** Alexander marches on India.

_____ **3.** Alexander burns down Darius's palace at Persepolis.

_____ **4.** Alexander is almost killed by an arrow.

The End of an Empire

As Alexander spread his control over the civilizations of the Mediterranean and Asia, he and his soldiers brought Greek ideas to these civilizations. In turn, soldiers brought back ideas and information from these eastern lands.

Alexander's dream was to unite the Asian and Mediterranean civilizations into one mighty state under his rule. He did not live to see this happen. In 323 B.C.E., when he was not quite 33 years old, Alexander died after a brief illness. In the 13 years following his father's death, he carved out one of the largest empires in world history. As a military leader, he had been a great planner, a heroic warrior, and a cruel conqueror who killed and destroyed. He had been king of the Greeks, pharaoh of Egypt, ruler of Persia, and master of an empire that stretched over 2 million square miles. But without his leadership, Alexander's empire quickly fell apart. His generals fought one another for control. Finally, what was left of Alexander's empire was divided into three regions: Syria, Macedonia, and Egypt.

THINK ABOUT IT

Now that you have read about his career, do you think that Alexander deserves to be called "the Great"? Why or why not? Write your answer on a separate sheet of paper.

■ PRACTICE 62: The End of an Empire

Circle the letter of the correct answer to each of the following questions.

1. How did Alexander's conquests lead to an exchange of ideas between the east and the west?
   a. He set up schools in the cities that he had conquered.
   b. He divided his empire into three regions (Syria, Macedonia, and Egypt) that could exchange ideas.
   c. His army brought Greek ideas to the lands they conquered and brought back ideas from Asia when they returned home.
   d. He wrote books about the lands he conquered.

2. What was Alexander's dream?
   a. to unite the civilizations of Asia and the Mediterranean into one state, under his rule
   b. to have an empire that covered millions of square miles
   c. to be the ruler of Syria, Macedonia, and Egypt
   d. to return home and live quietly

The Hellenistic Age

Alexander's empire spread Greek culture throughout much of the ancient world. As it spread, it blended with Middle Eastern and Eastern cultures, creating a Hellenistic culture. The Greek name for the country of Greece is *Hellas*. The word *Hellenistic* means "Greeklike." The Hellenistic Age began about 330 B.C.E., when Alexander was in the midst of creating his empire. It lasted until about 30 B.C.E., when the Greeks became part of the Roman Empire.

One of the major achievements of the Hellenistic Age was Alexandria, the city that Alexander had built in Egypt. The city's great buildings included its palace, Alexander's tomb, a school and huge library, a zoo, an athletic stadium, a racecourse, and a theater. The city had two harbors. In one was the famous Pharos (lighthouse) at Alexandria, one of the Seven Wonders of the Ancient World. Alexandria was a city that valued learning. It drew people from all over the Mediterranean and Asia.

■ PRACTICE 63: The Hellenistic Age

Decide if each statement below is true (**T**) or false (**F**). Write the correct letter on the line before each statement.

_____ **1.** The word *Hellenistic* means "for Helen of Troy."

_____ **2.** The Hellenistic Age lasted from c. 330 B.C.E. to c. 30 B.C.E.

_____ **3.** One of the major achievements of the Hellenistic Age was the city of Alexandria in Greece.

TIP

When you study for the Unit Review, try the SQ3R strategy: Survey-Question-Read-Recite-Reread. (1) Survey (look at) the heading for each section in the lesson. (2) Turn the heading into a question. The question for this page could be "What is the Hellenistic Age?" (3) Read the section to answer your question. (4) Recite the answer to all your questions. (5) Reread sections as needed so you can recite all the answers.

UNIT 2 REVIEW

Circle the letter of the correct answer to each of the following questions.

1. Unlike other early civilizations, the civilizations in ancient Greece rose up _____.
    a. along the coast and on islands
    b. in river valleys
    c. high in the mountains
    d. beside deep rivers

2. What is the source of most of our knowledge of the Trojan War?
    a. wall paintings
    b. two epic poems, the *Iliad* and the *Odyssey*
    c. history books that we know were written by Homer
    d. Mycenaean writings discovered by archaeologists in Troy

3. Which of the following statements best describes ancient Greek city-states?
    a. They were usually located next to deep rivers for trading.
    b. Each contained an agora, where people came to buy and sell goods and to discuss news and ideas.
    c. They were usually located in Asia Minor.
    d. They were ruled by the working classes.

4. What ancient Greek city-state is considered to be the birthplace of democracy?
    a. Sparta
    b. Athens
    c. Corinth
    d. Plataea

5. Why did Solon reform the laws of Athens in 594 B.C.E.?
    a. to give the rich more power
    b. to make Athens into a military state
    c. because Athens had no set of laws at that time
    d. to prevent civil war

6. Why do we focus on Athens when we study the Golden Age of Greece?
   a. Most of what we know of the period comes from Athens.
   b. Athens ruled the rest of Greece.
   c. Nothing much was happening elsewhere in Greece.
   d. All the best work of this period was done in Athens.

7. What did Herodotus do that led to his being called the father of history?
   a. He fought in the Greek-Persian Wars and then wrote about them.
   b. He was the first to write a complete history of Greece.
   c. He wrote the first historical narrative and reported events fairly.
   d. both *a* and *b*

8. Which Greek philosopher believed in the idea of "moderation in all things"?
   a. Socrates
   b. Plato
   c. Aristotle
   d. Homer

9. Why did Alexander cut the Gordian knot?
   a. to help the Persians solve a complex problem
   b. to show Greece his power and to help them take the ancient Gordion chariot
   c. to show his power and to prove that he was meant to be the conqueror of Asia
   d. both *b* and *c*

10. What effect did Alexander's empire building have on Eastern and Western civilizations?
   a. The Asian and Mediterranean civilizations became one mighty state.
   b. There was an exchange of ideas between Eastern and Western civilizations.
   c. Cities named after Alexander became centers of art and learning throughout Eastern and Western civilizations.
   d. Asia was divided into three regions.

UNIT 2 APPLICATION ACTIVITY
Democracy in Action

Athens is considered the birthplace of democracy. A democracy is a government in which the people rule through free elections and a system of representation. In Athens and in other Greek city-states, every male citizen could be part of the "assembly." The assembly met only when there was something important to decide. Otherwise, the day-to-day task of governing was in the hands of a small group of people.

Find out about your local government. How is it like ancient Athens? How is it different? Use the section below and on the next page to take notes on what you find out.

1. How is your community governed?

   _____

   _____

   _____

   _____

   _____

2. How are your local government officials chosen?

_____

_____

_____

_____

_____

3. How often are local elections held? Who can vote?

_____

_____

_____

_____

_____

4. How does your community decide on important issues that affect all of you?

_____

_____

_____

_____

_____

Optional Activity: Use the information you have collected to create a brochure on your local government. Family, neighborhood, and community members may be interested in receiving copies of this brochure.

UNIT 3

Ancient India and China

LESSON 9: Ancient India: The First Civilizations

> **GOAL:** To understand the characteristics and history of early Indian civilizations, including the Indus River Valley people and the Aryan invaders who took control of ancient India

WORDS TO KNOW

Buddhism	Hinduism	subcontinent
castes	reincarnation	Vedas
epic	sharecroppers	

NAMES TO KNOW

Aryans	Buddha	Indus Valley people

PLACES TO KNOW

Harappa	Indian subcontinent	Mohenjo-Daro

The Indian Subcontinent

Until the twentieth century, the world knew nothing of India's earliest history. But then archaeologists discovered evidence of a mysterious civilization that was about 4,500 years old. In this lesson, you will find out why this civilization was so mysterious. And you will learn about the invaders who took over this civilization. How did they change India? How did India change them?

To study ancient India, we must consider the whole Indian subcontinent, which is separated from the rest of the Asian continent by two mountain ranges. Think of the Indian subcontinent as a giant diamond divided in the middle by the Narmada River. The bottom half is often referred to as the Deccan Plateau. (A *plateau* is an area of elevated flatland.) This half is surrounded by three bodies of water. See if you can find them on the map on page 96.

The top half of the Indian subcontinent, often called Northern India, has two mountain ranges at its boundaries: The Himalayas are to the east, and the Hindu Kush are to the west. Northern India also contains three major rivers: the Ganges, the Brahmaputra, and the Indus. The name *India* comes from this last river, which flows down from the Kush and empties into the Arabian Sea. The Indus is

The Indian Subcontinent

important for another reason. It was in the valley of the Indus River that two ancient cities were discovered in the 1920s.

■ PRACTICE 64: The Indian Subcontinent

Decide if each statement below is true (**T**) or false (**F**). Write the correct letter on the line before each statement.

_____ **1.** The bottom half of the Indian subcontinent is surrounded by the Arabian Sea, the Bay of Bengal, and the Atlantic Ocean.

_____ **2.** India got its name from the Indus River.

A Lost Civilization—Found!

Thanks to archaeologists, we now know that India gave birth to one of the oldest civilizations in the world. Like the early civilizations of Sumer and Egypt, it began in a river valley.

In the 1920s, archaeologists in the valley of the Indus River began digging into what they thought was a huge burial mound. They called it Mohenjo-Daro, or "hill of the dead." Instead, they uncovered an entire giant city. Another ancient city, known as Harappa, was unearthed several hundred miles upstream. This civilization is sometimes called the Harappan civilization, after the city of Harappa. As the digging continued, hundreds of other sites were found in an area covering almost 500,000 square miles. Clearly, the Indus Valley people had a huge empire. Archaeologists have determined that the beginning of this civilization was around 2600–2500 B.C.E. They believe that it reached its height about 2000 B.C.E., and it continued to thrive until around 1700 B.C.E. The cities of Mohenjo-Daro and Harappa have been among the most studied of all the sites. What were these cities like when the Indus Valley people lived there?

Both cities had orderly streets laid out in a grid of straight lines. Thousands of people lived and shopped in the large brick buildings that made up each city. (Mohenjo-Daro had perhaps 40,000 people, Harappa perhaps 20,000.) Almost every house was connected to sewers and a water supply. In other words, the Indus Valley people knew all about plumbing! They were also skilled craftspeople who left behind finely made cups and vases of silver, bronze, copper, and lead. It is clear that the inhabitants of these cities traded with other cultures. Persian coins have been found at these sites. Pieces of jewelry with beads made of jasper, jade, and turquoise have also been found. None of these stones are native to the valley of the Indus River. It seems that the Indus Valley people also liked to play games. Marbles and dice (with markings just like the dice of today) have been found in the ruins of these cities.

■ PRACTICE 65: A Lost Civilization—Found!

Decide if each statement below is true (**T**) or false (**F**). Write the correct letter on the line before each statement.

_____ **1.** Like the early civilizations in Sumer and ancient Egypt, the earliest civilization in India began in a river valley.

_____ **2.** Archaeologists have found very few clues to the lifestyle of the people who lived in the valley of the Indus River.

A Mystery Yet to Be Solved

The Indus Valley people are still mostly a mystery to us. Scholars cannot figure out their writing, and we know nothing of their language. Some buildings that may be temples have been unearthed at Mohenjo-Daro. Yet, all in all, surprisingly little evidence of religious practices has been found. The fact that some homes are larger and grander than others points to a class system. But beyond these few hints, the social, religious, and political structure of the Indus Valley people is largely unknown.

Most mysterious of all is what could have happened to these people. The evidence shows that their cities were abandoned around 1700 B.C.E. All the crafts in the style of the Indus Valley people, engraved with their writing, date back before this time. What happened? No one knows for sure.

Some people believe that the Indus River flooded, killing many people and causing the rest to flee for their lives into the countryside. Others suggest that the Indus River changed course, causing a drought (a lack of rain resulting in the drying up of the land and bodies of water). Other scholars think that the people may have overused the valley's land, causing famine. A wave of illness might have wiped out the civilization. Still others feel that the Indus Valley people fell victim to invaders. Archaeological evidence does show that warlike tribes of the north invaded India, perhaps as early as 2000 B.C.E. Did they kill off or enslave the Indus Valley people? We do not know. But we do know that these invaders, known as **Aryans,** began a new era in the history of India.

TIP

As a reader of history, you need to be able to sort out facts from opinions. Look for words that writers often use to signal opinions. These include such words as *feel, believe, think, maybe, perhaps, might, it seems,* and *apparently.* Reread the third paragraph above. What clue words can you find?

■ PRACTICE 66: A Mystery Yet to Be Solved

Decide if each statement below is a fact (**F**) or an opinion (**O**). Write the correct letter on the line before each statement.

_____ **1.** Scholars have not been able to figure out the written or spoken language of the Indus Valley people.

_____ **2.** The Indus Valley people might have been killed off by illness.

_____ **3.** The Indus Valley people apparently had no religion.

_____ **4.** The Aryans invaded India from the north.

The Aryan Invaders

The Aryans were a tribe of warrior-nomads who were gifted horsemen. Their homeland was somewhere north of the Indian subcontinent. Around 2000 B.C.E., they began to migrate southward—through Anatolia, Persia, and the Hindu Kush. By 1500 B.C.E., they were settling in the Indus River valley, living in tribal villages and farming the fertile land around the river. These settlers counted their wealth in the number of cattle and sheep they owned and often raided one another's herds to increase that wealth.

What we know about these ancient Aryans comes from a collection of their poems and hymns known as the **Vedas,** the Sanskrit word for "knowledge." Sanskrit was the Aryans' spoken language, and it is the basis for many Indian languages spoken today. When the Aryans first invaded India, they had no written language. The Vedas were passed along from generation to generation by word of mouth. It was not until Sanskrit developed into a written language, centuries later, that the Vedas were actually written down.

Ancient Aryan literature also includes two epics. (An **epic** is a long story in poem form that celebrates the great deeds of a hero or heroes.) One epic is called the *Mahabharata*, or "Great Story." The other is called the *Ramayana*, and it tells of a king named Rama. These famous poems show the Aryans to be a warlike people, ruled by kings they called "rajas," who fought many wars to set up their kingdoms.

■ PRACTICE 67: The Aryan Invaders

Decide if each statement below is true (**T**) or false (**F**). Write the correct letter on the line before each statement.

_____ **1.** The Aryans were a warlike people who invaded India from the north.

_____ **2.** Once the Aryans were in India, they settled in the Indus River valley and began to farm.

_____ **3.** We learned about the Aryans through an ancient collection of their poems and hymns called the Vedas.

_____ **4.** The Vedas were written down by the Aryans in 1800 B.C.E.

From Classes to Castes

In early Aryan society, every man was the head of his household and had many roles: farmer, warrior, and even priest, leading his family in prayers and religious services. As tribes grew, they needed better-trained armies, so some men served only as soldiers. Others became priests, traders, or merchants. Some continued to be farmers. The Aryans had become a society with classes. In India, this class system was organized into a system with major groups called castes. The Aryans felt that they could use this caste system to control the people they had conquered.

The rules of the Aryan caste system were strict. A person was born into the caste of his or her parents and had to remain in that caste. People could marry only other people in the same caste. And they could do

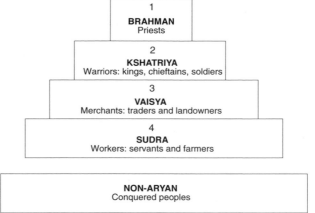

1
BRAHMAN
Priests

2
KSHATRIYA
Warriors: kings, chieftains, soldiers

3
VAISYA
Merchants: traders and landowners

4
SUDRA
Workers: servants and farmers

NON-ARYAN
Conquered peoples

only the kind of work that a person of their caste was supposed to do. The Aryan society had four major castes, as shown on the preceding page.

Many of the workers came from the non-Aryan people that the Aryans had conquered.

■ PRACTICE 68: From Classes to Castes

Circle the letter of the correct answer to each of the following questions.

1. Why did the Aryans create a caste system?
   a. so that each man could be the head of his household
   b. so that they could control the Indian population
   c. so that they could have a better-trained army
   d. so that farm workers could serve the people who were above them

2. Which of the following were in the first caste?
   a. kings
   b. merchants
   c. priests
   d. landowners

THINK ABOUT IT

What would be some advantages of living in a caste system? What would be some disadvantages? Write your answers on a separate sheet of paper.

Life in Ancient India

Ancient Indian life centered around farming villages. There were also city settlements, but none of these cities were as splendid as those of the Fertile Crescent, such as Babylon, Nineveh, Memphis, and Meroë. Neither did they equal the early Indus River valley cities of Mohenjo-Daro and Harappa.

The farming villages of ancient India were scattered throughout a countryside where lions, tigers, and elephants roamed. Some of the farmers in these villages were wealthy landowners who owned slaves and hired workers. A landowner sometimes rented out some of his farmland to **sharecroppers,** who gave much of what they grew (a share of their crops) to the landowner as rent payment.

■ PRACTICE 69: Life in Ancient India

Decide if each statement below is true (**T**) or false (**F**). Write the correct letter on the line before each statement.

_____ **1.** The center of life in ancient India was the Fertile Crescent.

_____ **2.** Sharecroppers did not own land; instead, they rented land and paid the landowner with part of their crops.

Hinduism

The word *Hindu* comes from an ancient Persian word meaning "a person of India." **Hinduism** is the major religion in India today and one of the oldest religions in the world.

After the Aryans settled in India, their beliefs blended with those of the native people of India. The result was a religion that was more a way of life than a set of religious beliefs. There was no single set of gods or goddesses to worship. (For Hindus, all gods and goddesses are different forms of the same god, so worshipers can choose the form they wish to worship.)

According to the Hindu religion, every person's soul has existed since the beginning of time and keeps seeking to reach perfection. When a person dies, the soul in that body is born again in a different body. This is known as **reincarnation.** Hindus believe that any person who lives a good life, performing the duties of his or her caste, may be rewarded in the next life by being born into a higher caste. On the other hand, a person who does not live a good life may be punished in the next life by being born into a lower caste or in the form of an animal.

By the sixth century B.C.E., Hinduism had spread across India. Around this time, c. 563 B.C.E., an Indian prince was born. He would grow up to establish another of the world's major religions—**Buddhism.**

IN REAL LIFE

Hinduism considers cows sacred because they represent all other creatures and give so much to humans—milk, meat, and leather, from which many products can be made. Cows wander among humans on the streets of India. Another Hindu custom involves the pottu, a dot in the middle of the forehead, that many Hindu women (and some Hindu men) wear. This symbolizes their "third eye," or spiritual sight.

■ PRACTICE 70: Hinduism

Decide if each statement below is true (**T**) or false (**F**). Write the correct letter on the line before each statement.

_____ **1.** Hinduism is one of the world's oldest religions.

_____ **2.** Hindus believe that every person's soul has existed since time began.

Buddhism

Siddhartha Gautama was born around 563 B.C.E. and died about 80 years later. His father was a king, which meant that Siddhartha belonged to the warrior caste, the second-highest caste. The young prince could have lived a life of luxury, but he chose not to. Instead, he spent six years as a wandering beggar. Then he began to preach, not in a temple or church but in a park filled with deer. He soon attracted many followers, especially in northern India, and he became known as **Buddha,** "the enlightened one." (An enlightened person is one who has great wisdom and knowledge.)

Buddha, who did not believe in the caste system, preached that to live a good life, a person must be patient and free from hatred and fear. Neither Buddha nor his followers ever organized a church or created a collection of sacred writings like the Hindu Vedas or the Hebrew Torah. Their goal was to set an example for others by living unselfishly and peacefully and by seeking enlightenment. Buddhism had enormous influence throughout the rest of Asia. Today, there are more than 300 million Buddhists in the world. However, although Buddhism began in India, it is not an important religion there today.

■ PRACTICE 71: Buddhism

Circle the letters of the correct answers to each of the following questions. (*Hint*: There is more than one correct answer to each question.)

1. Who was the founder of Buddhism?
    a. an Indian prince named Siddhartha Gautama
    b. a collector of the sacred writings of Buddhism
    c. a priest in a temple
    d. a wandering beggar who did not believe in the caste system

2. What is Buddhism?
    a. one of the world's major religions
    b. a collection of sacred writings
    c. a religion built around the idea of enlightenment
    d. a religion that believes in the caste system

3. Where did Buddha preach?
    a. in the temple
    b. in India
    c. in a church
    d. in an outdoor park

LESSON 10: Ancient Indian Empires and Dynasties

 GOAL: To understand the characteristics and history of India's earliest empires, which were founded by the Mauryan and Gupta dynasties

WORDS TO KNOW

edicts

missionaries

skin graft

vaccination

NAMES TO KNOW

Asoka

Chandragupta I and II

Chandragupta Maurya

Gupta dynasty

Kalidasa

PLACES TO KNOW

Magadha

Mauryan Empire

Chandragupta Maurya Takes Over

Between the fourth century B.C.E. and the fourth century C.E., India came under the rule of two powerful dynasties—the Mauryan and the Gupta. Both dynasties were set up by kings from the kingdom of Magadha. In this lesson, you will learn how each dynasty ruled over an Indian empire and how each had four different rulers. You will also learn about a period of time during one of the dynasties that some have called India's "golden age."

At this period, India was divided into many small kingdoms. Each had its own princely ruler, sometimes referred to as a raja. India's kingdoms were rich in precious metals and jewels, and its rajas lived in luxury. Such wealth attracted invaders.

Around the spring of 326 B.C.E., one of the most famous conquerors of the ancient world marched his army into northwestern India. His name was Alexander the Great. (You read about him in the second unit of this book, "The Ancient Greeks.") For a brief time, India was added to

Alexander's enormous empire. A few years later, Alexander died. A young Indian warrior rose up to drive the Greek army out of India. He was emperor of the kingdom of Magadha, located just south of the Ganges River in northeastern India. His name was Chandragupta Maurya, and he would go on to create the first great Indian empire.

■ PRACTICE 72: Chandragupta Maurya Takes Over

Decide if each statement below is true (**T**) or false (**F**). Write the correct letter on the line before each statement.

_____ **1.** Magadha was an Indian warrior who drove out the Greeks.

_____ **2.** Alexander the Great was the leader of the invading Greek army.

The First Indian Empire

Having defeated the Greeks, Chandragupta Maurya easily took control of kingdoms around Magadha. Eventually, he ruled the whole Punjab, as the northwest region of India was called. Thus, he began the Mauryan dynasty around 320 B.C.E. It lasted about 150 years. (Remember: A dynasty is a ruling family that passes control of the kingdom from one generation to the next.) Chandragupta Maurya is credited with being the first king to unite India under one rule, much like Menes is credited with doing in ancient Egypt.

Chandragupta Maurya expanded his empire to the Persian border and was able to defeat another invasion by the Greek army. Eventually, the Mauryan Empire covered most of the Indian subcontinent and parts of present-day Afghanistan.

Under Chandragupta Maurya, India enjoyed a period of peace and prosperity. Foreign trade expanded. India's trading partners now included China in the east and Greece and Rome in the west. When Chandragupta Maurya died in 297 B.C.E., a second Mauryan emperor came to the throne—Bindusara. Not much is known of his rule. On the other hand, much has been written about the reign of Bindusara's son, Asoka. Asoka's rule began sometime between 272 B.C.E. and 265 B.C.E. and lasted almost

40 years. The first major event in Asoka's reign was a war with the Kalinga people. It made a great impact on Asoka.

■ PRACTICE 73: The First Indian Empire

Decide if each statement below is true (**T**) or false (**F**). Write the correct letter on the line before each statement.

_____ **1.** During Chandragupta Maurya's reign, there was great peace and prosperity in India.

_____ **2.** Asoka's rule lasted almost 40 years.

Asoka, the Buddhist King

During the war between the Mauryans and the Kalinga, one bloody battle ended in the deaths of 100,000 soldiers and civilians. Such horrors turned the warrior-king Asoka against violence. As a result, he turned toward Buddhism, a religion that preaches nonviolence and respect for others. As ruler, Asoka allowed other religions to be practiced in India, but he made Buddhism the official religion of his empire.

Asoka's empire was divided into four provinces, each under a prince or governor. But the government was still organized around the king. Asoka saw himself in the role of a father. "All men are my children," he once said. He tried to improve the lives of his people. He had hospitals built to care for the sick and dying. Along his highways, he had shade trees and rest stops put up to shelter travelers. He had special herbs, used as medicine, planted in the countryside. To spread the word of Buddhism, Asoka had missionaries sent to Egypt and throughout Asia. (Missionaries tell other people about their religion and try to persuade them to believe the same things.)

When you read history, be on the lookout for a cause-effect relationship among events or ideas. The signal words *as a result* in the first paragraph under the heading "Asoka, the Buddhist King" indicate that one event (a bloody war) caused a certain effect (Asoka turning toward nonviolence). Other cause-effect signal words include *because, since,* and *due to* (to indicate causes) and *so* and *therefore* (to indicate effects). Of course, writers do not always include signal words. The reader sometimes has to figure out that one or more causes led to certain results.

■ PRACTICE 74: Asoka, the Buddhist King

Circle the letter of the correct answer to each of the following questions.

1. Why did Asoka turn to Buddhism?
   a. to win a war
   b. to become king
   c. because he disliked violence
   d. because the Kalinga forced him to

2. What did Asoka do to help his people?
   a. planted shade trees
   b. built hospitals
   c. sent out missionaries
   d. all of the above

Asoka's Edicts

About 12 years into his reign, Asoka began issuing public messages. The messages were carved on rock surfaces or on specially built stone pillars that were set up along the highway or in places where people got together. These edicts, or formal statements, were Asoka's way of speaking directly to his people. The edicts were mainly concerned with how people should behave toward one another.

Asoka's edicts set forth principles such as these:

- Do not commit violence against one another.

- Be tolerant of others.

- Respect priests and teachers.

- Be kind to your friends.

- Treat your servants fairly.

Some of these stone messages can still be seen in India today.

Asoka's rule lasted 37 years. After he died, the Mauryan Empire began to fall apart. By 150 B.C.E., India was once again a land of many separate kingdoms.

THINK ABOUT IT

What do you think of the edicts of Asoka that are listed above? Do you think they would have helped his people live better lives? Why or why not? Write your answers on a separate sheet of paper.

■ PRACTICE 75: Asoka's Edicts

Decide if each statement below is true (**T**) or false (**F**). Write the correct letter on the line before each statement.

_____ **1.** Asoka spoke to his people through edicts carved on pillars and rocks.

_____ **2.** Asoka's messages basically told people the news of the kingdom.

The Gupta Dynasty

After Asoka's death, India returned to being a collection of kingdoms. Buddhism, which Asoka had made the official religion, gradually faded away. (It would, however, take hold in other parts of Asia, such as China and Japan.) Hinduism regained its importance in India. The Hindu priests restored the caste system.

The first Indian empire, as you have read, was begun by a king from the kingdom of Magadha named Chandragupta Maurya. The next great Indian empire was also begun by a king from Magadha. His name, too, was Chandragupta. He was called **Chandragupta I** because he established what is now called the **Gupta dynasty.** Chandragupta I came to power in Magadha around 320 C.E. He increased his power and his empire by marrying Princess Kumaradevi, whose family ruled a neighboring kingdom. By the end of his reign, about 10 years later, his kingdom in northern India was large enough to earn him the title maharaja, or "king of kings." His son, Samudragupta, took over after Chandragupta I and began a conquest to make the kingdom bigger still, turning it into the Gupta Empire.

Around 380 C.E., the third Gupta king, **Chandragupta II,** took the throne. He is probably the best known of the Gupta kings. During his reign, India had what has been called a golden age. On the next page are some achievements of this period. This golden age of the Guptas ended after the death of the fourth Gupta king, around the year 467 C.E. This period is still remembered today as perhaps the greatest age in Indian history.

■ PRACTICE 76: The Gupta Dynasty

Decide if each statement below is true (**T**) or false (**F**). Write the correct letter on the line before each statement.

_____ **1.** Under Asoka, Islam became the official religion of India.

_____ **2.** Chandragupta I began the Gupta dynasty.

_____ **3.** Samudragupta's conquests led to the Gupta Empire.

_____ **4.** India's "golden age" ended around 647 C.E.

_____ **5.** Under Chandragupta II, India became weak.

The Golden Age in India

India's ideas and achievements were carried beyond its borders. Arab traders brought Indian spices, cloth, carpets, and jewelry to China, Southeast Asia, parts of Europe, the Middle East, and Africa. They also brought tales of what India had accomplished.

A Golden Age in India

Area	Some Achievements
Art	■ The *Mahabharata* is finally completed. This ancient Aryan epic first began to be written down around 300 B.C.E. ■ Kalidasa writes poetry and plays. He is considered one of the world's great writers. ■ Indian architects and sculptors develop styles for art. These styles became the models for Hindu temples and sculpture.
Science	■ Indian scientists develop the idea that matter is not solid but is made up of tiny molecules. This idea is at the heart of modern atomic theory.
Mathematics	■ The Indians create a numbering system. Taught to Arab traders, this system became the basis of the Arabic numbers we use today.
Medicine	■ Doctors give patients shots to keep them from getting certain diseases. The idea of using vaccination to fight disease did not become part of Western medicine until about 1,400 years later. ■ Doctors perform operations in medical centers. Their operations include setting broken bones, delivering babies, and repairing damaged skin using a skin graft.

■ PRACTICE 77: The Golden Age in India

Decide if each statement below is true (**T**) or false (**F**). Write the correct letter on the line before each statement.

_____ **1.** Kalidasa was an architect.

_____ **2.** Indians did not develop vaccinations until 1400 B.C.E.

■ IN REAL LIFE

As you can see, India's achievements during its golden age were remarkable. What we think of as classical Indian art was established. The basis for our numbering system, which uses what we call Arabic numerals, was actually created in India. Certain ideas that we think of as modern—such as atomic theory, vaccinations, and plastic surgery (skin grafts)—existed way back in the fourth century B.C.E., in India.

Lesson Review

To review the two dynasties and empires covered in this lesson, study the webs below.

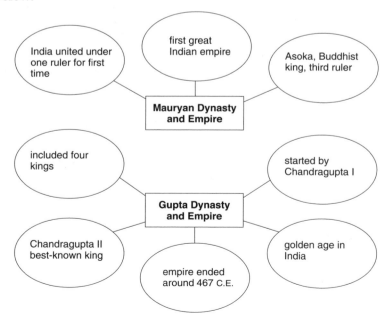

India united under one ruler for first time

first great Indian empire

Asoka, Buddhist king, third ruler

Mauryan Dynasty and Empire

included four kings

started by Chandragupta I

Gupta Dynasty and Empire

Chandragupta II best-known king

golden age in India

empire ended around 467 C.E.

LESSON 11: Ancient China:
The First Civilizations

GOAL: To understand the characteristics and history of early Chinese civilizations, including the Shang and Zhou dynasties

WORDS TO KNOW

bronze casting	feudal system	oracle bones
Confucianism	herbs	philosophy
dialect	monarchy	Taoism

NAMES TO KNOW

Confucius	Shang dynasty
Mandate of Heaven	Zhou dynasty

The Beginning of Chinese Civilization

In 1927, in an area that is now part of the city of Beijing, archaeologists dug up a skeleton of an early human that they called Peking (Beijing) Man. The skeleton served as evidence that there were early humans in China as long as 350,000 years ago.

TIP

There are two systems used to spell Chinese words with the Western alphabet. You can see both in the first paragraph under the heading "The Beginning of Chinese Civilization." The older system refers to the capital of China as Peking. The newer method, the pinyin system, spells it "Beijing." The pinyin system uses an alphabet that the Chinese created in 1956. Most modern texts, including this book, use pinyin spellings.

Chinese legends tell us that Chinese civilization began around 3000 B.C.E. with the Xia dynasty. Legends are stories that are believed to be based on truth but that cannot be proved. There is, in fact, no archaeological or historical evidence to support these legends. But there is evidence that Chinese civilization began in the valley of the Huang He, or Yellow, River. The earliest dynasty that we have evidence of is the Shang dynasty. It began somewhere between the nineteenth and sixteenth centuries B.C.E. and ended in the twelfth century B.C.E.

The Shang Dynasty, c. 1600 B.C.E.

■ PRACTICE 78: The Beginning of Chinese Civilization

Decide if each statement below is true (**T**) or false (**F**). Write the correct letter on the line before each statement.

_____ **1.** Chinese civilization first arose in the Huang He River valley.

_____ **2.** "Shang" is the pinyin spelling of the capital of China.

Fortune-Telling Leads to Writing

Archaeologists have found remains of the Shang people that date as far back as 2400 B.C.E. But it is hard to figure out exactly when the Shang ruling family came to power. Some historians date it as far back as 1900 B.C.E. Others place it as late as 1600 B.C.E. The written records we have may be inexact about such dates. But they do tell us something about the Shang dynasty, its kings, and its people.

Ancient Chinese records are written on **oracle bones.** In early China, it was customary for people to go to fortune-tellers with questions about the future. These questions might be about their luck for the coming week (their week lasted 10 days), whether they would have good fortune on a hunt, or perhaps whether their prayers would be answered.

Before a prediction could be made, the fortune-teller had to prepare an oracle bone. First, he or she bored holes into the shoulder bone of an animal or into the shell of a turtle. Next, the fortune-teller heated the oracle bone until it cracked into T-shaped markings. The fortune-teller's prediction depended on whether he or she thought the cracks were lucky or unlucky. Finally, the fortune-teller scratched words into the bone. These words noted the question, the answer, and details about the period of time when the question was asked. These scratchings are the earliest examples of Chinese writing.

TIP

When you read history, pay attention to the sequence of events. Writers do not always list events in order. When they do not, they often use signal words to help readers figure out the sequence. Look at the first sentence in the third paragraph under the heading "Fortune-Telling Leads to Writing." The word *before* signals that something happened before a prediction could be made (an oracle bone was prepared and heated). As you read, pay attention to signal words, such as *first, after, while, then, next,* and *finally.* Specific dates, of course, also help the reader figure out historical sequences.

■ PRACTICE 79: Fortune-Telling Leads to Writing

Match each event that took place in ancient Chinese fortune-telling with a term of sequence from below. Write the letter of the correct term on the line before each event.

a. first   **b.** second   **c.** third   **d.** fourth

_____ **1.** The fortune-teller interpreted the cracks.

_____ **2.** A person came to a fortune-teller with a question.

_____ **3.** The fortune-teller wrote details on the oracle bone.

_____ **4.** An oracle bone was bored with holes and heated until cracks formed.

Chinese Dialects and Chinese Writing

Ancient oracle-bone writing took the form of pictographs—pictures that stood for ideas and objects. Modern Chinese writing is not very different from its ancient beginnings. Why did the Chinese stay with this form of writing?

The Chinese people have always spoken many different dialects. A **dialect** is the form of language spoken by people in a particular geographical region. Dialects can be so different from each other that two people speaking two dialects of the same language may be unable to understand each other. But no matter what a Chinese person's dialect is, he or she is able to read and understand a single writing system. How is this possible?

The Chinese writing system is not based on an alphabet in which letters stand for the sounds in words. (Do not be confused by the pinyin alphabet. It is only used to spell Chinese words in English.) Instead, Chinese writing is made up of thousands of characters that grew out of the early pictographs of Chinese fortune-tellers. These characters represent— alone or in combination—all the objects, ideas, and relationships needed to put thoughts into writing. So no matter what dialect a writer speaks, the written thought will be understood. Imagine that you are a speaker of English who wants to tell someone who does not speak or read English the following: When three is multiplied by two, the answer is six. If you wrote $3 \times 2 = 6$, both of you would be able to read those characters and understand exactly what was meant.

■ PRACTICE 80: Chinese Dialects and Chinese Writing

Circle the letter of the answer that correctly completes each of the following statements.

1. People in China have always used many different _____ .
   a. languages
   b. dialects
   c. alphabets
   d. writings

2. Modern Chinese writing _____ .
   a. uses the pinyin alphabet to spell words in Chinese
   b. is exactly like the ancient Chinese pictographs that were used in telling fortunes
   c. is made up of thousands of characters that stand for objects and ideas
   d. is similar to English writing

Ancient Chinese Medicine

Chinese medicine is as old as Egyptian and Mesopotamian medicine. According to legend, the first Chinese medical book was written in about 2700 B.C.E. Chinese doctors continued to add to this store of knowledge. Over the centuries, they compiled more than 16,000 medicines.

Most ancient Chinese cures relied on herbs. Herbs are plants that are used as medicines or to flavor food. The most important medicinal herbs for the Chinese were ginseng and ephedra. (The Chinese used the plant's fluid, or *mahuang*, which we know as ephedrine.) Other cures came from a variety of other sources, including fossilized mammoth bones, musk ox stomachs, scorpions, and powdered tiger bones.

Several of these ancient treatments and practices are still in use today. For example, the early Chinese believed in the value of eating right and exercising to keep the body healthy. Long before Western medicine began using vaccines, and even before doctors in ancient India were developing their vaccines, Chinese doctors had a treatment based on the principle of vaccination. They removed small amounts of germs from a sick person and gave them to a healthy person to help the healthy person fight off the full strength of the disease. Other ancient Chinese practices involved massage and acupuncture, which are still in use today.

IN REAL LIFE

Ephedrine was brought to the United States from China in the 1920s by a doctor working in Beijing. It was found to shrink blood vessels and stop heavy bleeding. It is now also used to help people who have asthma. For a while, it was used as a weight-loss drug, but it was found to be too dangerous for this purpose.

■ PRACTICE 81: Ancient Chinese Medicine

Decide if each statement below is true (**T**) or false (**F**). Write the correct letter on the line before each statement.

_____ **1.** Chinese medical knowledge can be traced back to ancient times.

_____ **2.** Most ancient Chinese cures required herbs, which were made from powdered animal bones.

_____ **3.** Some Chinese treatments, such as acupuncture, massage, and vaccination, are still used today.

The Shang Dynasty and Its Achievements

The Shang kings ruled over a land that stretched east from Mongolia to the Pacific Ocean. Like many other civilizations, China under the Shang dynasty was a society of classes. The noble class, which was made up of the rich and powerful, ruled over the common people (craftspeople and farmers). They also ruled over slaves.

Most people in Shang China were farmers. They grew crops, such as millet, and raised animals, such as chickens and pigs. Some also kept silkworms, which spun threads that could be used to make the cloth that we call silk.

A major achievement of the Shang period was the development of **bronze casting.** This was a process that involved making a mold around clay, scraping out the clay, and filling the mold with bronze that had been heated to the melting point. Shang bronze casters used this process to create sculptures, pots, bowls, and parts of chariots.

The Shang dynasty began to lose its power late in the twelfth century B.C.E. Its army was fighting native tribes in the east and nomads in the north. The nomads were ruled by the royal house of Zhou. Around 1111 B.C.E., the Zhou army defeated the Shang.

■ PRACTICE 82: The Shang Dynasty and Its Achievements

Circle the letter of the answer that correctly completes each of the following statements.

1. Most people in Shang China were _____.
   a. craftspeople
   b. farmers
   c. slaves
   d. nobles

2. A major achievement of Shang China was _____.
   a. farming
   b. raising silkworms
   c. defeating the Zhou
   d. developing bronze casting

The Zhou Dynasty Takes Over

As you have just read, the Zhou dynasty defeated the Shang around 1111 B.C.E. The Zhou went on to establish a dynasty that lasted longer than any other in China's history.

The Zhou dynasty adopted many of the ways of the Shang, including the art of bronze casting. But the Zhou also introduced changes, such as the creation of a Chinese feudal system. Throughout the country, feudal states were set up in key locations. Each state was run by a feudal lord. The Zhou king had given this noble the land and the power to run it. The lord lived in a walled city, protected by his troops. The people in his state (which could include lands around the city or just the city itself) worked for the lord. The lord, in turn, worked for the Zhou king.

The Zhou kings claimed that they had been given something called the Mandate of Heaven. (A mandate is a command that gives someone the right to do something.) Zhou Chinese believed that their kings had been selected by the gods to rule the country. This belief is very similar to the belief that rose up later in Medieval Europe, "the divine right of kings." Laying claim to the Mandate of Heaven was a way for each new Zhou leader to persuade the Chinese people to accept him and his rule.

Of course, this mandate could also be used against a king. If disaster happened during his reign, for example, the people could claim that the ruler had lost the mandate. They were then justified in rebelling against him. Such things would happen later in the Zhou dynasty. But for the first 200 years or so, Zhou China enjoyed peace and prosperity.

■ PRACTICE 83: The Zhou Dynasty Takes Over

Decide if each statement below is true (**T**) or false (**F**). Write the correct letter on the line before each statement.

_____ 1. The feudal system was an organization of states run by lords who were loyal to the king.

_____ 2. The Mandate of Heaven described who could and could not be a feudal lord.

Achievements of the Zhou Dynasty

Although the Zhou dynasty began with a period of peace and prosperity, it went on to have many periods of unrest and uprisings. Various Zhou states fought against one another for control of the throne. For this reason, the Zhou dynasty is generally divided into two major periods, as shown in the diagram below.

Even with all this unrest, however, much was accomplished during the Zhou dynasty. For example, the government took care of the sick and the elderly. Also, public works were built from tax money. These works included irrigation systems to water crops, dams to control flooding, and highways to connect the empire.

WESTERN ZHOU	EASTERN ZHOU
c. 1111–770 B.C.E.	770–221 B.C.E.

Archaeologists have recovered many beautiful art objects that were created during this period, such as bronze mirrors, bronze and marble statues, and ornaments decorated with turquoise and jade (a stone that is often green). Musical instruments have also been found, such as bells, pipes, drums, flutes, and stringed instruments.

Across Zhou China, centers of trade sprang up. Written records and archaeological evidence show that the wealthy bought and sold goods such as bronze and gold jewelry, silk, and ceramics. There was also heavy trade in iron weapons and tools.

■ PRACTICE 84: Achievements of the Zhou Dynasty

Decide if each statement below is true (**T**) or false (**F**). Write the correct letter on the line before each statement.

_____ **1.** At the beginning of the Zhou dynasty, there was a time of peace and prosperity.

_____ **2.** There was not much trade during the Zhou dynasty.

_____ **3.** Archaeologists have found many beautiful works of art from the Zhou dynasty.

_____ **4.** The Eastern Zhou period came after the Western Zhou period.

Cultural Change

Between the eighth century B.C.E. and 221 B.C.E., Zhou China struggled through bloody wars, a changing society, and a flood of new ideas. Out of all this, a unified China emerged.

The greatest change during this time was the breakup of the Chinese feudal system. During the first centuries of the Zhou dynasty, feudal states and lords had grown in power. It became harder and harder for a single royal house to keep control. One set of nobles plotted against another. Battles broke out. Bit by bit, the feudal system fell apart. In the end, the

Zhou feudal system was replaced by a monarchy. A **monarchy** is a central government ruled by a king.

As feudalism fell away, there was great social change. Farmers and merchants who had previously worked for their feudal lords now worked for themselves. The upper class no longer consisted of just kings, nobles, and warriors, but also of great thinkers and teachers. And soldiers were no longer drawn from the upper class alone. In feudal times, nobles were trained in warfare, learning to handle weapons and horse-drawn chariots. Gradually, noble warriors gave way to professional soldiers who traveled mostly on foot. Battles were now fought by armies of foot soldiers, with some cavalry support.

Political and social change was accompanied by a flood of new ideas. One of the great thinkers of this time was named K'ung Fu-tzu. He is better known by his Latin name—**Confucius.** You will learn about Confucius and his ideas in the next section.

■ PRACTICE 85: Cultural Change

Decide if each statement below is true (**T**) or false (**F**). Write the correct letter on the line before each statement.

_____ 1. Under the feudal state, soldiers were drawn only from the upper classes.

_____ 2. Under the monarchy, all soldiers were noblemen.

_____ 3. Under the feudal state, farmers and merchants worked for themselves.

_____ 4. Under the monarchy, teachers and thinkers could be members of the upper class.

Confucius and Confucianism

K'ung Fu-tzu ("Great Master Kung"), better known as Confucius, was born in 551 B.C.E. He is probably the most famous person of ancient China.

His teachings, known as **Confucianism,** became the model for official and personal behavior in China—a model that lasted almost 2,000 years, well into the twentieth century.

Confucius, like others of his day, saw the feudal system collapse. And, like others, he worried what would come next. He developed a **philosophy,** or approach to life, that focused on the need for order. He taught that everyone had a place in society, that people needed to respect one another, and that they needed to respect authority.

At the center of Confucianism is a quality called *qen* (pronounced "chen"). The word means showing kindness and love to others as well as having a sense of duty toward others. Anyone can develop *qen*. Confucian society was not based on social classes but on learning. A man did not achieve great leadership by being born into the noble class. He did it by becoming a wise and learned person who then set an example for his people.

▨ THINK ABOUT IT

Why do you think Confucianism was so popular with the people of the late Zhou dynasty? (*Hint*: Remember what changes were happening in China at the time.) Write your answer on a separate sheet of paper.

■ PRACTICE 86: Confucius and Confucianism

Decide if each statement below is true (**T**) or false (**F**). Write the correct letter on the line before each statement.

_____ **1.** Confucianism became the model for Chinese behavior for about 2,000 years.

_____ **2.** Confucius developed a philosophy that focused on the collapse of the feudal system.

_____ **3.** In Confucianism, a leader follows the example that his people set.

Taoism and Lao-Tzu

Next to Confucianism, Taoism was the most important Chinese philosophy of this period. It arose around the same time as Confucianism. It got its name from the Chinese word *tao*, which can be translated as "the road" or "the way."

Confucianism was concerned with social order and social conduct. Confucius saw himself as an adviser to heads of state, instructing them on how to behave properly as they ran the government. Taoism did not concern itself with leaders and governments. In fact, it taught that the best government was the one that governed the least. The Taoist philosophy focused on the individual. Each person, it taught, should lead a simple life, living in harmony with nature. Because Taoism scorned wealth and power, it appealed to the common people.

The teachings of Taoism are sometimes linked to a person named Lao-tzu ("the old Master"). Lao-tzu was a philosopher who supposedly lived at the same time as Confucius. Some people believe he was actually a man named Lao Tan, who was an archivist (keeper of records) during this period. Whether he was real or not, Lao-tzu is often honored by Taoists as a founder of Taoism.

■ PRACTICE 87: Taoism and Lao-tzu

Decide if each statement below is true (**T**) or false (**F**). Write the correct letter on the line before each statement.

_____ 1. *Tao* is a Chinese word that means "the road" or "the way."

_____ 2. Historians have proved that Lao-tzu developed Taoism.

_____ 3. Taoism focuses on social order and social conduct.

_____ 4. The goal of Taoism is to live simply, in harmony with nature.

LESSON 12: Ancient China: The Qin and Han Dynasties

GOAL: To understand the characteristics and history of ancient China's later dynasties, the Qin and the Han

WORDS TO KNOW

civil service	empress dowager	standardization
emperor	mandarins	weights and measures

NAMES TO KNOW

Great Wall of China	Qin dynasty
Han dynasty	Shih Huang-ti

PLACE TO KNOW

Silk Road

The Qin Dynasty Brings Order

The two dynasties that came after the Zhou made important contributions to China—and to the world. In this lesson, you will learn about the contributions of these two dynasties—the Qin and the Han.

The last part of the Zhou dynasty has been given the name Warring States Period. The winners of this struggle for control of China were the Qin. They were a warlike people from northwestern China.

In 221 B.C.E., the Qin dynasty began with Shih Huang-ti, who claimed the title of emperor. The new emperor quickly moved to unite and bring order to his empire. He began by making himself the only source of power. He divided the country into districts and appointed a governor to oversee each district. But all the taxes that the governors collected from the people in their districts went to the emperor. The last of the feudal system in China was now gone. A monarchy was officially in its place.

Shih Huang-ti made a number of other important reforms. He had a system of highways built so that his troops could move easily from one place to another. He also brought standardization to the huge country. Emperor Shih Huang-ti decreed that the same system of writing be used throughout the country. He wanted his commands to be understood by everyone. He also standardized trade by ordering the people to use the same system of weights and measures everywhere in China. And everyone had to use the same round bronze coins.

■ PRACTICE 88: The Qin Dynasty Brings Order

Decide if each statement below is true (**T**) or false (**F**). Write the correct letter on the line before each statement.

_____ **1.** Shih Huang-ti did little to unite and bring order to his empire.

_____ **2.** During the Qin dynasty, the same system of weights and measures was used throughout China.

The End of the Qin Dynasty

To protect his country from northern invaders, Emperor Shih Huang-ti had hundreds of thousands of workers build a giant wall. This double wall, which could be patrolled by troops, was started around 214 B.C.E. Ten years later, the wall stretched more than 1,000 miles to the west, from the Yellow Sea to the edge of Tibet. It is known as the **Great Wall of China.**

The emperor also did things that he felt would protect the minds of his subjects. He dealt harshly with any thinkers who spoke out against him. And he made sure that the only books that the public could read were about "safe" subjects that did not threaten to create unrest, such as gardening and herbal medicine.

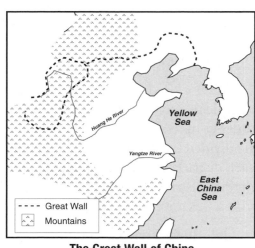

The Great Wall of China

Shih Huang-ti died around 210 B.C.E. while touring his empire. His younger son took the throne. The son was a weak emperor who ruled for just four years. In all, the Qin dynasty lasted only 15 years.

IN REAL LIFE

The Qin dynasty may not have lasted long, but it had two long-lasting effects: the Great Wall of China, which was later extended and which is a major tourist attraction in China today; and the Qin (pronounced "chin") name, which became associated with the name of the country it ruled so briefly—China.

■ PRACTICE 89: The End of the Qin Dynasty

Decide if each statement below is true (**T**) or false (**F**). Write the correct letter on the line before each statement.

_____ **1.** Shih Huang-ti had the Great Wall of China built as a tourist attraction.

_____ **2.** The emperor tried to control his people by punishing those who spoke out against him and by limiting the kinds of books the public could read.

The Han Dynasty

The **Han dynasty** began in 202 B.C.E. One after another, 12 members of the same ruling family (the Liu family) came to power. Then, in 9 C.E., the line was broken when an outsider named Wang Mang took control of the throne. He reigned until around 25 C.E., when the royal house of Liu was restored to the throne. From then until 220 C.E., 14 rulers from the house of Liu were in power. In 220 C.E., the Han dynasty was overthrown. A China that had been united under the Han was then broken into three different kingdoms.

The Han dynasty is always thought of as a single dynasty. But the brief break in the line of rulers has led historians to split the dynasty into two sections, as shown on the next page.

The Han Dynasty	
Xi (Western) Han c. 202 B.C.E. – 9 C.E.	Tung (Eastern) Han 9–220 C.E.

The Han dynasty is often considered a model for monarchs to follow. Han rulers are given credit for 400 years of strong rule with only a few short periods of unrest and disorder. In fact, the opposite is true. There were more times of struggle, violence, and confusion during the Han dynasty than there were times of peace and order. But no one disagrees with the statement that, during the Han dynasty, there were great changes and major achievements.

■ PRACTICE 90: The Han Dynasty

Decide if each statement below is true (**T**) or false (**F**). Write the correct letter on the line before each statement.

_____ **1.** During the Han dynasty, there was great peace and order with only a few short periods of violence and unrest.

_____ **2.** There were many changes and great achievements during the Han dynasty.

_____ **3.** All of the rulers of the Han dynasty were from the Liu family.

Han Law and Government

Possibly the greatest contribution that the Han dynasty made to China was in the area of civil service. Civil service can be thought of as the business of running a government. It includes those branches of government that are not legislative (lawmakers), judicial (courts of law), or military. Civil servants are hired to do government jobs.

One of the problems the Han government faced was finding honest men to work in the civil service. (These civil servants are called mandarins by people in the West.) The Han government developed a system to bring young men into the civil service and to make sure that the best people got promoted. The system offered young men jobs as clerks. These jobs were open to all men, rich or poor. (The civil service was not open to women.) They could earn a living as they received training, and they had a chance to prove themselves. Those who did the best job were given more responsibility.

The Han government was clearly a monarchy. The center of power was the emperor—or, in some cases, the empress dowager. The empress dowager was the favorite wife of the emperor (who usually had several wives). Her son was expected to become the next emperor. Sometimes, there was no son to take the throne or the son was young and weak. In these cases, the empress dowager was the real power. For example, after the first Han emperor died in 195 B.C.E., his widow Kao-hou ran the government until her death.

■ PRACTICE 91: Han Law and Government

Match each description with a term from the list below. Write the letter of the correct term on the line before each description.

    a. mandarins   **b.** empress dowager   **c.** civil service

_____ **1.** Perhaps the greatest contribution the Han dynasty made to China was in this area.

_____ **2.** This is the Western name for China's civil servants.

_____ **3.** She was the emperor's favorite wife, who sometimes ran the government until a son could take over.

Industry and Trade

The Han government controlled industry and trade in various ways. Government agencies were set up around 117 B.C.E. to oversee the mining (digging up), manufacturing (turning into products), and selling of metal. The standardization of coins, begun in the Qin dynasty, was completed by the Han. In 112 B.C.E., the minting, or making, of coins was limited to state agencies.

In the early years of the Han dynasty, the Great Wall of China was not well cared for. But later on, when there were threats of invasion from the north by the Xiung-nu people of Central Asia, the wall was repaired. Troops were stationed along its length. And more work was done to extend the wall to the northwest. By about 100 B.C.E., travelers and merchants felt protected by the wall all the way across China to the Taklimakan Desert.

At this point, new trade routes around the desert were set up. They came to be known by the single name Silk Road. These routes ran from China, across Asia, all the way to the Mediterranean. Chinese exports, such as silk, could thus be carried all the way to Europe. The Han government controlled this export trade. In spite of such trade, contact between China and the rest of the world was limited. (Most of the merchants dealing in Chinese goods were Arabic.) Some officials from Japan did come to the Han court (where the emperor lived) around 57 C.E. About 97 C.E., a group of Chinese officials tried but failed to visit the West. Visitors from Rome came to China by ship in 166 C.E.

■ PRACTICE 92: Industry and Trade

Circle the letter of the correct answer to each of the following questions.

1. Which of the following is NOT a part of industry and trade that the Han government controlled?
   a. the mining of metal
   b. the minting of coins
   c. the Xiung-nu people to the north
   d. export trade

2. What was the Silk Road?
   a. a path along the Great Wall of China
   b. routes around the Taklimakan Desert
   c. one long road from China to Rome
   d. a silk-covered path for the emperor

Cultural and Technological Developments

The growth of the Han government and its civil service depended on the development of education, literary achievements, and technology. The government needed to keep records and send out communications. But the only writing materials were wooden strips and pieces of silk. Around 105 C.E., a major development in world history occurred in China: the invention of paper.

THINK ABOUT IT

Why was the invention of paper so important? What advantages does paper have over ancient writing materials—Sumerian stone tablets, Egyptian papyrus, and Chinese wooden strips and silk? Write your answers on a separate sheet of paper.

The written vocabulary of the Chinese grew during the Han dynasty. The first Chinese dictionary, which was put together around 100 C.E., included more than 9,000 characters. The Han government ordered the works of Confucius to be collected and published. Other great books of this period include the *Shih Ching* ("Classic of Poetry") and the *I Ching* ("Classic of Changes"). Han scientists wrote textbooks on subjects such as chemistry and zoology.

Along with paper, there were other important inventions and discoveries. Magnetic rocks (lodestones) came to be used as compasses to determine direction. Water clocks and sundials were used to keep time. Mathematicians divided the year into 365 1/4 days, the measurement that we use today. Han Chinese also invented the rudder to steer ships, the wheelbarrow, the suspension bridge, the metal stirrup, and the fishing reel.

During the Han dynasty, a new religion arrived from India—Buddhism. Buddhist missionaries spread the new faith to the Chinese people. It later became the main religion of China.

■ PRACTICE 93: Cultural and Technological Developments

Decide if each statement below is true (**T**) or false (**F**). Write the correct letter on the line before each statement.

_____ **1.** A major development in world history, the invention of silk, occurred in China in 105 C.E.

_____ **2.** Missionaries traveling the Silk Road brought Confucianism to China.

A Time of Confusion

By the end of the second century C.E., the Han dynasty had all but disappeared. No longer was there a strong central government. China had entered a period of unrest and warfare, as one warlord and his army fought against another. Out of this fighting, the Three Kingdoms rose up: the Wei in the north, the Shu in the west, and the Wu in the south and east.

For a brief time, from 265 C.E. until around 317 C.E., a dynasty known as the Western Qin united the country again and brought peace. But after a while, powerful princes began to fight with the government and with one another. There was widespread famine. Nomads were invading from the north. Finally, about 20 years into the fourth century, China split apart.

The Eastern Qin took control of southern China. Northern China was divided into many small states run by a series of short-lived dynasties. Many of these dynasties were set up by nomad invaders, including the Xiung-nu, the Mongolians, and the Tibetans. This period in northern China is usually called the Sixteen Kingdoms.

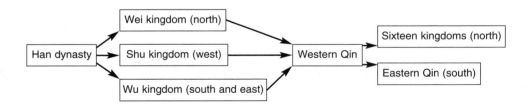

Through all of these changes, however, China remained united as a culture. For one thing, the Buddhist Age of China began in the fourth century, in both the south and the north. Buddhism united the Chinese under a common philosophy and way of looking at life. For another thing, the invaders who were occupying the north took up Chinese ways.

■ PRACTICE 94: A Time of Confusion

Circle the letter of the correct answer to each of the following questions.

1. What was happening to the Han dynasty at the end of the second century?
   a. It was getting stronger.
   b. It was disappearing.
   c. It was in a state of unrest.
   d. both *b* and *c*

2. Who took control of southern China?
   a. the Southern Qin
   b. the Western Qin
   c. the Northern Qin
   d. the Eastern Qin

UNIT 3 REVIEW

Circle the letter of the correct answer to each of the following questions.

1. How was ancient India's earliest civilization different from the early civilizations of Sumer and ancient Egypt?
   a. It began in a river valley.
   b. It had a system of writing.
   c. The inhabitants traded with other cultures in the ancient world.
   d. The inhabitants left their cities behind and disappeared.

2. Which of the following best describes Hinduism?
   a. It is an ancient Persian religion.
   b. It is a belief in a certain set of gods and goddesses.
   c. It is based on the teachings of Buddha.
   d. It is a blend of Aryan religious beliefs and the religious ideas of the native Indian people.

3. The Mauryan and Gupta dynasties were similar in many ways. Which of the following statements about these dynasties is false?
   a. A king from Magadha began both dynasties.
   b. During both dynasties, there was a golden age in India.
   c. Indian products were traded in China during both dynasties.
   d. The first king of both dynasties was named Chandragupta.

4. What was one of the great medical achievements of the fourth century B.C.E. in India?
   a. the use of vaccinations to prevent disease
   b. the setting up of hospitals and roadside shelters
   c. the creation of the number system on which our modern-day number system is based
   d. the treating of the wounded during the war with the Kalinga

5. What is the first dynasty in China for which there is archaeological and historical evidence?
   a. the Xia dynasty
   b. the Shang dynasty
   c. the Zhou dynasty
   d. Peking Man

6. Which of the following is a major achievement of the Shang dynasty?
   a. bronze casting
   b. irrigation systems
   c. fortune-telling
   d. dialects

7. How are Confucianism and Taoism similar?
    a. They are both popular philosophies that began in China during the Zhou dynasty.
    b. They were both models for official and personal behavior in China.
    c. They both teach that the best government is one that governs least.
    d. They both teach that people must respect authority.

8. What important structure was first built during the Qin dynasty?
    a. the Silk Road
    b. the feudal system
    c. the Great Wall of China
    d. the system of weights and measures

9. Why is the Han dynasty divided into Western and Eastern Han?
    a. For a brief time, between the two divisions, there was a break in the line of Han emperors.
    b. There were different rulers in Western and Eastern China during the Han dynasty.
    c. Powerful princes fought against one another, splitting China into two kingdoms.
    d. The Han dynasty lasted for such a long time.

10. What major development in world history happened around 105 C.E.?
    a. Buddhism, a major world religion, came to China in that year.
    b. The Great Wall of China was finally finished.
    c. Paper was manufactured in China.
    d. The first civil service came into existence.

UNIT 3 APPLICATION ACTIVITY
What Confucius Said

The sayings of Confucius are gathered together in a collection called the Analects. Below are some sayings from this collection that have been translated into English. What does each one mean? Imagine that you are explaining each saying to a young child. Write the saying in your own words, in the space provided.

■ What you do not wish for yourself, do not do to others.

_____

_____

_____

_____

_____

■ Virtue is not solitary. It always has neighbors.

_____

_____

_____

_____

_____

- It is in the cold of winter that you see how green the pines and cypresses are.

_____

_____

_____

_____

_____

- A promise easily made may be hard to keep.

_____

_____

_____

_____

_____

Optional Activity: Confucius also said, If a man can steer his life straight, the tasks of government should be no problem for him. If he cannot steer his own life straight, how could he steer other people straight? Think of politicians who are in the news at the moment. Does this saying apply to any of them? Write your opinion on a separate sheet of paper. Use examples to support your opinion.

UNIT 4
The Ancient Romans

LESSON 13: Ancient Italy and the Early Republic of Rome

GOAL: To learn about the early civilizations of ancient Italy, notably the Etruscans and the Latins, and to understand their impact on the early development of Rome

WORDS TO KNOW

citizen	republic	tribune
consuls	Senate	veto
founded	status	
imperial	treaty	

NAMES TO KNOW

Aeneas	King Pyrrhus	Tarquin dynasty
Etruscans	Latins	Twelve Tables
Gauls	Romulus and Remus	

PLACES TO KNOW

Alps	Rome	Tiber River

The Italian Peninsula

The city of Rome came to rule the Mediterranean world. How did such a city begin? What was Italy like in the early days of Rome? What great civilization rose up—and disappeared?

Look at the map on the next page. Can you see what appears to be a high-heeled boot "kicking" the island of Sicily? This is the peninsula of Italy. It is long (about 760 miles) and narrow (100 to 150 miles across). As you can see, the Apennine Mountains stretch along the eastern side of the peninsula. The volcano Mount Vesuvius is in this range.

Italy is separated from the rest of Europe by another mountain range called the Alps. This range contains the second-highest mountains in

Europe. (The highest are in the Caucasus Mountains of Eastern Europe.) The Alps served as protection from northern invaders in the early days of ancient Rome.

Italy contains rich farmland. Some of the best is in the region of two major rivers—the Po and the Tiber. It was on the Tiber River that the city of Rome was founded, or first established.

Ancient Italy, c. 600 B.C.E.

■ PRACTICE 95: The Italian Peninsula

Decide if each statement below is true (**T**) or false (**F**). Write the correct letter on the line before each description.

_____ **1.** Italy is separated from the rest of Europe by the Apennine Mountains.

_____ **2.** Italy contains very little good farmland.

The Legendary Founding of Rome

The Romans had two legends about the founding of their city. One legend centered on the Trojan prince **Aeneas.** He was supposedly a mighty warrior during the Trojan War. After the Trojans were defeated by the Greeks, Aeneas fled. He and his followers searched for a new home. They settled in central Italy, where the city of Rome later arose. The great Roman poet Virgil wrote of Aeneas in his epic poem the *Aeneid.*

The other legend told of twin brothers. They were said to be the sons of the god of war. Their names were **Romulus and Remus.** As babies, they were thrown into the Tiber River by their wicked great-uncle, Amulius. He had hoped to drown the boys, but they were saved by a mother wolf.

When they grew up, the twins overthrew Amulius. They then founded the city of Rome. But a quarrel led Romulus to slay Remus. The surviving twin became Rome's first king and gave the city its name.

THINK ABOUT IT

What do these legends tell us about what the ancient Romans valued? Consider what Aeneas, Romulus, and Remus had in common. Write your answer on a separate sheet of paper.

You have seen what the legends have to say about the founding of Rome. But what do the historical and archaeological records tell us about the early days of ancient Rome?

■ PRACTICE 96: The Legendary Founding of Rome

Match each description with a name from below. Write the letter of the correct name on the line before each description.

a. Troy **b.** Remus **c.** Romulus

_____ **1.** where Aeneas and his followers came from

_____ **2.** the twin who gave his name to the city of Rome

_____ **3.** the twin who was slain

Early Italy and Early Rome

The historical record of Italy (and of Rome) begins around 700 B.C.E. Several groups of people were living in ancient Italy by this time. Most of them lived in agricultural villages and small towns. They raised crops and animals. (The name *Italy* comes from a word that means "calf land.")

One group of these ancient people was the **Latins.** They had begun migrating into Italy from central Europe as far back as 2000 B.C.E.

They had settled in an area south of the Tiber River. By 1500 B.C.E., they had set up a cluster of towns on seven hills overlooking the Tiber. Over time, these towns combined to form the city of Rome. The year of Rome's birth as a city-state is usually given as 750 B.C.E. At this point, the young city was in an excellent position to control the best trade routes between northern and southern Italy.

Rome was in Latin territory. Thus, the language of Rome was Latin. But Rome itself was always a multicultural city. Of the many cultures that were there, two had the most influence on early Rome. One of these was the Greek culture. The Greeks had colonized southern Italy and the island of Sicily. The other major influence was the Etruscan culture. While the historical and archeological record of the ancient Greeks is rich in detail, we know very little about the Etruscans. But what little we do know is fascinating.

■ PRACTICE 97: Early Italy and Early Rome

Match the events below with the dates on the time line. Write the letter of the correct event on the line after each date.

a. A cluster of towns is set up on the Tiber.

b. The historical record of Italy begins.

c. Latins begin migrating into Italy.

d. The city-state of Rome is "born."

c. 2000 B.C.E.   1. _____

c. 1500 B.C.E.   2. _____

c. 750 B.C.E.   3. _____

c. 700 B.C.E.   4. _____

The Etruscan Civilization

The Etruscans were the most powerful group in ancient Italy. Theirs was the first great civilization on the peninsula. Historians are not sure where these people first came from. By the time Rome was established, they were living in a region known to the Latins as Etruria. The land of Etruria was rich in copper and iron ore, and it was covered with forests. The Etruscans used their resources well. They were expert metalworkers. They used the wood from the forests to build their homes and their ships. They were great sailors—and master pirates.

The Etruscans believed that death was a gateway to another world filled with pleasures. Like the Egyptians, the Etruscans stocked their tombs with food, drink, and treasures. Their goal was to create stone houses for the dead that were copies of the wood-and-clay houses they lived in. This meant that each of their cities was really two cities—an acropolis for the living and a necropolis for the dead. (The Greek word *necropolis* means "a city-state of the dead.")

The Etruscans' homes did not survive. Their language has faded away as well. (The language of Rome was the language of the Latins.) Scholars have made progress in figuring out the written language of the Etruscans. But gaps in understanding the language remain. The necropolises—the tombs—have survived. So what we know of the Etruscans comes from the homes they built for their dead.

■ PRACTICE 98: The Etruscan Civilization

Decide if each statement below is true (**T**) or false (**F**). Write the correct letter on the line before each statement.

_____ **1.** The first great civilization in ancient Italy was the Latin civilization.

_____ **2.** The land of Etruria was rich in resources.

_____ **3.** Each Etruscan city was really two cities—one for the living and one for the dead.

_____ **4.** What we know of the Etruscans comes from their writings.

The Legacy of the Etruscans

Etruscan tombs are filled with wall paintings. These paintings show people enjoying themselves. Scholars have used their paintings to learn about their culture. Many paintings show the Etruscans at feasts—eating, drinking, singing, and dancing. They are also shown fishing, hunting, and playing in sports contests. Historians believe that Etruscan women had an almost equal status in society. They are shown side-by-side with men—feasting, fishing, hunting, and competing in contests. Historians also believe, based on the paintings, that most of the work in Etruscan society was done by slaves.

Because of the wall paintings, historians have also discovered something else: what we thought were Roman inventions were often borrowed from the Etruscans. For example:

- **Togas**—The wrapped robes that the Romans wore were actually an Etruscan form of dress.

- **Layout of cities**—Roman military camps—which became the center of many European towns that still stand today—were built on an Etruscan model.

- **Alphabet**—The Etruscan alphabet was created from the Greek alphabet. The Romans based their alphabet on the Etruscan one.

- **Mythology**—We once thought that the Romans borrowed their mythology directly from the Greeks. They actually borrowed it from the Etruscans, who borrowed from the Greeks.

Gods of Rome and Greece					
Roman	*Greek*	*Roman*	*Greek*	*Roman*	*Greek*
Jupiter	Zeus	Vesta	Hestia	Venus	Aphrodite
Juno	Hera	Mars	Ares	Apollo	Apollo
Neptune	Poseidon	Mercury	Hermes	Diana	Artemis
Hades	Pluto	Minerva	Athena	Vulcan	Hephaestus

■ PRACTICE 99: The Legacy of the Etruscans

Decide if each statement below is true (**T**) or false (**F**). Write the correct letter on the line before each statement.

_____ **1.** Women had a low status in Etruscan culture.

_____ **2.** The Etruscans borrowed many ideas from the Romans.

IN REAL LIFE

The Etruscans may be gone, but their legacy lives on today through the Romans. Our language uses the Roman alphabet, adding the letters *j* (the Romans used *i*), *u* (the Romans used *v*), and *w*. We have also named all the planets in our solar system except Earth after Roman gods. And the popular television show and movie series *Star Trek* has a race of aliens named after the Roman god Vulcan.

Rome Becomes a Republic

Between about 600 B.C.E. and 509 B.C.E., Etruscan kings ruled Rome. They introduced Etruscan and Greek ideas to the city. We know little about these kings. We do know that the last three kings were part of what is called the **Tarquin dynasty.** (The city of Tarquinii was a major city in Etruria.) Soon after 500 B.C.E., the Tarquin dynasty lost power. Why? Certain Roman historians of later years claim that a young Roman woman was attacked by a group of drunken Etruscan men. She then killed herself in shame. This led the people of Rome to rise up against Etruscan rule. But many modern historians believe that the last Etruscan king led the city into war and lost. This left Rome without leadership.

Whatever the cause, Rome became a **republic** around 509 B.C.E. A republic is a form of government that allows people to rule themselves by voting for representatives. These representatives stand in for the people who elected them to office and look out for their interests.

■ PRACTICE 100: Rome Becomes a Republic

Circle the letter of the correct answer to each of the following questions.

1. Who were the first rulers of Rome?
   a. Etruscan kings
   b. Greek soldiers
   c. Egyptian kings
   d. Persian dynasty

2. Which of the following statements does NOT describe a republic?
   a. People rule themselves.
   b. Representatives are elected to office.
   c. A king decides who should be elected to represent the people.
   d. Representatives look out for the interests of the people.

The Early Republic

As the new state of Rome grew during the Early Republic (c. 509–280 B.C.E.), new government positions were added, and old ones were changed. At the top of the government, in place of a king, were two consuls. Each consul had equal power. This meant that one could check on the other, so that neither one could gain too much power. The consuls were usually generals who led Roman armies into battle. They were elected each year by the soldiers who made up the military assembly.

The Senate made many of the most important decisions for Rome. It was composed of members from Rome's leading families. Once a man became a senator, he served for the rest of his life. (When consuls left office, they became senators.)

During the Early Republic, two different assemblies had the power to elect men to office, pass laws, and make decisions—the military assembly and the civilian assembly. Only an adult male Roman citizen could attend assemblies. Only he could vote for officials. Roman women had very few political rights.

In the fifth century B.C.E., another important office was added—the tribune. Roman society was traditionally divided into an upper class, called *patricians*, and a lower class called *plebeians*. Tribunes were supposed to look out for the rights of the plebeians. Each year, the plebeian (civilian) assembly elected tribunes. These officers helped balance the Senate, which was filled with patricians. Tribunes could veto, or vote down, a law passed by the Senate that they felt was unfair. (*Veto* means "I forbid" in Latin.)

Around 450 B.C.E., the first Roman code of law was created. It was called the Twelve Tables because it was written on 12 bronze tablets. These tablets were put on public display so that every Roman would know the law of the land.

■ PRACTICE 101: The Early Republic

Decide if each statement below is true (**T**) or false (**F**). Write the correct letter on the line before each statement.

_____ **1.** In the Early Republic, two consuls ruled the state of Rome.

_____ **2.** Tribunes could not vote down the laws passed by the Senate.

_____ **3.** The plebeian assembly passed laws.

_____ **4.** The Twelve Tables were a Roman code of law.

Roman Expansionism Leads to War

Toward the end of the fifth century B.C.E., it was clear Rome wanted to be an imperial nation. This means that Rome wanted to expand its power. The Romans began by expanding their power into the Etruscan states. Around 400 B.C.E., an invading tribe of Celts (the Romans called them Gauls) swept in from northern Europe. They conquered Rome in 390 B.C.E. and sacked it, stealing the treasures of the captured city. Slowly, the Romans were able to build up their military and take the city back again. But it would be more than 300 years before the Romans could completely settle the score by conquering Gaul.

TIP

When you come across a word you do not know, read on. The word may be defined later. Or you may see that you do not need to know the word to understand what you are reading. For example, the word *sacked* in the first paragraph under the heading "Roman Expansionism Leads to War" is defined for you (*sack* means "steal the treasures of a captured place"). But if you need to know a word and there is no definition, look at the context—the sentences around the word—for clues. The word *imperial* is not defined in the first paragraph. But the next sentence tells you that it has something to do with expanding power.

As Rome's power grew, it ran up against another power. The city-state of Carthage had been built on the North African shore of the Mediterranean by the Phoenicians. Both Carthage and Rome wanted control of the rich Mediterranean sea trade. Carthage had a strong navy. Rome had a well-trained army. The two powers signed a peace **treaty** in 348 B.C.E., but they kept an eye on each other. Meanwhile, neither side ruled the Mediterranean.

During the 40 years after this treaty was signed, Rome increased its power on the Italian peninsula. To do so, the Romans fought against their neighbors in central Italy, the Samnites. In the end, Rome won. The final victory, which occurred around 290 B.C.E., gave Rome control of northern and central Italy. At this point, the Romans turned toward the Greek city-states of southern Italy.

■ PRACTICE 102: Roman Expansionism Leads to War

Decide if each statement below is true (**T**) or false (**F**). Write the correct letter on the line before each statement.

_____ **1.** Rome signed a treaty with the city-state of Carthage in 348 B.C.E.

_____ **2.** Rome fought against the Samnites to gain control of northern and central Italy.

The Pyrrhic War

In the south, the Greek city of Thurii was having trouble with a Samnite tribe. The city called on Rome for help. The Roman navy came to aid Thurii. In the process, the navy started a war with the Greek city of Tarentum. Tarentum turned to the Greek mainland for support. King Pyrrhus, who ruled over the Greek region of Epirus, responded. He was one of the great generals of the ancient world.

Pyrrhus arrived in southern Italy in 280 B.C.E. He brought with him 20 elephants and a well-trained army of 25,000 men. Twice Pyrrhus defeated the Romans in what became known as the Pyrrhic War. But his losses in these two battles numbered about 7,500 soldiers—almost one third of his entire army. The Greek historian Plutarch tells the following story:

After the second battle, Pyrrhus was congratulated for his victory. The general replied that one more victory like that would kill him.

Ever since, such a win with huge losses has been called a "Pyrrhic victory." This term is still used today. In 275 B.C.E., Pyrrhus and his army were finally beaten by the Romans. The king returned to Greece. At this point, the Republic of Rome controlled most of the Italian peninsula.

■ THINK ABOUT IT

What did King Pyrrhus mean by his reply? What is a Pyrrhic victory? Write your answers on a separate sheet of paper.

■ PRACTICE 103: The Pyrrhic War

Decide if each statement below is true (**T**) or false (**F**). Write the correct letter on the line before each statement.

_____ **1.** In the process of aiding the city of Thurii, the Roman navy started a war with the city of Tarentum.

_____ **2.** During the Pyrrhic War, about 7,500 Roman soldiers were killed.

LESSON 14: Rome: The Middle Republic

GOAL: To trace the growth of the Republic of Rome as it fought Carthage for control of the Mediterranean and to understand the Roman culture of this period

WORDS TO KNOW

aqueducts	Greco-Roman	population
authority	influence	rival
concrete	just	

NAMES TO KNOW

Hamilcar Barca	Hannibal

Rome and Carthage Go to War

During the Middle Republic of Rome (c. 264–133 B.C.E.), Rome came to rule the Mediterranean world. How did it happen? What was Roman culture like during this period?

After the Pyrrhic War, the Republic of Rome controlled most of the Italian peninsula. But the Romans wanted to expand their power beyond their borders and to rule the Mediterranean world. Their main rival in this region was the city-state of Carthage, which had been founded long ago on the coast of North Africa by the Phoenicians.

In earlier times, Rome and Carthage had been friendly. But they were now about to begin a series of wars. These three wars came to be known as the Punic Wars. (The word *Punic* comes from a Latin word that means "Phoenician.")

Rome and Carthage at time of Punic Wars

How did these wars start? Roman historians claimed that Carthage broke the peace treaty between Rome and Carthage by marching on Greek colonies in Sicily. But many modern historians now believe that Rome began the war by invading Sicily. According to the treaty, Sicily was under Carthaginian rule. Whatever the cause, the two powers went to war in 264 B.C.E.

■ PRACTICE 104: Rome and Carthage Go to War

Decide if each statement below is true (**T**) or false (**F**). Write the correct letter on the line before each statement.

_____ **1.** Rome wanted to control all of the Mediterranean world.

_____ **2.** Rome fought Sicily in the Punic Wars.

The Punic Wars

Much of the First Punic War was fought at sea. Both sides lost many ships and soldiers. After the Romans won a battle at sea on March 10, 241 B.C.E., it was clear that Carthage had lost the war. They were forced to hand Sicily over to the Romans. Afterward, the Carthaginian leader Hamilcar Barca tried to rebuild his city's power. Around 237 B.C.E., he began to create a rich empire in Spain. When he died in 228 B.C.E., his son-in-law, Hasdrubal, continued Hamilcar's work. So did Hasdrubal's son Hannibal.

Hannibal had grown up hating Rome. He had spent his young life preparing to fight the Romans. In 221 B.C.E., he was given command of the Carthaginian army in Spain. In 219 B.C.E., he attacked the town of Sagunto on the east coast of Italy. In response, Rome demanded that Carthage turn Hannibal over to Rome or be prepared to go to war. Carthage would not surrender Hannibal. In 218 B.C.E., the Second Punic War began.

Hannibal decided to bring the war into Italy. He entered the peninsula by an unexpected route. He put together a force of 20,000 foot soldiers and 6,000 horses. Although not the first to use them in war, Hannibal also had perhaps 60 elephants. These elephants could be thought of as "walking tanks." He marched his army across the Pyrenees of Spain and then across the Alps. The march took about six months. His troops took Rome completely by surprise.

Rome had a hard struggle. Hannibal was a brave and clever general. Then King Philip V of Macedonia joined the Carthaginians in 214 B.C.E. to fight against Rome. But the Romans held out. In 204 B.C.E., a Roman army under Scipio boldly crossed the Mediterranean to attack Carthage. Hannibal had to leave Italy to defend his city. But it was too late. Carthage was forced to surrender in 201 B.C.E. It turned its empire in Spain and the Mediterranean over to the mighty Republic of Rome.

■ PRACTICE 105: The Punic Wars

Decide if each statement below is true (**T**) or false (**F**). Write the correct letter on the line before each statement.

_____ **1.** Hannibal and his troops took six months to march over the mountains to surprise Rome.

_____ **2.** Carthage surrendered its empire in Spain and the Mediterranean to Hamilcar Barca.

Roman Imperialism and "Just Wars"

The Romans celebrated their triumphs. Their soldiers and generals were national heroes. They celebrated victory in battle by staging giant parades through Rome. As a culture, the Romans were always ready to go to war.

The Roman people believed that their gods would support them if their cause was just, or right and fair. They had to be sure each war was a "just war." This means that they could not attack another nation without good reason. Historians point out, however, that the Romans often teased, pushed, or forced their enemies into attacking first. Then the Romans felt free to "fight back." And they almost always won. After the Second Punic War, Rome engaged in a series of wars in the east, north, south, and west that lasted for years.

The Third Punic War was fought between 149 B.C.E. and 146 B.C.E. It ended with the city of Carthage being taken again by the Romans. But this time, Carthage was completely crushed. All its people were made slaves, and the great city of Carthage was burned to the ground.

In the west, Roman armies were almost constantly fighting for control in Spain. These wars finally ended in 133 B.C.E. with Rome again the winner.

THINK ABOUT IT

The Romans believed that all their wars were "just wars." Do you think they were? Do you think that any wars can be considered just? Why or why not? Write your answers on a separate sheet of paper.

■ PRACTICE 106: Roman Imperialism and "Just Wars"

Decide if each statement below is true (**T**) or false (**F**). Write the correct letter on the line before each statement.

_____ **1.** The Romans believed that all their wars had to be just.

_____ **2.** At the end of the Third Punic War, Rome destroyed Carthage.

Running the Empire

After they destroyed Carthage and conquered Spain, the Romans were left with an empire that spread across the Mediterranean. It included Roman provinces in Sicily, Sardinia-Corsica, Spain, Africa (Carthage), Macedonia, and Asia (northwestern Anatolia). In these Roman provinces, there were people of many different cultures. The Romans did not try to turn these people into Romans. Instead, Rome let the people in each province go about their business. But, the provinces were under the **authority** of Roman governors. The governors' duties were to keep order, protect against outside invaders, and collect taxes for Rome. Each governor had the use of Roman troops to help him carry out his duties.

By the second century B.C.E., the Republic of Rome controlled the Mediterranean world. As you can see from the map on page 156, it took

Rome about 360 years to grow from a small city-state into a gigantic empire. The Roman culture was built around war. Because of this, Rome had turned itself into one of the greatest imperial powers in world history.

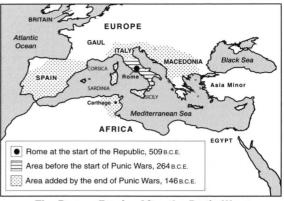

The Roman Empire After the Punic Wars

This expanding empire created changes in the Republic of Rome. Life in the Middle Republic was not the same as life in the Early Republic.

■ PRACTICE 107: Running the Empire

Circle the letter of the correct answer to each of the following questions.

1. What part of Africa was part of Rome's Mediterranean empire?
   a. Sardinia
   b. Egypt
   c. Carthage
   d. Greece

2. Who was in charge of the Roman provinces?
   a. Roman governors
   b. a Roman king
   c. foreign governors
   d. Roman troops

A Greco-Roman Culture

During the Middle Republic, people from all over the empire poured into Rome. The city and the Republic came under the influence of many cultures. But the culture that had the greatest influence on the Republic of Rome was the Greek culture. In fact, it was a Greco-Roman culture that the Romans passed along to later European civilizations.

The Greek influence can be seen in many ways: Wealthy Romans liked to collect Greek art and Greek books. Most nobles—including almost every senator—could speak and write Latin and Greek. The first histories by Roman historians were written in Greek, not Latin. Most of the writers of Latin literature were foreigners who imitated Greek styles of writing. (None of the writers of this time, however, produced works equal to those of the great Greek writers.) And many public and private buildings were built in the Greek style of architecture.

However, other forms of Greek learning were not well received in Rome. Romans were suspicious of Greek medicine and Greek philosophy. They felt that these areas of study involved "new ways of thinking." Such thinking was seen as dangerous to the traditional Roman way of life.

TIP

When you study history, it is useful to look for the main ideas that a writer is discussing. Look at headings or titles as you read. These often point to the main idea of a section. Then read each paragraph and try to figure out if there is a single idea the writer is trying to get across. Sometimes this idea may be a sentence in the paragraph. Find the sentence that describes the main idea in each paragraph under the heading "A Greco-Roman Culture."

■ PRACTICE 108: A Greco-Roman Culture

Decide if each statement below is true (**T**) or false (**F**). Write the correct letter on the line before each statement.

_____ **1.** Most Roman nobles could speak and write Greek.

_____ **2.** Many Roman buildings were built in the Greek style.

_____ **3.** Greek medicine was very popular in the Roman culture.

Economic and Social Change in the Middle Republic

The Roman army was almost always at war somewhere in the empire—increasing its power or keeping order. The army always seemed to find enough men to fill the ranks. In part, this is because Rome allowed foreigners and freed slaves to become citizens and join the army.

The expanding empire brought other changes to Rome. The expansion led to a greater **population.** This created a need for more goods. Many of the goods went to the wealthy, who demanded more and more luxury. As the Roman Empire grew, the rich grew richer—and the poor grew poorer.

An expanding population meant more building and rebuilding across the empire. Around 200 B.C.E., a wonderful new building material was discovered in central Italy. It was made from mixing crushed stone, lime (a white powder often made by crushing limestone), and sand with water. When this mixture dried, it was very strong. (Today, we call it **concrete.**)

The Romans used concrete to make their buildings and the **aqueducts** that carried the city's water supply. Concrete was also used to make Roman roads. The ancient Romans are famous for their roads. These roads were built on a layer of sand and stones that was covered with concrete. On top was a smooth layer of flat stone blocks. The long, straight roads of the Romans connected many parts of their mighty empire.

IN REAL LIFE

Many Roman roads, such as the Appian Way, still exist in Europe today. There is a saying that "all roads lead to Rome." Today, the saying is used to talk about something that is the center of importance. In the ancient world of the Mediterranean, that center was the city of Rome.

■ PRACTICE 109: Economic and Social Change in the Middle Republic

Decide if each statement below is true (**T**) or false (**F**). Write the correct letter on the line before each statement.

_____ **1.** The Roman army often did not have enough men.

_____ **2.** As the Roman Empire grew, the rich got richer, and the poor got poorer.

LESSON 15: Rome: The Late Republic

GOAL: To recognize the shift from external to internal warfare and to appreciate its impact on Rome's Late Republic

WORDS TO KNOW

abolished	frontier	revolt
assassinated	gladiator	triumvirate
dictator	opponents	
discipline	reform	

NAMES TO KNOW

Cato	Julius Caesar	Sallust
Cicero	Marius	Spartacus
Cleopatra	Mark Anthony	Sulla
Gracchi brothers	Octavian	Virgil
Horace	Pompey	

PLACE TO KNOW

Rubicon River

War Inside Rome

What happens to a culture that believes in war when there are no more major wars to fight? Can its people live in peace?

War and military glory were a major part of Roman life. Winning the Punic Wars against Carthage had brought power and riches to Rome. The Romans considered the Carthaginians to be worthy opponents. There was glory in fighting such worthy armies. There was honor in beating a general like Hannibal.

After its empire had been established, however, Rome's major opponents became tribes that lived along the frontier—the edges of the empire. The Romans referred to these tribes as barbarians (from the Latin word *barbarus*, which means "foreign"). To the Romans, these people were not civilized. Battles with the barbarians did not take the form of large-scale wars. Instead, the Romans fought many small battles along the frontier.

Ancient historians feel that this change in warfare—from major wars to small battles—marks the beginning of the Late Republic (133–31 B.C.E.). As you will see, the end of major wars outside of Rome led to war inside of Rome, as Romans fought against Romans.

■ PRACTICE 110: War Inside Rome

Decide if each statement below is true (**T**) or false (**F**). Write the correct letter on the line before each statement.

_____ **1.** The ancient Romans considered the Phoenicians to be worthy opponents.

_____ **2.** During the Late Republic, the Romans stopped fighting major wars and began to fight small battles.

■ IN REAL LIFE

Have you ever heard someone called a barbarian? The Romans' attitude toward the enemies they called the barbarians added a new meaning to their word *barbarus*. They used the word *barbarian* to describe people whose culture was strange and uncivilized in their eyes. This is the meaning that we have inherited from the Romans.

The Reforms of the Gracchi Brothers

The wealthy citizens of Rome were happy with things as they were. But other people of Rome were not. Many small farmers had lost their land during the wars and now owned nothing. Many people who had become part of the Republic of Rome were not allowed the rights of citizenship. And many poor people could not afford the high prices that were being charged for grain and other goods.

Two brothers—Tiberius Gracchus and Gaius Gracchus—led **reform** movements to try to bring about some needed changes. The older of the **Gracchi brothers,** Tiberius, started a reform movement in 133 B.C.E. that led to his death. His younger brother took up the fight in 123 B.C.E. The Gracchi brothers' reforms included a law that allowed small farmers to resettle on public land. Another law used money from taxes to provide free grain for the poor. A third reform involved controls on the power of the Senate. Although these and other Gracchi reform laws were passed, many senators were against them. In 121 B.C.E., Gaius Gracchus, too, was killed. Many of his followers were executed. In the years after Gaius's death, most of the Gracchi brothers' reforms were **abolished,** or undone, by the Senate.

■ PRACTICE 111: The Reforms of the Gracchi Brothers

Circle the letter of the correct answer to each of the following questions.

1. Who tried to bring about reform in the Late Republic?
   a. the wealthy
   b. the senators
   c. the Gracchi brothers
   d. the Barbarians

2. Which of the following was NOT a reform of the Late Republic?
   a. land for farmers
   b. free grain for the poor
   c. controls on the Senate's power
   d. free health care

Marius Reforms the Army

Small wars kept breaking out along the Roman frontier in Africa and in the North. Because these wars called for many small armies, it was hard for the Romans to keep all of the armies supplied with soldiers. But an army general named Gaius **Marius** came up with a solution. He looked for any men he could find who seemed to be good fighters. It did not matter to him whether these people were citizens or not. It did not matter if they were from the "better" classes or from the poorer classes. His men were not volunteers. He paid them to be soldiers. Soon, other generals were following Marius's example.

TIP

Have you ever heard the word *mercenary*? A mercenary is a hired soldier. The word can also mean "greedy."

The Senate passed laws to keep soldiers' pay low. To make up for this, soldiers were able to keep what they won during battles. The more battles they won, the richer they became. And winning battles often depended on the general in charge of the troops.

The result was that the Roman armies were no longer made up of well-to-do citizens who volunteered to fight for the glory of the Republic of Rome. Instead, the armies were filled with men who fought for money and were loyal only to their generals, not to Rome. It was only a matter of time before a general (and his loyal army) decided he wanted more power and glory—even if it meant fighting another Roman general.

■ PRACTICE 112: Marius Reforms the Army

Decide if each statement below is true (**T**) or false (**F**). Write the correct letter on the line before each statement.

_____ **1.** In the Late Republic, the Romans had a hard time finding enough soldiers.

_____ **2.** Gaius Marius only wanted soldiers who were citizens of Rome.

Sulla Becomes Dictator

Around 88 B.C.E., various Roman generals were hoping to get command of the troops in the eastern part of the empire. This was the sort of assignment that could ensure a man's career success. Marius, the general who had reformed the Roman army, was one of those leaders. But the assignment went to Sulla, a man who had trained under Marius. Sulla was successful in the East and became a famous military hero in Rome.

Lucretius Cornelius Sulla believed in law and order. He felt that the Roman people needed a strong government and a strong Senate. He did not believe in reforms. But when he returned to Italy from the East, he found that Rome was in the hands of reformers. He and his loyal army seized control of Rome in 82 B.C.E. Sulla had himself made **dictator** and had his political enemies put to death. He passed new laws to give the Senate more power over Rome. In doing so, he undid more of the Gracchi reforms. As far as Sulla was concerned, Rome was now in good hands. So in 79 B.C.E., he retired from public office.

Sulla's retirement left the door open for various Roman generals to fight one another for control of Rome. Two of these generals were **Pompey** and Crassus.

■ PRACTICE 113: Sulla Becomes Dictator

Decide if each statement below is true (**T**) or false (**F**). Write the correct letter on the line before each statement.

_____ **1.** Around 88 B.C.E., Marius was given the eastern command, an assignment that many generals wanted.

_____ **2.** Sulla believed that the Roman government, including the Senate, should be strong.

_____ **3.** When Sulla returned, he found Rome in the hands of his enemies.

_____ **4.** Sulla had himself made dictator and passed laws that took all power away from the Senate.

Pompey and Crassus Share Power

Around 73 B.C.E., Roman troops were busy fighting in various parts of the empire. Few troops were left in Rome. A small slave **revolt,** which should have been easy to stop, grew and grew until it became a major problem. The revolt was started by a **gladiator** named **Spartacus.** Gladiators were fighters who were paid to fight one another for the entertainment of the Roman public. Often the fight did not end until one man was dead.

Crassus volunteered to lead special troops against the rebellious slaves, who now numbered in the thousands. He succeeded in stopping the revolt. At this point, around 71 B.C.E., Pompey returned from Spain. He and his troops killed the remaining rebels. Pompey and Crassus each claimed victory, and each demanded to be made consul (head of the Roman government). In the end, they both became consuls. But it was not a friendly alliance. The two men did not trust each other.

Under their rule, the Senate underwent a change. Many senators were replaced by favorites of either Pompey or Crassus. These new senators were greedy for power and money. They were not interested in public service or watching out for the people of Rome.

Pompey spent much of his time away from Rome, adding new provinces to the Roman empire. While Pompey was absent, Crassus tried to make his position stronger. He feared that Pompey, as a returning military hero, would seize all the power. When Pompey returned to Rome, he and Crassus continued their uneasy rule. Meanwhile, another Roman general was waiting for his chance to gain control of Rome. His name was **Julius Caesar.**

■ PRACTICE 114: Pompey and Crassus Share Power

Decide if each statement below is true (**T**) or false (**F**). Write the correct letter on the line before each statement.

_____ **1.** The slave revolt that began in 73 B.C.E. was led by Pompey and Crassus.

_____ **2.** Under Pompey and Crassus, the Senate became filled with men who were greedy for power and money.

Julius Caesar Rises to Power

Julius Caesar was a talented general who could walk a political tightrope—seeming to support two opposite views. Seeing how Pompey and Crassus distrusted each other, Caesar made a show of support for Pompey. At the same time, he helped Crassus.

Caesar first gained fame by conquering Gaul. (The regions that he conquered covered most of modern-day France and Belgium, as well as parts of the Netherlands, Germany, and Switzerland.) Pompey started to see Caesar as a rival. While Caesar was overseeing the new province of Gaul, Pompey moved against him. In 49 B.C.E., the Senate (filled mainly with Pompey's supporters) ordered Caesar to return to Rome. Caesar knew that if he came alone, he would be killed. Instead, he returned with his troops and stationed himself on the Italian border, north of the Rubicon River. He knew that once he crossed the river into Italy, he would be declaring war against Pompey. But his troops were young and fresh, while Pompey's troops had not seen action for a long time. Caesar crossed the Rubicon and invaded Italy.

Pompey knew that he had lost. He fled to Greece and then to Egypt. Caesar was now in control of Rome. He promised the people of Rome, who had grown tired of war, that he would bring them peace. To those who were tired of dishonest, greedy politicians, he promised fair government. To the poor, he promised homes, jobs, and food. He did not keep all these promises.

THINK ABOUT IT

Do Caesar's promises sound familiar? Do politicians of today make such promises as they run for office? How often do politicians follow through on the promises they make? What might keep a politician from following through? Is it always politicians' fault if they do not keep promises? Write your answers on a separate sheet of paper.

■ PRACTICE 115: Julius Caesar Rises to Power

Decide if each statement below is true (**T**) or false (**F**). Write the correct letter on the line before each statement.

_____ **1.** Caesar was a politician, but he wanted to be a general.

_____ **2.** Caesar promised Romans peace and fair government.

Caesar's Rule Ends in Death

When Pompey fled to Egypt with his troops, Caesar followed, bringing his army with him. While in Alexandria, the 54-year-old Caesar met the 22-year-old **Cleopatra.** She was fighting with her brother Ptolemy for control of the Egyptian throne. Caesar helped her become queen. He then went on to defeat Pompey's forces. (Pompey himself had been killed by this time.) Pompey's sons, who had fled to Spain, put together an army. In a bloody battle in 45 B.C.E., Caesar again was the winner.

During these battles with Pompey's forces, Caesar had acted as dictator of Rome. Roman law allowed a ruler to do so in time of war. Now the war was over. As Caesar had promised, he had brought peace to Rome. But he remained a dictator. And even though he had made many promises of reform, he really made only one change—to the calendar. He had it based on a year lasting 365 1/4 days, in a form that has now been used for centuries.

■ IN REAL LIFE

Our calendar is similar to the Julian calendar of Julius Caesar. The names of our months all have Roman origins. Some are named for Roman festivals, some for Roman gods and goddesses, some come from Roman numbers, and two are named for Roman rulers. One of these is July, which is named for Julius Caesar. January is named after Janus, the god of gates and doorways, who is often drawn as having two faces, looking both ways. Can you figure out why the first month of the year is named after this god? Write your answer on a separate sheet of paper.

Many wealthy Romans feared Caesar. They thought that he had too much power and was planning to make himself king. Sixty of them got together to plan his death. Claiming to be fighting for liberty, they assassinated Caesar on March 15, 44 B.C.E.

■ PRACTICE 116: Caesar's Rule Ends in Death

Decide if each statement below is true (**T**) or false (**F**).Write the correct letter on the line before each statement.

_____ **1.** Caesar put Cleopatra on the throne of Egypt.

_____ **2.** The army put together by Pompey's sons defeated Caesar.

The Triumvirate Takes Over

The people of Rome were shocked by Caesar's death. The army had been loyal to him, and many senators had admired him. The assassins were forced to run away from Rome. **Mark Anthony,** Caesar's second-in-command, took over for Caesar. But soon a challenger appeared. He was **Octavian,** Caesar's adopted son. In the beginning, Anthony and Octavian battled for power. Then they agreed to work together. Adding a third man, Lepidus, they formed a three-man ruling team known as a **triumvirate.**

TIP

When you come across a term you need to remember, look to see if there is anything familiar about the word. In the word *triumvirate*, for example, the prefix *tri-* may be familiar. Think: How many people are in a *trio*? How many sides does a *triangle* have? You will notice that the word *triumvirate* is defined as a "three-man ruling team." The *tri-* at the beginning of the word should help you remember how many rulers make up a triumvirate.

For five years, the triumvirate of Anthony, Octavian, and Lepidus ruled the Roman Empire. Around 42 B.C.E., the three men divided the empire into three parts. Lepidus got the smallest piece. Octavian got Italy. And Anthony got the eastern part of the empire. Anthony, who had settled in Alexandria with Cleopatra, wanted to rule all of Rome. But he wanted to do so from Egypt, at Cleopatra's side. Octavian had other plans. He easily defeated Lepidus and took his share of the empire. Then Octavian moved on Anthony. In 31 B.C.E., he beat Anthony's forces in the sea battle of Actium. By 27 B.C.E., Octavian was master of the Roman world. He was about to become its first emperor.

■ PRACTICE 117: The Triumvirate Takes Over

Match each description with a name or group of names from below. Write the letter of the correct name or group of names on the line before each description.

a. Anthony

c. Anthony, Octavian, and Lepidus

b. Anthony and Octavian

d. Octavian

_____ 1. Caesar's adopted son who became master of Rome in 27 B.C.E.

_____ 2. the triumvirate that ruled Rome for five years

_____ 3. wanted to rule Rome from Egypt

_____ 4. fought in the battle of Actium

The Culture of the Late Republic

The Late Republic of Rome was a time of war. There were wars along the frontiers to stop barbarian invaders. There were wars of conquest, as provinces such as Gaul were added to the empire. And there were wars between Roman generals, who fought for control of Rome. In spite of all this warfare, there were major developments in Roman culture during this time.

Earlier Roman culture had borrowed much from the Etruscans and the Greeks. Now Rome began to claim certain areas as its own: oratory (speech making), law, and history. In addition, great philosophical works and beautiful poetry were produced.

- **Oratory**—Speech makers, such as Cato and Cicero, became famous for their ability to win over an audience. Cicero's speeches, in particular, were masterpieces of organization and logic. The Roman art of speaking well led the Romans to value proper spelling and good grammar. Sons of wealthy Romans learned these skills in school. Any young man who hoped for a political career needed to be a skilled speech maker.

- **Law**—The Romans of this period played a large part in turning the study and practice of law into a discipline. Men began to train for and study law. Laws themselves had to fit into a logical system, based on a set of legal principles.

- **History**—Roman historians detailed the wars and conquests of the Late Republic. Sallust is the best known of these historians. Caesar himself wrote an account of his conquests in Gaul. Cornelius Nepos is known for his biographies.

- **Philosophy**—Cato and Cicero also wrote well-received philosophical works. A popular philosophical movement of the time was called *epicureanism.* The Greek philosopher Epicurus believed that achieving happiness was the greatest good of all. His followers believed in living a life of pleasure.

- **Poetry**—One of Rome's two greatest poets was Virgil, who wrote about the founding of Rome in his epic the *Aeneid.* The other great Roman poet was Horace, who wrote humorous poetry as well as more serious works. A third poet, Catullus, was famous for short poems that poked fun at the politicians of his day. The poet Lucretius argued for epicurean philosophy in verse.

■ PRACTICE 118: The Culture of the Late Republic

Circle the letter of the correct answer to each of the following questions.

1. Which term refers to the skill of making speeches?
   a. philosophy
   b. oratory
   c. poetry
   d. legality

2. Which of these men became famous for making stirring speeches?
   a. Virgil and Horace
   b. Sallust and Caesar
   c. Cato and Cicero
   d. Catullus and Lucretius

3. What is the *Aeneid*?
   a. an epic poem about the founding of Rome
   b. a history of the Late Republic's wars
   c. a set of legal principles
   d. a guide to philosophy

4. What is Sallust best known as?
   a. a philosopher
   b. a poet
   c. a lawyer
   d. a history writer

LESSON 16: The Roman Empire

GOAL: To understand the transformation of Rome from a republic to an empire; to trace the rise of Christianity within the Roman Empire

WORDS TO KNOW

Augustine Age	persecuted
Christianity	representative government
civilian	Romance languages
crucified	tolerated
military dictatorship	tyrant
Pax Romana	

NAMES TO KNOW

Augustus	Jesus Christ
Constantine	Marcus Aurelius
Diocletian	Nero

PLACES TO KNOW

Coliseum	Constantinople	Forum

The First Emperor of Rome

It is 27 B.C.E. Octavian, the adopted son of Julius Caesar, is master of the Roman world. He is about to put an end to the Republic of Rome and replace it with . . . what?

After Octavian's victory at Actium, Cleopatra and Mark Anthony killed themselves. Octavian quickly added Egypt to the Roman Empire. Then he turned his attention to Rome. For years, the state had been battered by a series of wars. Various generals had fought one another for control of Rome. Octavian wanted to bring order, but not through military force.

His goal, he said, was to set up "the best civilian government possible."

In January of 27 B.C.E., the Senate voted to give Octavian the name *Augustus,* meaning "honored." He was now known as Imperator Caesar Augustus, or simply Augustus. For the rest of his rule, he held only offices that had always existed in Rome (although he often held several at once, year after year). And he was careful never to claim the power of emperor. But, in fact, he was the first emperor of Rome. He was the only commander of the army. Soldiers swore loyalty to him, not to their generals.

IN REAL LIFE

Imperator and *Caesar* were part of Augustus's name. But because of him, these two names have come to stand for powerful leadership. From Imperator comes the English word *emperor.* The German language changed Caesar into the title *kaiser,* which is used to refer to German and Austrian emperors. And the Russians changed Caesar into *czar* (also spelled *tsar*), a title for their emperors. *Czar* is also an English word that refers to anyone with a lot of power.

■ PRACTICE 119: The First Emperor of Rome

Decide if each statement below is true (**T**) or false (**F**). Write the correct letter on the line before each statement.

_____ **1.** Augustus proudly claimed the title and power of emperor.

_____ **2.** The English word *emperor* comes from the Latin term *imperator.*

The Beginning of the Pax Romana

If his days in the triumvirate are included, Augustus ruled the Roman world for 56 years—until 14 C.E. His rule was one of the longest in European history. When he took on the role of emperor, his aim was to set up the best civilian government that he could. Augustus lived up to his goal.

Augustus began by looking for the best people to fill government jobs. Often, these people were not from the upper classes. Some were merchants. Some were freed slaves. Some were even slaves from the royal household. What was important to Augustus was that they could do the job well. He checked on the governors in charge of the provinces throughout his empire. He wanted to make sure that they were doing their jobs and that the taxes they collected were fair.

Almost single-handedly, Augustus was able to restore peace to Rome, bring unity to the empire, and raise everyone's spirits. Thus began a period known as the **Pax Romana** ("Roman Peace"). Rome's earlier history was filled with warfare. The Roman army was always fighting battles somewhere in the empire, sometimes even in and around Rome. But during the Pax Romana, no major wars were fought.

THINK ABOUT IT

How would you rate Augustus as a leader? If he were running for president of the United States, would you vote for him? Why or why not? Write your answers on a separate sheet of paper.

■ PRACTICE 120: The Beginning of the Pax Romana

Decide if each statement below is true (**T**) or false (**F**). Write the correct letter on the line before each statement.

_____ **1.** Augustus ruled for 56 years.

_____ **2.** Pax Romana means "a pox upon Rome."

_____ **3.** Augustus looked only in the upper classes for people to fill government jobs.

The Accomplishments of the Augustine Age

Under Augustus, the Roman Empire continued to expand. In the South, the Red Sea and the Arabian Desert came under Roman control. In Africa, more of Egypt, as well as the kingdoms of Numidia and Mauretania, were added. In Europe, the empire took over more of Spain and extended its borders into Germany. In the East, kingdoms such as Syria and Judea were added. The Roman army's role now was to keep the peace throughout the empire. It no longer stirred up wars along the frontier or around Rome. Pirates and thieves were kept in check. Trade flourished. Goods from as far away as India were exchanged. In fact, the Mediterranean world was better linked together through trade than ever before.

Augustus also made improvements in the city of Rome. He ordered new buildings to be put up, including government offices, public baths, and libraries. "I found Rome brick," he once said, "and left it marble." The culture of the **Augustine Age** reached a high level of excellence, thanks to its emperor. And this culture spread throughout the empire. The Mediterranean world was a Roman world—filled with Roman roads, Roman architecture, Roman art, and Roman literature.

As emperor, Augustus had complete power. But he did not abuse this power. He was never a **tyrant.** When he died in 14 C.E., the Senate pronounced him *divus*—a god. He was considered a god on Earth who had restored peace to Rome, improved the government everywhere, raised people's hopes, and brought glory to Rome. None of the emperors who came after him would live up to Augustus's example.

■ PRACTICE 121: The Accomplishments of the Augustine Age

Decide if each statement below is true (**T**) or false (**F**). Write the correct letter on the line before each statement.

_____ **1.** Under Augustus, the Roman army stirred up battles along the frontier.

_____ **2.** Under Augustus, the Mediterranean world was better linked together through trade than ever before.

_____ **3.** Under Augustus, Roman culture reached a high level of excellence.

_____ **4.** After his death, Augustus was declared a god by the Senate.

The Emperors and Empire After Augustus

To show thanks for the Pax Romana, Romans were encouraged to practice "emperor worship." At an emperor's death, the Senate would vote whether to make the title of *divus* ("god") official, as they had with Augustus. Often, they did. But some emperors were such cruel and greedy rulers that, instead, the Senate voted to condemn them.

Ruling Family/ Emperor's Name	Years of Rule/ Made a God or Condemned?	Comments About His Rule
Julio-Claudians		
Tiberius	14–37 C.E. Condemned	Although a good soldier and administrator, he was always unpopular with the people and the Senate.
Gaius (known as "Caligula")	37–41 C.E. Condemned	He had a short and violent rule. He was a cruel and greedy tyrant. He was assassinated.
Claudius I	41–54 C.E. Made a god	A man with physical problems, including a stutter, he was never popular. But he ruled well, enlarging the empire (adding Britain) and improving Rome.
Nero	54–68 C.E. Condemned	Another cruel tyrant. During his rule, Britain revolted under Queen Boudicca. There was a great fire in Rome, which Nero blamed on the Christians, followers of a new religion. He killed himself.

(continued)

Flavians		
Vespasian	69–79 C.E. Made a god	Not a native Roman or a noble. He managed to restore order after Nero's horrible reign.
Titus	79–81 C.E. Made a god	Vespasian's son. He was a popular ruler. During his short rule, Mount Vesuvius erupted and buried the towns of Pompeii and Herculaneum.
Domitian	81–96 C.E. Condemned	Titus's brother. He was a strict ruler, and he maintained order. Seen as a tyrant. He was assassinated.
Antonines		
Nerva	96–98 C.E. Made a god	An elderly senator, his rule was short. He adopted Trajan, a Spaniard, as his successor.
Trajan	98–117 C.E. Made a god	Considered a good ruler, he kept the empire in harmony. Under him, the empire reached its peak.
Hadrian	117–138 C.E. Made a god	A Spaniard, he was adopted by Trajan. He was against further expansion, and he improved the existing empire. He also developed Rome's civil service.
Antoninus Pius	138–161 C.E. Made a god	Adopted son of Hadrian. He was a Gaul with a Spanish wife.

(continued)

| Marcus Aurelius | 161–180 C.E. Made a god | Adopted son of Antoninus. Though he was co-emperor with his brother, Lucius Verus, he was the real power. He spent much time in the field, battling barbarians. |
| Commodus | 180–192 C.E. Condemned | Marcus's son. He became emperor at age 19. A cruel and greedy tyrant, he was assassinated. |

In 192 C.E., the Roman army took over, claiming the right to elect their commanders as emperors. They did not choose good rulers.

During the reign of the Antonine emperors, the Roman Empire reached its peak. On the right is a map of the empire at this time.

The Roman Empire, c. 117 C.E.

While these emperors ruled Rome, a new religion was born. Some Roman emperors tolerated this religion. Others persecuted its followers. But Christianity continued to grow.

■ PRACTICE 122: The Emperors and Empire After Augustus

Decide if each statement below is true (**T**) or false (**F**). Write the correct letter on the line before each statement.

_____ **1.** Claudius I was a poor but popular ruler.

_____ **2.** During the reign of the Antonine emperors, the Roman Empire reached across Africa, Europe, and Asia.

The Rise of Christianity

Today, Christianity is one of the world's major religions. It began in the eastern part of the Roman Empire, in a region called Palestine. The religion developed around the life and teachings of Jesus Christ. He was a Jew who preached in Palestine. Although he preached love and peace, he was considered a dangerous rebel. He was crucified in 30 C.E. When it began, Christianity was only one among many new religions to spring up in the various provinces of the Roman Empire. But a group of men called the apostles began to spread the teachings of Jesus throughout the empire. They claimed that Jesus was the son of the only god and that he had died to save his people. Soon, the apostles were attracting many followers to Christianity.

In general, the Romans were tolerant of the customs and religions of the many people in their empire. They were a bit suspicious of the Jewish religion, though, mainly because it was monotheistic. That is, the Jews worshiped only one god. The Romans, in contrast, worshiped many gods, including their emperors. But the Romans respected the fact that the Jewish religion was quite old and that the Jews tried to live in peace with the Romans. The Romans did not feel this way about the new monotheistic religion of Christianity.

■ PRACTICE 123: The Rise of Christianity

Decide if each statement below is true (**T**) or false (**F**). Write the correct letter on the line before each statement.

_____ **1.** The Jewish religion developed around the life and teachings of Jesus Christ, a Jew who preached in Palestine.

_____ **2.** Men known as apostles spread the Christian religion throughout the Roman empire.

_____ **3.** The Romans were generally not at all tolerant of other religions.

_____ **4.** The Romans believed in many gods, but the Jews and Christians were monotheistic.

Romans Versus Christians

During the rule of **Nero,** Christians began to be persecuted by the government of Rome. When a fire raged through Rome in 64 C.E., Nero blamed it on the Christians.

Under **Marcus Aurelius,** the persecution continued. The Romans were angry that the Christians refused to worship the state gods in general, and the emperor in particular. Persecution of the Christians sometimes took the form of cruel contests. Christians were sometimes killed by gladiators or wild animals for the entertainment of the Roman public.

After the Antonine emperors, there was a series of soldier-emperors. They were poor rulers. Under them, the empire grew weaker. Wars broke out. The empire began to fall apart.

■ PRACTICE 124: Romans Versus Christians

Match each description with a name from below. Write the letter of the correct name on the line before each description.

        a. Nero   **b.** Marcus Aurelius

_____ **1.** He began the persecution of the Christians when he blamed them for a fire in 64 C.E.

_____ **2.** He continued the persecution of Christians, which included having them killed by gladiators or wild animals.

The Empire Is Divided . . . and Reunited

Rome was saved by a strong emperor named Diocletian. He came to power in 284 C.E. In an attempt to restore order to Rome, he reorganized the government. At its head, Diocletian placed four rulers: Two older men, each with the title Augustus, made the decisions for the state of Rome; two younger men, each with the title Caesar, carried out these decisions.

The Divided Roman Empire

Diocletian then divided the empire into two parts—East and West. He took the eastern part. But, in truth, there was really only one leader— Diocletian. He made all the important decisions. In his drive to restore order, he passed many laws to regulate people's lives. His rule has been described as a military dictatorship.

When Diocletian retired in 305 C.E., there was a struggle for power. The winner was named Constantine. He declared himself a Christian in 312 C.E. and made Christianity the official religion of the empire. As he took control of the Roman empire, he decided to rule both halves, the East and the West. But he did not rule from Rome. Instead, he built a new capital in the ancient Greek city of Byzantium. He called it Constantinople ("the city of Constantine"). From now on, the city of Rome would no longer be the center of the Mediterranean world.

■ PRACTICE 125: The Empire Is Divided . . . and Reunited

Match each description with an emperor from the list below. Write the letter of the correct emperor on the line before each description. (*Hint*: Each emperor may be used more than once.)

a. Diocletian   b. Constantine

_____ **1.** He united the empire.

_____ **2.** He divided the empire into two parts.

_____ **3.** He made Christianity the official religion.

Gifts from Rome

All in all, the ancient Romans ruled the Mediterranean for more than 1,000 years. The Pax Romana, more than 200 years of peace without a major war, was Rome's gift to the people of the Mediterranean world. And this Roman peace—maintained by Roman soldiers—allowed people, goods, and ideas to move freely across the Roman Empire along Roman roads. Ancient Rome continues to have an effect on our world today.

■ **Buildings and Engineering**—Some of Rome's greatest achievements were its buildings. The Forum was Rome's main square. It was the center of the empire—the point from which all roads began and all roads were measured. The Coliseum was a gigantic arena where public entertainment was staged. The Baths of Caracalla drew people who wanted to swim or soak in hot baths. All these structures survive today. The Romans are also admired for their sewer systems and their aqueducts. Their long, straight, well-built roads are world famous. Many Roman structures survive today because they were built of concrete, a Roman invention.

■ **Laws and Government**—Many of the laws that we value today can be traced to Rome. For example, Roman law said that a person is innocent until proved guilty. It also said that a person cannot be forced to testify against himself or herself. The Romans also helped develop the idea of **representative government.** (The U.S. government is a representative democracy, a blending of Roman and Greek ideas.)

- **Language**—The Romans spoke Latin, a language that is no longer spoken. But Latin is the basis of what we call the **Romance languages** (French, Spanish, and Italian). And Latin, along with Greek, has contributed much to English.

■ PRACTICE 126: Gifts from Rome

Decide if each statement below is true (**T**) or false (**F**). Write the correct letter on the line before each statement.

_____ **1.** The Romans ruled the Mediterranean world for about 200 years.

_____ **2.** During the Pax Romana, there were no major wars in the Mediterranean world.

UNIT 4 REVIEW

Circle the letter of the correct answer to each of the following questions.

1. A Roman legend says that Rome was founded by two twins named Romulus and Remus, who had been _____.
   a. warriors in the Trojan War who fought with Aeneas
   b. written about in the epic poem the *Aeneid*
   c. almost drowned as babies but were saved by a mother wolf
   d. the first two kings of Rome

2. In the Republic of Rome, what was a consul?
   a. one of the two men who were at the head of the government
   b. a member of the military assembly
   c. an officer who represented the rights of the plebeians
   d. a member of the Senate

3. What caused the Pyrrhic War?
   a. Romans were fighting the Samnites, who asked King Pyrrhus for help.
   b. The Roman navy, coming to help the city of Thurii, started a war with the city of Tarentum, which got help from King Pyrrhus.
   c. King Pyrrhus invaded Italy so that he could gain control of the Italian peninsula.
   d. The city of Carthage wanted control of the Mediterranean sea trade.

4. What were the Punic Wars?
   a. a series of wars that Rome fought throughout its empire
   b. three wars between Carthage and Rome
   c. two wars between Macedonia and Rome
   d. sea battles fought around Sicily

5. What culture had the greatest influence on the Roman culture?
   a. Carthaginian
   b. Gallic
   c. Phoenician
   d. Greek

6. How did the Romans find enough men to supply their army with soldiers?
   a. They used slaves that they had taken in war.
   b. They allowed foreigners and freed slaves to become citizens because citizens could join the army.
   c. They paid people from all over the empire to come to Rome.
   d. They made their soldiers into heroes and staged victory parades in the city of Rome.

7. How did Gaius Marius change the Roman army?
    a. He took soldiers only from the upper classes of Roman society.
    b. He paid men who were good fighters to be soldiers, no matter what class they were from.
    c. He required men to volunteer to be in the Roman army.
    d. He made sure his soldiers were loyal to the Republic of Rome, not to their generals.

8. What was the only important reform that Caesar made when he ruled Rome?
    a. He reformed the army.
    b. He got rid of all the dishonest, greedy politicians.
    c. He reformed the calendar, basing it on a year made up of 365 1/4 days.
    d. He passed a law that allowed small farmers to resettle on public land.

9. What was one reason for the Romans' dislike of Christianity?
    a. The Christians worshiped gods that were different from the ones Romans worshiped.
    b. The Romans were never tolerant of new religions, and Christianity was a new religion.
    c. The Christians set fire to Rome in 64 C.E. and drove Emperor Nero to kill himself.
    d. The Christians refused to worship the Roman gods, including the emperors who had been made into gods.

10. One principle of ancient Roman law that we still value today is _____.
    a. the Pax Romana
    b. the idea of a representative democracy
    c. that a person is innocent until proved guilty
    d. that a person cannot be forced to testify against himself in a court of law

UNIT 4 APPLICATION ACTIVITY
Social Satire

Quintus Horatius Flaccus, known as Horace, was one of Rome's great writers. He was a master of satire. Satire is writing that makes fun of human weaknesses. Were the ancient Romans' weaknesses different from our own? You be the judge. Below is a passage translated from the *Satires* of Horace.

Mankind for the most part, fooled by its own false desires, says, "There's no such thing as enough. You are worth only as much as you have." And what can you do with a person like this? Oh, well! Wish him to hell and farewell, since he's headed that way by choice. Like the man they tell of in Athens, filthy but rich, who hated the voice of the people and kept saying, "So! The citizens hiss at me! Ah! But I applaud myself alone at home when I gaze on the coins in my strongbox."

—Horace, *Satires* 1•1

(Smith Palmer Bovie, translator)

Do you think Horace's words fit our society today or not? Write your thoughts on the lines below.

_____

_____

_____

_____

_____

_____

_____

_____

_____

_____

UNIT 5
Europe in the Middle Ages

LESSON 17: An Empire Divided: The East

 GOAL: To identify the people, places, and events involved in the fall of Rome, the split of the Roman Empire, and the growth of the Byzantine Empire

WORDS TO KNOW

Justinian Code   multiple causes

NAMES TO KNOW

Justinian I   Theodora   Theodosius

PLACES TO KNOW

Byzantine Empire   Hagia Sophia

Why Rome Fell

The Roman Empire was the greatest empire the world had ever seen. It stretched across three continents. It lasted for five centuries, from 27 B.C.E. to 476 C.E. It made important contributions in government, philosophy, architecture, and other areas. The influence of Rome is seen throughout the Western world today.

But Rome could not last. Today, we say that Rome fell, or ended. Why did such a great empire fall?

There is no one, single reason why Rome fell. In fact, the fall of Rome is a good lesson in the idea of multiple causes. Multiple causes means that more than one condition triggers an event. There were many reasons for the fall of the Roman Empire. For centuries, historians have debated these causes. There is widespread agreement on several of them.

1. Rome fell because it grew **too large.** The Roman Empire was a geographic giant. It stretched across three continents. It included mountains, deserts, seacoasts, and forests. When it was hot in one place in the empire, it was snowing in another. The Romans did make great improvements in transportation and communication. But the vast size of the empire made it difficult for its leaders to keep track of everything that was going on.

2. Rome fell because of a **weak government.** The Romans tried to control a huge empire with a government that had been created to rule a small city-state. Many historians think that the Romans never created a government that was really suited for running such a large empire. Also, selfish leaders often made decisions to benefit themselves and their friends instead of the people and the empire as a whole.

3. Rome fell because of **economic problems.** Rome grew rich at first because it conquered other peoples and took their wealth. When this growth slowed and then stopped, there were no new sources of wealth. The government then imposed heavy taxes, which hurt the economy. There was never enough tax money to pay for everything the Romans wanted. For example, there was not enough money to keep the famous Roman roads repaired. This caused a decline in trade, which further hurt the economy.

4. Rome fell because of **slavery.** The Romans held slaves. In some parts of the empire, there were more slaves than any other class of people. Because there were so many slaves, there were always thousands of people who were unhappy. Often, slaves revolted against their owners.

5. Rome fell because of **social problems.** Over the centuries, the people of Rome seemed to lose their patriotism. They took less and less interest in their government. They cared more for themselves than for their empire. For example, Roman soldiers often deserted their posts just when they were needed the most.

6. Rome fell because of **revolutions.** The Roman Empire included many different peoples. Many of these groups did not want to belong to the empire. Over the centuries, there were many revolts against Roman rule. These revolts took a toll on the government, the military, and the economy.

7. Rome fell because of **invasions.** Toward the end of the empire, tribes of barbarians who lived on the Roman frontier, or border, invaded the empire.

As you can see, there were many reasons for the fall of Rome. Remember that all of these causes developed slowly, over centuries. But toward the end of the empire, all of these conditions were going on at the same time.

The traditional date given for the fall of Rome is 476 C.E. This was the year a barbarian commander overthrew the last emperor in Rome. By then, all of the multiple causes had taken their toll. The fall of Rome did not happen in just one day or one year. The Roman Empire, which took centuries to build, took hundreds of years to disintegrate.

■ PRACTICE 127: Why Rome Fell

Fill in each of the following empty boxes with a reason for the fall of Rome.

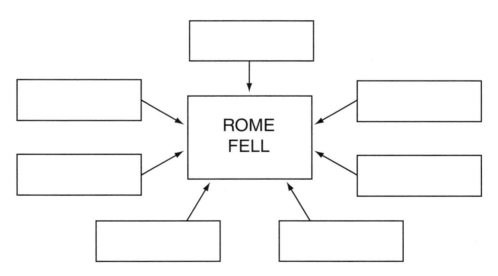

Dividing the Empire

In 476 C.E., enemies of Rome finally overran the great city. But before this happened, the Roman Empire was already in trouble. There were serious problems in the government and with the economy. Romans were losing confidence in their empire.

By the 200s C.E., the Roman Empire was on the verge of collapse. During this period, there were twenty different emperors in 50 years. The army was not defending the frontier well. Increasing taxes were taking a heavy toll on the economy. Roads were falling to ruin. And inflation was making most of the people very poor.

All of the signs pointed to the collapse of the Roman Empire. In fact, the empire might well have collapsed in the 200s C.E. except for two important emperors: Diocletian and Constantine. They are two of the most famous rulers in history.

Diocletian was born poor. But he was talented and determined. He rose to become a general in the army. His success made him very popular. With the support of the army, he became emperor in 284 C.E.

Diocletian realized that the Roman Empire was simply too big for one person to rule. His solution was to divide the Roman Empire into two. This division was not an official division. In other words, the Roman Empire was still one in name. But for all practical purposes, it became the Roman Empires. Diocletian appointed a co-emperor to rule the western part of the empire. Diocletian ruled the eastern half of the empire.

Although Diocletian shared his power, he was still in charge. A powerful ruler, he fought against invaders and restored law and order to the empire. Diocletian's system of having two emperors worked well for about 50 years. But soon a rivalry grew between the two halves of Rome. The rivalry erupted in a civil war. Diocletian retired in 305 C.E.

The Roman Empire: East and West

Constantine came to power the next year, 306 C.E. Constantine is famous for protecting Christianity in Rome. He said that once, while leading his army into battle, he saw a vision: a blazing cross in the sky. With the cross appeared the words *Hoc Signo Vinces.* The words mean "By this sign you shall conquer." When he saw this vision, Constantine swore his allegiance to Christianity and the Christian God. He won the battle. From that time on, he always protected Christians. This helped Christianity to grow quickly throughout the empire.

Constantine is also famous for the founding of the city Constantinople, which means "city of Constantine." It was the new capital of the empire, and it centered power in the eastern part of the empire. Constantinople still exists, although under a different name. Today, it is the city of Istanbul, the largest city in Turkey.

TIP

Often, you can help yourself remember events by using word tricks. In other words, think about how related words are similar or different. For example, a word trick that will help you easily remember that Constantine founded Constantinople is to remember how similar the names are. Alexander and Alexandria is another example of this kind of word trick.

Like Diocletian, Constantine was a strong emperor. He was so powerful, in fact, that in 324 C.E., he became the sole emperor. Rome was once again under the leadership of one man. Even after Constantine's death, in 337 C.E., Rome remained stable for 50 years.

But the forces of decline, which you read about earlier, were taking their toll. Theodosius, the emperor who followed Constantine, was the last emperor to lead a single Rome. When he died, in 395 C.E., the empire was split between his two sons. There were now officially two Roman Empires—the East Roman Empire and the West Roman Empire. They ended up having very different histories.

■ PRACTICE 128: Dividing the Empire

Decide if each statement below is true (**T**) or false (**F**). Write the correct letter on the line before each statement.

_____ **1.** By 200 C.E., the Roman Empire was rich and thriving.

_____ **2.** It was Diocletian who first divided the Roman Empire.

_____ **3.** Diocletian is famous for being the protector of Christianity in Rome.

_____ **4.** After Theodosius died, the Roman Empire was split into two empires.

The Byzantine Empire

By 400 C.E., there were two Roman Empires, East and West. The West, which was struggling with problems ranging from inflation to invasion, grew weaker and weaker. Meanwhile, the East grew stronger and stronger. It had better armies and a stronger government than the West. But the key reason for its strength was its wealth. Most of the trade and wealth of the Roman Empire was centered in the East.

Over time, the East Roman Empire developed into the **Byzantine Empire.** It was called this because its capital, Constantinople, was built on the site of the old Greek city Byzantium. The Byzantine Empire lasted about 1,000 years, from 395 C.E. to 1453 C.E. Remember this: The people of the Byzantine Empire still called themselves Romans. This will help you remember that the Byzantine Empire preserved, or kept alive, many of the great advances of Roman civilization.

The Byzantine Empire is important for several

The Byzantine Empire in the 500s

reasons. The Byzantines protected Europe from invasions by the Arabs and others. They preserved Greek and Roman philosophy, literature, and ideas about government. Above all else, they became the link between the great achievements of the ancient world and those of modern Europe.

The Byzantine Empire reached its greatest size in the 500s. It covered much the same area as the Roman Empire. It stretched across North Africa, southern Europe, and the eastern Mediterranean.

The Byzantine Empire was a Christian empire. Its first emperors were Christian, and its official religion was Christianity. As the empire spread, so did Christianity. Missionaries converted the new members of the empire. In fact, the growth of Christianity under the Byzantines is one of the main reasons why Christianity is the most widespread religion today. The Eastern Orthodox Church, with its millions of members, is a direct descendant of the Christian Church of the Byzantine Empire.

Christianity played a large part in Byzantine art, music, and architecture. The Byzantines produced wonderful works, which are still celebrated today. They greatly influenced the religious art of later peoples. One of the most famous buildings in the world is the Hagia Sophia, a magnificent church built in Constantinople. It is in the shape of a cross, and it has a huge, beautiful dome. People still visit it today.

The Hagia Sophia

■ PRACTICE 129: The Byzantine Empire

Circle the letter of the correct answer to each of the following questions.

1. Which of the following is NOT a reason why the East Roman Empire was stronger than the West Roman Empire?
   a. It had better armies.
   b. It was never invaded.
   c. It had a stronger government.
   d. It was the center of wealth and trade.

2. How long did the Byzantine Empire last?
- **a.** about 1,000 years
- **b.** about 500 years
- **c.** about 100 years
- **d.** about 10,000 years

3. What parts of Byzantine life did Christianity influence?
- **a.** art
- **b.** music
- **c.** architecture
- **d.** all of the above

Justinian and Theodora

The greatest emperor of the Byzantine Empire was Justinian I, who ruled from 527 to 565. Few other rulers in history accomplished as much as Justinian did.

Justinian wanted the Byzantine Empire to be as great and as grand as the old Roman Empire. He began a series of wars to recapture what had been the West Roman Empire. Many victories against the Vandals and Goths expanded the empire. Justinian was careful to secure the territory that he captured. Trade flourished, and the empire grew in wealth. Justinian was so successful that he brought the empire to its height.

Justinian also did much to promote Christianity during this period. Although many religions were practiced in the Byzantine Empire, Justinian wanted to organize his empire under the one faith.

Justinian was also a great builder. Under his direction, many wonderful structures were built. Many, including the Hagia Sophia, still stand. Justinian built monasteries to promote Christianity. He also built harbors, fortresses, and other public buildings.

Perhaps Justinian's most important accomplishment was his creation of the Justinian Code. The Justinian Code was an organized collection of laws. Justinian directed ten of the wisest men in the empire to collect and organize the most important laws of old Rome. These laws were assembled into one document. Along with the laws were explanations of the legal ideas that supported them and cases to help explain them. The Justinian Code preserved Rome's great legal contribution. But the code also had greater effects. It served as the basis for the laws in many countries. In fact, many of the laws that we live under today are related in some form to those of the Justinian Code.

Justinian could not have accomplished all that he did without his wife, Theodora. Their marriage is one of the great love stories of all times. Theodora was a poor peasant. Her father trained bears in a traveling circus. As a girl, Theodora became an actress, a profession that many people looked down on. Despite laws that prohibited high officials from marrying people of her class, Justinian married Theodora.

As the empress, Theodora became very powerful, co-ruling with Justinian. She wrote to foreign leaders, met with foreign diplomats, and built hospitals and churches. She also saw to it that women in the empire were treated well. At her insistence, Justinian changed the law so that husbands could not beat their wives. She made sure that wives could get a divorce if they wanted to. She also saw to it that laws keeping women from owning property were changed. Before Theodora, widows were forced to give up their children. Theodora made sure that that law was changed, too.

Once, when rebels threatened to overthrow him, Justinian wanted to flee. Theodora insisted that they stay and fight. They won and, thus, were able to continue to make the many contributions that they had started. Theodora died of cancer in 548. Justinian was devastated, and he made no more lasting accomplishments.

■ THINK ABOUT IT

You have just read some fascinating facts about Theodora. She accomplished many things. You probably noticed that most of her accomplishments had to do with helping women. Based on this fact, what can you guess about how women were treated in the Byzantine Empire before Theodora became powerful? Write your answer on a separate sheet of paper.

■ PRACTICE 130: Justinian and Theodora

Circle the letter of the correct answer to each of the following questions.

1. Which of the following did NOT occur during the rule of Justinian I?
   a. People began to practice many different religions.
   b. Many wonderful structures were built, including the Hagia Sophia.
   c. A collection of laws was organized.
   d. Trade flourished.

2. What was the Justinian Code?
   a. a collection of the most important laws of Rome
   b. an oath taken by Justinian's army
   c. a secret document of the Byzantine Empire
   d. a secret password used by Justinian and Theodora

3. Which of the following is NOT an accomplishment of Theodora?
   a. A law was changed to state that men could not beat their wives.
   b. A law was passed stating that wives could divorce their husbands.
   c. A law was changed to state that only men could own property.
   d. Widows were given the right to keep their children.

4. What happened when rebels threatened to overthrow Justinian?
   a. Theodora wanted to flee, but Justinian insisted that they stay and fight.
   b. Justinian wanted to flee, but Theodora insisted that they stay and fight.
   c. Theodora and Justinian decided to flee the country.
   d. The rebels conquered Justinian and took over the Byzantine Empire.

End of the Byzantine Empire

The Byzantine Empire lasted another 900 years after the death of Justinian. But it never regained the greatness it had known.

The empire soon began to decline. The costs of wars and great building projects had left the empire almost bankrupt. Worse, the empire suffered from invasions on all sides. Attackers included Lombards, Slavs, Avars, Persians, and Arabs. These wars lasted for centuries and took a terrible toll on the people of the empire.

During the 800s, the Byzantine Empire enjoyed short-lived success. It drove back the Arabs and other enemies. But within 200 years, the empire was losing wars again. This time, the Ottoman Turks were threatening the Byzantines. The emperor turned to Europe for help. The Europeans responded by launching the Crusades (which you will read about later).

But the Crusades failed to protect the Byzantine Empire from its enemies. In 1453, the Ottoman Turks captured Constantinople. The Byzantine Empire was no more.

IN REAL LIFE

Today, people sometimes use the word *byzantine* to mean "complicated" or "intricate." For example, someone might refer to "a byzantine way to run the government." This use of the word reflects the culture of the Byzantines. They had a complex style that can be seen in the design of their domed churches, the patterns of their decorative arts, and the mysteries of their religion.

■ PRACTICE 131: End of the Byzantine Empire

Decide if each statement below is true (**T**) or false (**F**). Write the correct letter on the line before each statement.

_____ **1.** The Byzantine Empire lasted 500 years after the death of Justinian.

_____ **2.** The Persians, Slavs, and Avars all invaded the Byzantine Empire.

_____ **3.** When the Ottoman Turks threatened his empire, the Byzantine emperor turned to the Arabs.

_____ **4.** The Ottoman Turks captured Constantinople in 1453.

LESSON 18: An Empire Divided: The West

GOAL: To identify the people, places, and events involved in the rise of the Frankish kings and Charlemagne's empire; to understand the Viking invasions and explorations

WORDS TO KNOW

Franks   Vikings

NAMES TO KNOW

Charlemagne	Erik the Red	Pepin the Short
Charles Martel	Leif Eriksson	

PLACES TO KNOW

Greenland	Tours
Iceland	Vinland

Frankish Kings

The Roman Empire collapsed in 476. But it had been in decline for hundreds of years before then. One of the main reasons for its decline was that it was invaded by many peoples. These peoples included the Vandals, Burgundians, Visigoths, and Ostrogoths.
As Rome weakened, these peoples strengthened. They moved into many areas that had been part of the West Roman Empire. They took over the towns and the countryside. They plundered the wealth of Rome. Many of them established small kingdoms. What had been one empire became a patchwork of kingdoms.

The Franks

The most successful of these peoples were the Franks. The Franks first invaded the Roman Empire in the 300s. They settled in northwest Europe. By 500, they ruled a great area in the region.

One of the greatest Frankish kings was Charles Martel. He was a strong military ruler whose name means "Charles the Hammer." His greatest military victory was at Tours, in what is now France, in 732. There, he defeated Spanish Moors who were trying to invade. This victory proved to be very important. The Spanish Moors were Muslims, who were trying to bring their religion into Christian Europe. Charles Martel's victory at Tours helped to make sure that Europe would remain Christian.

After Charles Martel died, his son took over. The son was Pepin the Short. Like his father, he was a strong ruler. His greatest maneuver was to form an alliance with the pope, the leader of the Christian Church in Europe. This alliance strengthened Frankish rule. Although this was a great achievement, Pepin's greatest legacy is being the father of one of the greatest kings who ever lived: Charlemagne.

THINK ABOUT IT

History can change in the blink of an eye. For example, think about the Battle of Tours. Think about who fought in this battle and where it was fought. Think about the religious beliefs of each side. Now consider this: How might the world be different today if the Muslims had won the Battle of Tours? Write your answer on a separate sheet of paper.

■ PRACTICE 132: Frankish Kings

Circle the letter of the correct answer to each of the following questions.

1. Which of the peoples who conquered Rome were the most successful?
   a. the Vandals
   b. the Ostrogoths
   c. the Franks
   d. the Visigoths

2. Why was Charles Martel's victory at Tours important?
   a. It separated Spain and France.
   b. It encouraged the Roman people to become Muslims.
   c. It opened trade routes.
   d. It helped to make sure that Europe would remain Christian.

3. With whom did Pepin the Short make an alliance?
   a. the ruler of the Spanish Moors
   b. Charlemagne
   c. the pope
   d. none of the above

Charlemagne

Charlemagne, the son of Pepin the Short, became king of the Franks in 768. He ruled until 814. Few other kings in history have been as successful as Charlemagne was.

In the nearly 350 years since the fall of Rome, Europe had been a poor, dangerous, and divided place. Despite the advances made by Charles Martel, Pepin the Short, and other Frankish kings, Europe was still greatly divided. There were many small kingdoms, which were often at war with one another. There were few towns, little trade, and almost no industry. Charlemagne changed much of that.

Charlemagne had little education. But he was extremely intelligent. He read and spoke Latin, the language of learned people. (He could not write it, however, even though he tried to learn.) Charlemagne was a tall man—over 6 feet—and he was strong and active. He loved riding horseback and other sports. Overall, he was an impressive man. His personal power matched the power he wielded as king.

Charlemagne's Empire

As soon as he took the throne, Charlemagne began to expand his kingdom. He conquered many peoples throughout western Europe. At its height, Charlemagne's kingdom stretched across almost all of Europe.

Throughout his reign, Charlemagne worked to improve conditions in Europe. He helped the economy by creating markets and by issuing money. He encouraged farmers to grow food more efficiently. Perhaps most important, he established feudalism, a system of government that lasted for hundreds of years. (You will read more about feudalism later.)

A devout Christian, Charlemagne encouraged and sometimes forced Christianity on the peoples he conquered. Charlemagne also worked hard to make sure that courts of law were just. He established schools throughout his empire. He built many libraries. In short, Charlemagne changed the face of Europe.

By the time he died, in 814, Charlemagne ruled almost all of western Europe. For the first time since the fall of Rome, nearly 350 years earlier, a great and unified empire provided order for life in Europe.

TIP

As you read, look for paragraphs that summarize the main idea of a lesson. For example, in the last paragraph under the heading "Charlemagne," the main idea is that Charlemagne's empire united western Europe for the first time in centuries. By remembering just this one idea, you have learned a very important fact about history.

■ PRACTICE 133: Charlemagne

Decide if each statement below is true (**T**) or false (**F**). Write the correct letter on the line before each statement.

_____ **1.** Charlemagne established feudalism, a new way to organize government.

_____ **2.** Charlemagne was a cruel dictator who abolished all courts of law.

_____ **3.** By 814, Charlemagne ruled almost all of western Europe.

Northern Invaders

Charlemagne's empire was split among his three sons after his death. Divided into three parts, the great empire grew weak. This weakness was taken advantage of by many invaders. The fiercest and most famous of these were the Vikings. The Vikings lived in what is now Norway, Sweden, and Denmark. They were also called the Danes and the Norse, or Norsemen. About the time of Charlemagne's death, a famine, or lack of food, struck northern Europe where the Vikings lived. This famine was caused by changes in the weather, which made it harder to grow crops. It was also caused by a rapid increase in the Viking population. There simply was not enough farmland or food to go around. As a result, the Vikings went out in search of new land and treasure.

From the 700s to the 1000s, the Vikings sailed in three directions. One group headed south, raiding the British Isles and western Europe. Another group headed east, invading eastern Europe. A third group headed west, across the Atlantic Ocean.

Wherever they went, the Vikings spread terror. They were cruel in their warfare. They often murdered women and children. They took what they wanted from their opponents and burned the rest.

IN REAL LIFE

Throughout history, famine has encouraged many groups to leave their homelands. In the 1840s, for example, a potato famine struck Ireland. About 1.5 million people left Ireland during that time. Many of these people came to the United States. The potato famine is one reason why there is a large Irish population in the United States today.

■ PRACTICE 134: Northern Invaders

Decide if each statement below is true (**T**) or false (**F**). Write the correct letter on the line before each statement.

_____ **1.** The rapid increase of the Viking population and changes in weather resulted in a famine in northern Europe.

_____ **2.** Vikings were also called Norsemen.

Skilled Seafarers

The Vikings are famous not only for being fierce invaders, but also for their shipbuilding and navigation.

Viking ships possessed great beauty. They stood 50 to 100 feet long and about 20 feet wide. These wooden ships had a lovely, curved shape. And their appearance was more than matched by how beautifully they sailed. They were stable in rough, open seas. They glided smoothly in calm, shallow coastal areas and rivers. They could be driven by sail or by oars. Larger Viking ships could easily carry dozens of people and tons of supplies over vast distances.

The Vikings decorated the front of their ships with carvings of horses, birds, and fierce imaginary beasts. These carvings came to symbolize the power of the Vikings.

The Vikings were as skilled in navigation as they were in shipbuilding. They used the sun and the stars to help them find their way. When sailing along the coast, they used landmarks. One method Vikings used for navigating involved the releasing of ravens. Ravens are birds that can find land well. Whenever a Viking ship became lost, the crew would release a raven and follow it to land. The raven was so important to the seafaring Vikings that they included a picture of one on their flag.

■ PRACTICE 135: Skilled Seafarers

Choose a word or words from below to complete each sentence. Write the letter of the correct word on each line.

a. ravens   **b.** sails   **c.** landmarks   **d.** oars

1. Viking ships could be powered by _____ or _____.

2. When sailing along the coasts, the Vikings used _____ to navigate.

3. The Vikings sometimes released _____ to help them find land.

Leif Eriksson

In the late 800s, Vikings sailed west to **Iceland,** a large island in the North Atlantic Ocean. Within the next 100 years, about 25,000 Vikings settled in Iceland.

In 982, a Viking named **Erik the Red** sailed farther west. He traveled from Iceland to **Greenland.** Erik the Red then returned to Iceland and told of his discovery. Hundreds of people followed him to Greenland and settled there.

Viking Territories

Several years later, another Viking attempted to sail from Iceland to Greenland. He got lost but sighted more land to the west. This is the first known sighting of North America by a European.

After the good farmland in Greenland was used up, Vikings began to think about the mysterious land to the west. Around 1000, one of Erik the Red's sons, **Leif Eriksson,** set out to find this new land.

Leif Eriksson succeeded. He landed somewhere in North America. (He probably landed in what is now Canada, although some people think he landed in what is now the state of Maine.) The Vikings named the land they found **Vinland,** which means "wine land." They called it this because they found many wild grapes, from which they made wine, growing there.

Historians believe that the Vikings established many settlements in North America. But the only remains found so far are in Newfoundland. One of the great mysteries of history is where in North America the Vikings walked—a full 500 years before Christopher Columbus set foot on the continent.

So, why is Columbus given credit for discovering America for the Europeans? Why do we not celebrate Leif Eriksson Day instead of Columbus Day? The answer is that the Vikings never shared their knowledge of North America with the rest of Europe, as Columbus and his followers did.

■ PRACTICE 136: Leif Eriksson

Number the following places to show the order in which the Vikings arrived there.

_____ Greenland

_____ northern Europe

_____ North America

_____ Iceland

Viking Home Life

Most people think of the Vikings simply as warriors and invaders. They were, in fact, a fierce and warlike people. But the Vikings were more than just warriors.

Most Vikings were farmers. They grew crops and raised animals. They also hunted for their food. Other Vikings were metalworkers or woodcarvers.

Most Viking families lived in small one-room houses. These houses were built of stone or wood, with roofs of straw or sod. Their main feature was a hearth, which provided heat and a way to cook food. At mealtime, the father sat in a special chair, while the mother and children sat on small, rough benches.

The Vikings were a very religious people. They told the story of their religion through myths. These myths tell of their many gods, including Thor and Odin. Odin was the king of all gods. Thor was the god of the sky. Thor could hurl thunderbolts, make storms, and send the winds. He was very important to the Vikings, who depended on the weather for raising crops and for sailing.

If you think that Odin and Thor have little to do with you today, think again. Wednesday was named for Odin ("Odin's day"), and Thursday was named for Thor ("Thor's day"). This is a good example of why studying history is important. Much in our lives today was shaped, in some way, by the peoples of long ago.

■ PRACTICE 137: Viking Home Life

Circle the letter of the correct answer to each of the following questions.

1. Which of the following was a common occupation for Vikings?
    a. warrior
    b. farmer
    c. woodcarver
    d. all of the above

2. How did most Viking families live?
    a. in large stone houses
    b. in tents made from animal skins
    c. in small one-room houses
    d. in wooden forts with many other families

3. Which statement best describes the Vikings' religious beliefs?
    a. They believed in many gods.
    b. They learned about their gods from the Bible.
    c. They believed in only one all-powerful god.
    d. The Vikings had very few religious beliefs.

LESSON 19: Life in the Middle Ages

GOAL: To identify and explain the terms *Middle Ages*, *feudalism*, and *manorialism*; to describe the impact of Christianity and the Crusades on life in western Europe

WORDS TO KNOW

archbishops	fief	page
bishops	knights	parishes
cathedrals	lord	peasants
chivalry	manor	pope
convents	manorialism	sacraments
crusaders	medieval period	serf
Dark Ages	Middle Ages	squire
diocese	monasteries	vassals
excommunicate	monasticism	village priest
feudalism	nobles	

NAME TO KNOW

Pope Urban II

PLACES TO KNOW

Holy Land   Palestine

EVENT TO KNOW

Crusades

Bridge of History

Knights in shining armor. Damsels in distress. Castles with moats. All of these images come to mind when you hear the term Middle Ages. But what exactly were the Middle Ages?

The Middle Ages is the name given to a period of the history of western Europe. Before the Middle Ages, much of western Europe was part of the Roman Empire. After the Middle Ages, western Europe was controlled by large kingdoms. So the Middle Ages are a very special time. They bridge the gap between ancient times and modern times.

The Middle Ages are also called the **medieval period.** The word *medieval* comes from the Latin words for "middle" and "age." People also sometimes call this period the **Dark Ages,** because life was hard and most people had little learning.

So, there are three names for this period in western European history: the Middle Ages, the medieval period, and the Dark Ages. They all refer to the same time, from 500 C.E. to about 1500 C.E. (The term *Dark Ages* usually refers only to the time between the fall of the Roman Empire and about 1000 C.E.) That makes it easy to remember: The Middle Ages lasted an even 1,000 years. You should also remember that the Middle Ages refers only to western Europe.

■ PRACTICE 138: Bridge of History

Decide if each statement below is true (**T**) or false (**F**). Write the correct letter on the line before each statement.

_____ **1.** The Middle Ages happened in western Europe.

_____ **2.** The Latin Ages is another name for the Middle Ages.

_____ **3.** The Middle Ages occurred between 500 C.E. and 1500 C.E.

_____ **4.** The Middle Ages are also called the Dark Ages because the preceding era was called the Light Ages.

Feudalism

As you have read, Charlemagne succeeded in uniting western Europe during the 800s. His empire did not last, however. After it fell apart, Europe was again divided into many small kingdoms.

These kingdoms were ruled under a form of government that Charlemagne had started. This form of government was called **feudalism.** By 1000, feudalism was the way of life throughout western Europe. It lasted for many centuries.

What exactly was feudalism? Feudalism was a system of government under which most Europeans lived in the Middle Ages. Under feudalism, Europe was ruled by **nobles,** or people of high social rank. Nobles who were loyal to a king were called **vassals** of the king. The king was their **lord.** The king gave each vassal a **fief,** or an estate of land, in exchange for his loyalty. A fief included the land, the buildings, and even the **peasants—** poor, working people—who lived there. Kingdoms in the Middle Ages were divided into hundreds of fiefs.

Each fief was ruled by a vassal of the king. Most vassals had titles such as baron or earl or duke. Within their fiefs, these rulers had supreme power over the people and the land. They collected taxes, served as judges in legal disputes, and supervised the farming of the fief. Many of them were so powerful that they had their own castles.

Relationships under feudalism were often complicated. For example, a baron who became a vassal to a king controlled a fief in exchange for his loyalty to the king. The king was the baron's lord. Meanwhile, the baron had his own vassals. Each of his vassals was given a fief in exchange for loyalty to the baron. Thus, the baron was both a vassal and a lord at the same time.

▨ IN REAL LIFE

No doubt you know the story of Robin Hood. In this story, an evil sheriff rules while King Richard is away at the Crusades. The sheriff taxes the peasants and forces them to work for him. The peasants live in such poor conditions that Robin Hood and his band of thieves (or "Merry Men") steal from the sheriff to give money to the poor. The stories and movies that tell the tale of Robin Hood are filled with daring adventures. It is not known whether Robin Hood was a real man or if he is simply a legend. Either way, the tale of Robin Hood adds a little excitement to the dreariness of the Middle Ages.

During the Middle Ages, there were thousands of feudal relationships. Europe was governed through these feudal relationships.

The people who had no say in these arrangements were the peasants. Peasants had no economic or social power. For the most part, they led a very poor existence. They lived in huts, worked from dusk to dawn, and were at the mercy of their rulers. Most people in Europe during the Middle Ages were peasants. You will read more about peasant life later.

■ PRACTICE 139: Feudalism

Use the words below to complete the following paragraph. Write the letter of the correct word on each line.

a. feudalism	**c.** lord	**e.** peasants
b. fiefs	**d.** nobles	**f.** vassals

The system of government used in the Middle Ages was called (1) _____. Under this system, a king would give (2) _____ estates of land called (3) _____ in exchange for their loyalty. The nobles would then be the (4) _____ of the king. The king would be their (5) _____. These people had control of these lands and the (6) _____ who lived on them.

Knights and Manors

Europe during the Middle Ages was a patchwork of dozens of kingdoms and thousands of fiefs. Often, the nobles who ruled the land went to war with one another. As a result, soldiers, especially those who rode horses, were extremely important during this time.

Everyone has heard of knights in shining armor—noble warriors who defended a princess's honor. Such things really did occur. Mostly, though, knights were fighting men who went into battle on horses. Only nobles could be knights. Most knights were lords of their own vassals. The knights were also vassals themselves—of kings and lords. Being a loyal vassal meant fighting for the king or lord and raising and leading his armies. Thus, feudalism was a military system as well as a government system.

To become a knight, a boy of noble birth went through three stages. The first stage was to become a **page.** When the son of a noble was about seven years old, he left his home to go and live in the house (or castle) of a knight. There he learned to ride a horse and to fight with a sword, a knife, and other small weapons.

When the boy turned 16, he became a **squire.** That was the second stage toward becoming a knight. As a squire, the boy served as a personal servant to the knight in whose home he lived. He assisted the knight in battle and even took part in battle himself. During this time, the squire learned all he could about becoming a fighting man.

During this time, the boy also learned the code of **chivalry.** The word *chivalry* comes from an old word that means "horse soldier." But chivalry came to refer to the code of conduct by which knights were supposed to live. Being chivalrous meant being loyal to one's lord, treating women with respect, keeping promises, and defending the church. Today, the word lives on. Being chivalrous means being especially respectful to women.

Any knight could make a squire a knight. Usually, though, the knight who trained the squire did the honors. Tapping the back of the squire's neck with a sword, the knight said "I dub you a knight." With that, the young man became a knight. Sometimes, these ceremonies were simple and quick. At other times, the ceremonies were elaborate and lasted for days. Once he became a knight, the young man was expected to be a chivalrous leader of fighting men for the rest of his life.

Feudalism was the government and military system of the Middle Ages. Kings ruled through their vassals. The king's vassals often ruled their own vassals. Through feudalism, the people of Europe were ruled.

Meanwhile, another kind of system developed. **Manorialism** was the economic system of the Middle Ages. This system was called manorialism because it was based on the manor. A **manor** was a large farm or estate. It included the manor house. This was a large home where the lord, or ruler, of the manor lived. It also included pastures, farm fields, small farm buildings, and usually an entire village. Remember, a fief was the land given to a vassal in exchange for his support. Small fiefs usually had only one manor. But a large fief could include many manors.

Each manor was self-sufficient. In other words, all of the things that people needed to live were made on the manor. This included food from farms and animals, clothing from leather, tools, and buildings. Manors traded with one another, but only for those things that they could not make themselves.

It should not surprise you to learn who did the work on the manor. It was the peasants. They lived in a small village, often along a stream, where there was a mill for grinding grain. The noble who ruled the manor kept up to half of the land of the manor for himself. The peasants worked his land for him, in addition to working their own land.

■ PRACTICE 140: Knights and Manors

Match each description with a term below. Write the letter of the correct term on the line before each description.

a. feudalism   **b.** manorialism   **c.** chivalry   **d.** manor

_____ **1.** the code of conduct by which knights were supposed to live

_____ **2.** the economic system of the Middle Ages

_____ **3.** a large farm or estate

_____ **4.** the system in which kings ruled Europe through their vassals

Peasants

We may think about kings and castles and knights in shining armor when we think of the Middle Ages. But most of the people of the time were peasants. As you will recall, peasants were poor people.

Most peasants were serfs. A **serf** was a peasant who was bound to the manor. Although serfs were not slaves, their lives were hardly any better than those of slaves. They could not leave the manor without the permission of the lord of the manor. They were required to pay heavy taxes to the lord, usually in the form of crops or animals. And they lived at the lord's mercy.

■ THINK ABOUT IT

The lives of peasants during the Middle Ages were unbelievably difficult. Why do you think the serfs and peasants led the hard lives that they did? Why did they not just move away to find better lives? Write your answers on a separate sheet of paper.

The life of a peasant was hard and short. Men, women, and children spent their days doing backbreaking work in the fields. They were required to farm the lord's fields as well as their own. At night, they returned to their homes—crude huts in the manor village. They usually ate only black bread, cabbage, turnips, and cheese. They rarely ate any meat, because the game animals and the fish of the manor belonged to the lord. One of their few pleasures was the drinking of beer or wine. After an exhausting day, they fell asleep on crude mattresses made of sacks stuffed with hay.

Such a hard life meant an early death. In fact, historians think that most peasants died by the time they were 30 or 40. A lifetime of malnutrition, hard labor, and disease took its toll.

Like many people who live in hard circumstances, peasants found some peace and hope in their religion, Christianity. In fact, Christianity was a central feature of life in the Middle Ages for both peasants and nobles.

■ PRACTICE 141: Peasants

Decide if each of the following statements is true (**T**) or false (**F**). Write the correct letter on the line before each statement.

_____ **1.** Most peasants were serfs.

_____ **2.** Peasants ate very well, and few died of malnutrition.

_____ **3.** Many peasants died at a young age because they led very hard lives.

_____ **4.** Peasants found some peace and hope in their hard lives by practicing Christianity.

The Church

By the Middle Ages, the Christian religion had spread throughout western Europe. Almost everyone was a member of the Church. Thus, as one historian put it, "Christianity and the Church touched the life of almost everyone during the Middle Ages." From baptism at birth to one's wedding ceremony to the last rites performed near death, the Church was a central feature in most people's lives.

Almost every village had a **village priest.** The priest was usually a peasant himself. But he was an important spiritual leader. He administered most of the **sacraments,** or special ceremonies, of the church for the peasants in his village. He also supervised their moral and religious training. Poor peasants turned to their priest in times of trouble and confusion. So village priests were also called parish priests. The areas that priests served were called **parishes.**

A group of parishes made up a diocese. **Bishops** were church officials in charge of dioceses. The headquarters of a diocese was in the largest town in an area. Often, these towns had **cathedrals**—large, beautiful churches that took years to build. Many stunning cathedrals built during this period are still standing.

Just as parish priests answered to bishops, bishops answered to **archbishops.** They, in turn, answered to the **pope.** The pope was the leader of the Church. He lived in Rome.

As you can see, the Church was highly organized, much like a government. In fact, the Church at this time had many powers that governments have today. The Church established laws for the people in the lands it held. It settled disputes. At times, the Church even raised armies and went to battle.

The Church became the largest landholder during the Middle Ages. Kings and nobles gave fiefs to nobles in exchange for their loyalty. Nobles often granted fiefs to the Church. As a result, the Church grew rich and powerful. The Church also held power because its officials could **excommunicate** people (cut them off entirely from the Church). Excommunication was a powerful weapon because the Church was so important to the people of Europe.

During the Middle Ages, some people came to believe that the best Christian life was one that was cut off from the world. These people became monks and nuns. Monks formed communities called **monasteries.** Nuns formed communities called **convents.** The term for this way of life is **monasticism.**

Monasteries played several important roles during the Middle Ages. For one thing, the monks were the most learned people of their time. They were scholars and teachers. Since printing was yet to be invented, their copying of books from the ancient world preserved much knowledge for future generations.

■ PRACTICE 142: The Church

Use the words below to complete the following paragraph. Write the letter of the correct word or words on each line.

a. bishop **c.** archbishop **e.** diocese

b. pope **d.** parish priest

The Church was a central figure in the lives of most Europeans in the

Middle Ages. In each village, the (1) _____ would perform the

sacraments for the members of his parish. A group of parishes was

called a (2) _____ and was headed by a (3) _____. The next step up in

the order of church officials was the (4) _____, to whom the bishop

answered. The leader of the Church was the (5) _____, who led from

Rome.

The Crusades

During most of the Middle Ages, the people of Europe took little interest in life outside of their kingdoms. Kings and nobles either fought or cooperated. Members of the Church sought to help their people. Peasants lived their hard lives. Then developments outside Europe began to threaten the Church. And life in Europe changed forever.

The Byzantine Empire in eastern Europe was a Christian empire. But during the Middle Ages, the empire was attacked by the Turks from Asia. The Turks were Muslims—they followed the religion of Islam. The Christians viewed the Muslims as a threat to their religion. What's more, the Turks came to control the Holy Land, or Palestine. This land, which lies at the eastern end of the Mediterranean, was (and is) important to Christians. It is the land told about in the Bible.

Pope Urban II, the leader of the Church in Europe, wanted to regain the Holy Land from the Muslim Turks. To help the Byzantine Empire, the pope called on the Europeans to fight the Muslims. He helped organize a military expedition to regain the Holy Land.

This Christian expedition became the first Crusade. There were eight major Crusades. They took place between 1096 and 1270. The kings, nobles, and peasants who joined the Crusades were called crusaders. They had two goals: to recapture the Holy Land from the Muslims and to help the Christian Byzantine Empire. Many crusaders also hoped for wealth and land. Others wanted adventure.

Overall, the Crusades failed. Although the crusaders controlled the holy land for a time, they could not maintain their control. The crusaders also failed to save the Byzantine Empire. They looted Constantinople, capital of the empire, in 1204. Then the empire fell to the Muslim Turks in 1453.

However, the Crusades had important effects on European life. Returning crusaders brought with them ideas and goods (spices, perfumes, and fabrics) that were new to the Europeans. Most important, the Crusades promoted trade between Europe and Asia. This trade eventually brought wealth to Europe. And that set the stage for a dramatic change in European life.

■ PRACTICE 143: The Crusades

Circle the letter of the correct answer to each of the following questions.

1. What event started the Crusades?
   a. The Byzantine Empire took over the Holy Land.
   b. The Turks attacked the leader of the Church in Europe.
   c. The Turks took over control of the Holy Land.
   d. Armies from Europe attacked the empire of the Turks.

2. The Crusades were a clash between two religions. What were these two religions?
   a. Christianity and Buddhism
   b. Islam and Judaism
   c. Judaism and Christianity
   d. Christianity and Islam

3. Where was the Holy Land?
   a. Palestine
   b. Turkey
   c. eastern Europe
   d. Constantinople

4. What was the most important result of the Crusades for Europe?
   a. increased trade between Europe and Asia
   b. control of the Holy Land by Europe
   c. defeat of the Turks
   d. better living conditions for the peasants

LESSON 20: The Rise of Nations in Europe

 GOAL: To describe how larger kingdoms replaced a patchwork of smaller kingdoms toward the end of the Middle Ages

WORDS TO KNOW

Black Death	Capetian dynasty	guilds
bubonic plague	due process of law	Magna Carta

NAMES TO KNOW

Charles V	King John
Hugh Capet	Otto I
Joan of Arc	William the Conqueror

PLACE TO KNOW

Holy Roman Empire

EVENTS TO KNOW

Battle of Agincourt	Battle of Hastings	Hundred Years' War

Feudalism in Decline

During the Middle Ages, kings granted nobles fiefs of land in exchange for their loyalty. The nobles held supreme authority within their fiefs. They controlled all of the manors, or farm estates, on their lands. This arrangement gave the nobles tremendous power over the peasants and serfs who lived on the land.

Slowly, over centuries, all of this changed. The main reason for this change was that the economy in Europe slowly improved. Europe during the Middle Ages was, as a rule, a very poor place. There was virtually no trade. Manors were mostly self-sufficient. However, toward the end of the Middle Ages, trade began to increase. This was largely a result of the contact that Europeans made with the outside world during the Crusades. Trade routes were thus developed between Europe and Asia.

The trade that developed included many kinds of goods. Some of them were luxury items from Asia, such as spices, dyes, and fine cloth. In exchange, Europeans traded things such as timber, fur, and wine.

As trade grew, the need arose for a place to make exchanges. At first, trade was conducted in small village markets. Over time, these markets grew. Soon, trade fairs were being held throughout Europe.

At the beginning of the Middle Ages, towns were small, few, and far between. Mostly, each was a tiny village that was part of a manor. As trade grew, towns began to grow. Traders and merchants did not need to live on farms. In the towns, they formed organizations called guilds. **Guilds** were designed to protect their members, establish prices and wages, and settle disputes between workers and their bosses. Many guilds grew very powerful. In fact, towns were often run by the guilds themselves.

IN REAL LIFE

Today, you are more likely to join a union than a guild. But there are still guilds performing many of the same tasks that they did in the Middle Ages. In London, for example, some of the same guilds that were begun in the Middle Ages still thrive: There is a mercers (general merchants) guild, an apothecaries (medicine) guild, a grocers guild, and many more!

Most towns of the time were small, with populations of about 5,000 people. But a few had populations of as many as 30,000 people. These were the huge cities of the day.

As towns grew, the manorial system began to break down. Fewer people needed to make a living off the land. Since the feudal system depended on manorialism, it began to break down, too. Peasants sold farm produce to people in towns. They paid their feudal lords with money instead of with labor. Feudal lords used the money to buy trade goods they wanted.

Europe was changing. The Crusades led to trade. And trade led to a new kind of economy based on business in towns instead of agriculture on manors.

■ PRACTICE 144: Feudalism in Decline

Circle the letter of the correct answer to each of the following questions.

1. What happened in Europe as a result of increased trade between Europe and Asia?
   a. Towns and cities grew.
   b. Guilds were formed.
   c. Feudalism and manorialism declined.
   d. all of the above

2. Why were guilds formed?
   a. to establish prices and wages
   b. to help with the Crusades
   c. to abolish manorialism
   d. all of the above

3. What caused the manorial system to begin to break down?
   a. wars in Europe
   b. the growth of towns
   c. the weakness of the guilds
   d. knights' taking over the government

William the Conqueror

The growth of trade was not the only thing that brought an end to feudalism. Political developments also played an important role.

In 1066, William of Normandy (in France) claimed the English throne. The nobles of England, however, refused to recognize him as their king. In response, William organized a fleet of ships and an army of loyal nobles and sailed to England. At the Battle of Hastings, he defeated the English nobles. He declared himself king of England. From then on, he was known as William the Conqueror.

William the Conqueror ruled England for nearly 20 years. During this time, he established a new type of feudalism in England. He organized the feudal system so that he, himself, held the authority. Elsewhere in Europe, the nobles were as powerful as or more powerful than the king. William made sure that he was in charge. To make sure the nobles would not organize against him, he gave them fiefs that were scattered all throughout England.

William was one of the first to organize power under a strong king instead of a patchwork of rival kingdoms. In doing so, he took the first steps toward unifying the country of England.

■ PRACTICE 145: William the Conqueror

Decide if each statement below is true (**T**) or false (**F**). Write the correct letter on the line before each statement.

_____ **1.** William of Normandy used force to become king of England.

_____ **2.** William the Conqueror gave his nobles fiefs that were scattered throughout England so that he could spread Christianity throughout England.

_____ **3.** William the Conqueror is important because he was one of the first to organize power under a strong king.

_____ **4.** William the Conqueror's brand of feudalism helped unify England.

The Magna Carta

William the Conqueror was careful to keep a strong rule in England. The kings who followed William further strengthened the ruler's power in England. William's son, Henry I, set up a government department to oversee the kingdom's finances. He further weakened the nobles by having cases tried in the king's courts instead of in the nobles' courts.

A later king, Henry II, raised a national army instead of relying on nobles for military service. He also arranged for clergy members to go to government courts. He worked at establishing the king's law as the common law of the land.

By this time, the king of England was very powerful—much more powerful than the nobles of England. The king who followed Henry II was his son, **King John.** King John tried to make the nobles pay heavier taxes than they had paid before. He also insisted on more military service from the nobles than they had had to provide in the past. Most important, he made decisions based on his own wishes, rather than on law and feudal tradition.

The nobles resented these changes. They revolted against King John. They forced him to sign a document called the **Magna Carta.** *Magna Carta* is a Latin phrase that means "great charter." The Magna Carta is one of the most important documents in history.

The Magna Carta was intended to require the king to uphold feudal law and tradition. It was designed to benefit the nobles. It did little to help the common people. But the Magna Carta had other important effects.

First, the Magna Carta limited the power of the king. It made him follow the law, not his own wishes. In other words, the Magna Carta put in writing the idea that the leader of the country was not above the law.

Second, the Magna Carta became the foundation for modern justice. Ideas in the Magna Carta affect our lives today. For example, the Magna Carta said that no one could be put in jail or have property taken away unless the law or a group of people (like a jury) allowed it. This idea is called **due process of law.** It is an important idea in the laws of many countries today, including the United States.

Third, the Magna Carta set the stage for other ideas of law that exist today. Five hundred years after its signing, the Magna Carta became a basis for the work of Sir William Blackstone. Blackstone was an English lawyer who wrote about English law. When the English colonists came to America, they brought Blackstone's ideas with them. In fact, the ideas in the Magna Carta—that the leaders of a country are not above the law, that people are entitled to due process, and that legal decisions can be made by juries—are included in the U.S. Constitution. In addition, the Magna Carta set up "no taxation without representation." The king must call a respresentational body to ask permission to institute a new tax thus providing the foundation for Parliament.

■ PRACTICE 146: The Magna Carta

Decide if each statement below is true (**T**) or false (**F**). Write the correct letter on the line before each statement.

_____ **1.** The Magna Carta was a document intended to limit the power of the king.

_____ **2.** Due process of law is the idea that the king should decide who will and who will not go to jail.

_____ **3.** Some of the ideas in the Magna Carta are in the U.S. Constitution.

_____ **4.** William the Conqueror was king when the Magna Carta was written.

The Capetian Dynasty

Despite the Magna Carta, the kings of England helped unify the land into a single country. From a patchwork of smaller kingdoms, England developed into a country. A similar process occurred in France.

France, like the rest of western Europe, was divided during the Middle Ages. Hundreds of nobles each had power over a certain region. There were French kings, but they were not much more powerful than the other nobles. The kings were basically nobles whom the other nobles chose to lead them in war. These independent nobles were powerful. For example, William the Conqueror, who invaded England, was a French noble.

The power of the French nobles began to decrease in 987. In that year, the nobles chose Hugh Capet as their king. **Hugh Capet** was the first of the **Capetian dynasty**, a line of kings that continued almost to the end of the Middle Ages.

Over the years, the Capetian kings added to their lands. The new lands added to their power and influence. Equally important, each Capetian king had a son to pass the kingdom on to. This allowed the dynasty to continue.

French nobles went on the Crusades, leaving the kings free to increase their power at home. The kings became stronger, while the nobles became weaker.

Like England, France was becoming a single country instead of a collection of smaller kingdoms.

IN REAL LIFE

Can you think of a dynasty that exists today? Remember, a dynasty is a group of rulers from the same family. Have you ever heard anyone mention the "Kennedy dynasty"? In the United States, members of the Kennedy family (including John, Robert, and Edward) have served in government positions over many decades.

■ PRACTICE 147: The Capetian Dynasty

Decide if each statement below is true (**T**) or false (**F**). Write the correct letter on the line before each statement.

_____ **1.** The Capetian dynasty helped make France a single country.

_____ **2.** As the Capetians grew in strength, so did the French nobles.

_____ **3.** When the nobles left France on the Crusades, the kings were able to increase their power.

_____ **4.** The Capetians were successful because disease killed many of the French nobles.

The Hundred Years' War

The Hundred Years' War was not a single war. It was a series of wars between England and France. These wars took place over a period of 116 years, from 1337 to 1453. (So, the Hundred Years' War was really the One Hundred Sixteen Years' War.) Interestingly, the English won most of the battles, but the French won the war.

The French and the English went to war for many reasons. Mainly, both wanted to control land in what is now France. Both also wanted to control the wool trade in a part of France and to control the English Channel.

One of the most famous figures of the war was **Joan of Arc.** She led a French army against the English in 1429. The English captured her and burned her as a witch.

As one would expect in such a long war, there were many battles. One side would win a great battle. A period of peace would follow. Then the war would start again. For example, the English won the **Battle of Agincourt** in 1415. The peace treaty that ended this battle gave much of France to the English king. But after the king died, the French began the war again.

By the end of the war, England had lost all the French land that it had gained except for one small part. England soon lost even that. So the main result of the Hundred Years' War was the determining of the boundaries of England and France, which remain to this day.

The Hundred Years' War had another very important effect. The war strengthened the kings in each country and weakened the nobles. As a result, each country became more or less united. Where there were once hundreds of small kingdoms, there were now two whole countries.

■ PRACTICE 148: The Hundred Years' War

Decide if each of the following statements is true (**T**) or false (**F**). Write the correct letter on the line before each statement.

_____ **1.** The Hundred Years' War was fought between England and France.

_____ **2.** After the war, France and England were divided into many small kingdoms.

_____ **3.** The war weakened the power of both the French and the English kings.

_____ **4.** The French won the Hundred Years' War.

The Black Death

During the Hundred Years' War, a terrible disease spread across Europe. It killed millions of people in England, France, and the rest of Europe. The disease was called the **bubonic plague.** The plague caused spots of blood to appear under a person's skin. The spots then turned black. The bubonic plague is therefore also called the **Black Death.**

The Black Death took a horrible toll on the people of Europe. Historians think that it killed between one fourth and one third of the entire population of Europe.

The people who caught the plague died slowly and painfully. At first, they felt chills, fever, headaches, and other body pains. Their necks and other body parts swelled. These swollen parts often developed black, open sores. During the Middle Ages, there was no cure.

The germ that caused the plague was brought to Europe from Asia by traders. The germ was carried by rats and fleas. The plague spread fast and far because of poor sanitation. Conditions in Europe at the time were so unsanitary that rats and fleas infested almost everything. These conditions contributed to many other illnesses and deaths. But none were so famous or widespread as the Black Death.

■ PRACTICE 149: The Black Death

Circle the letter of the correct answer to each of the following questions.

1. When did the bubonic plague strike Europe?
   a. before the Hundred Years' War
   b. after the Hundred Years' War
   c. during the Hundred Years' War
   d. none of the above

2. Was the bubonic plague the only disease that thrived in unsanitary conditions during the Middle Ages?
   a. No, but it was the most famous and widespread.
   b. No, but it was the only fatal disease in Europe at the time.
   c. Yes; Europe was very healthy in the Middle Ages.
   d. No, but it was the only one that affected humans.

The Holy Roman Empire

Strong leaders and the Hundred Years' War helped to unite the separate nations of England and France. At the same time, the Holy Roman Empire sought to unite much of the rest of Europe.

The empire began in 962, when the first in a series of German kings became emperor. Throughout the empire's nearly 850 years of existence, the emperors tried to unite all Christians and lands of central Europe. They never quite succeeded.

The Church was one problem. The first emperor, Otto I, was crowned as a reward for his alliance with the pope. Although ties remained close throughout the Middle Ages, the empire and the Church often quarreled over questions of power.

Another obstacle was the size of the empire. Originally, the empire included what is now Germany, Austria, the western Czech Republic,

The Holy Roman Empire

northern Italy, Switzerland, eastern France, Belgium, the Netherlands, and Luxembourg. Because the empire was so big, emperors left nobles in charge of vast areas. Struggles broke out among the nobles. And the various peoples were never truly united under one ruler.

In the early 1500s, Charles V exerted his power as emperor and came close to uniting the empire. He was the last emperor to be crowned by a pope.

Events that followed the Middle Ages weakened and eventually ended the empire. These events included the Thirty Years' War, the Protestant Reformation, and Napoleon Bonaparte's rise to power in France.

Interestingly, the Holy Roman Empire was actually "neither holy nor Roman nor an empire," as the French writer Voltaire put it. But the emperors wanted to be considered *holy* so that they would have the support of the Church. They hoped to be as powerful as the *Roman* leaders had been. And they wanted to create an *empire*, though they were effectively unable to do so.

■ PRACTICE 150: The Holy Roman Empire
Decide if each statement below is true (**T**) or false (**F**). Write the correct letter on the line before each statement.

_____ **1.** The first person to be crowned emperor of the Holy Roman Empire was Otto I.

_____ **2.** The Holy Roman Empire began in 962.

_____ **3.** The emperors were unable to unite the empire because of various struggles for power.

_____ **4.** The emperors wanted the empire to be known as holy so that they would have the support of the Church.

_____ **5.** Charles V came closest to uniting the empire.

A Time of Great Change

Just before the Middle Ages, western Europe was part of the Roman Empire. At the end of the Middle Ages, western Europe was divided among the large nations of England and France and the Holy Roman Empire. There were also several smaller kingdoms.

The Middle Ages was a time of many important developments. As you have read, feudalism was the government and military system of the time. Manorialism, with manors run by lords and worked by serfs, was the economic system.

Both feudalism and manorialism began to decline as trade with Asia increased after the Crusades. Towns grew, and kings (especially in England and France) grew more powerful. The time of smaller kingdoms was giving way to the time of modern nations.

All of these developments (and others) mark the Middle Ages. It is a favorite time in history for many people today. The romance of the time— images of knights in shining armor and beautiful castles—are still with us. The reality of the time was more complex. But it is just as fascinating.

■ PRACTICE 151: A Time of Great Change

Decide if each statement below is true (**T**) or false (**F**). Write the correct letter on the line before each statement.

_____ **1.** Feudalism and manorialism became stronger after the Crusades.

_____ **2.** At the end of the Middle Ages, Europe was made up of mostly small kingdoms.

_____ **3.** Many people today find the romance of the Middle Ages fascinating.

_____ **4.** Trade with Asia was a powerful force for change in the later years of the Middle Ages.

UNIT 5 REVIEW

Circle the letter of the correct answer to each of the following questions.

1. What date is usually given for the fall of Rome?
   a. 476 B.C.E.
   b. 276 C.E.
   c. 376 B.C.E.
   d. 476 C.E.

2. Which of the following words best describes the Byzantine Empire?
   a. Asian
   b. small
   c. Christian
   d. poor

3. Why was the Battle of Tours important?
   a. It stopped the Muslim advance into Christian Europe.
   b. It made Charlemagne king.
   c. It ended the Roman Empire.
   d. It made the pope an ally of the Frankish kings.

4. Where did the Vikings come from?
   a. northern Europe
   b. southern Europe
   c. eastern Europe
   d. western Europe

5. Who first sailed to North America?
   a. Thor
   b. Erik the Red
   c. Leif Eriksson
   d. Christopher Columbus

6. What form of government existed during most of the Middle Ages?
   a. fiefs
   b. manorialism
   c. vassals
   d. feudalism

7. Which of the following was a result of the Crusades?
   a. less contact between Europeans and other peoples
   b. the beginnings of manorialism
   c. the beginnings of feudalism
   d. more trade between Europe and Asia

8. What caused feudalism and manorialism to decline?
   a. increased trade and wealth
   b. the growth of towns
   c. more powerful kings
   d. all of the above

9. Why was the Capetian dynasty important?
   a. It started the Holy Roman Empire.
   b. It helped make France a single country.
   c. It helped make England a single country.
   d. It divided France into smaller kingdoms.

10. What fraction of Europe's population did the Black Death kill?
    a. about one tenth
    b. about one third
    c. about three quarters
    d. about nine tenths

UNIT 5 APPLICATION ACTIVITY
Women's Rights in the Byzantine Empire

Theodora, the wife of Emperor Justinian, was extremely active during her husband's rule. In fact, much of the success of the Byzantine Empire was a result of her work. A special concern of Theodora was how the women in the empire were treated.

Look at the list of laws below. These are all laws that Theodora insisted should be passed.

- A law making it illegal for a husband to beat his wife

- A law allowing women to divorce their husbands

- A law allowing women to own land and other valuable property

- A law allowing widows to keep and raise their children

Choose one of the laws listed above. Then imagine it is your job to try to convince Emperor Justinian to pass this law. Write a letter explaining why this law is necessary and how it will benefit his empire as a whole. Think carefully about your reasons. Take notes on the lines below. Then write your letter on another sheet of paper.

_____

_____

_____

_____

_____

_____

_____

_____

UNIT 6

The Middle East and the Rise of Islam

LESSON 21: The Rise of Islam

GOAL: To understand the beginnings and spread of Islam; to learn important terms associated with Islam and its history

WORDS TO KNOW

Allah	diverse	Muslims
caliphs	geography	
disciples	Islam	

NAMES TO KNOW

Abu Bakr	Umar
Muhammad	Umayyads
Rightly Guided Caliphs	

PLACES TO KNOW

Islamic Empire	Mecca	Muslim Empire
Islamic world	Medina	

EVENTS TO KNOW

Battle of Tours	Hegira

Geography of the Mediterranean

A lot of what you do when you study history is learn *what* happened and *when* it happened. But you should not forget a third thing—*where* things happened. In fact, learning where things happened is just as important as learning what happened and when it happened.

Why is learning the "where" of history so important? The answer is that the location of events in history is like the stage in a play. The stage is where everything takes place.

The term we use to describe where things happen is **geography.** Used this way, the word *geography* means "a description of the land where historical events occur." The geography of the area you are going to read about here is among the most interesting in the world.

Look at the map below. This map shows most of the areas you will read about in this unit. It shows the Mediterranean, the area where Islam developed.

Areas of the Mediterranean Sea

The land shown in the map covers parts of three continents: Europe, Asia, and Africa. These land areas surround the Mediterranean Sea.

Along the European coast, the land is rugged and beautiful. There are many small mountain chains. There are also beautiful beaches near the coast. Inland, there are thick forests. The climate here is mild: warm summers and cool winters. Because there is plenty of rain, many different kinds of plants grow.

The coasts of Asia and Africa in this region are also mild. But most of this land is desert. Deserts are not just big areas of sand. They include rugged mountains and vast, rocky areas. The climates of these deserts are hot. At night, though, the air can be freezing cold.

The land and climates of this area are very **diverse,** or varied. More than 1,000 years ago, the population of this region was also diverse. The region was home to hundreds of different groups of people. They spoke different languages, had different cultures, and practiced different religions.

Important developments in history changed much of this. Despite the diversity in geography, climate, and population, a religious movement united this region and changed world history forever. You are about to read about this dramatic change.

■ PRACTICE 152: Geography of the Mediterranean

Decide if each statement below is true (**T**) or false (**F**). Write the correct letter on the line before each statement.

_____ **1.** *Geography* is the term used to describe the "where" of history.

_____ **2.** The population of this region is still very diverse today.

_____ **3.** More than 1,000 years ago, all the people around the Mediterranean spoke the same language.

The Founding of Islam

One of the most influential people who ever lived was **Muhammad.** Muhammad was the founder of the religion known as **Islam.**

Muhammad was born around 570 in the town of **Mecca,** in what is now Saudi Arabia. Like other boys, he learned to tend sheep and camels. But when he was a young adult, a great event changed his life. While he was meditating in a cave, a vision of an angel came to him. The angel called on Muhammad to be God's messenger on Earth.

At first, Muhammad was doubtful about his vision. He told only his wife about it. But she encouraged him. Soon, Muhammad had more visions. He began to preach in public.

Some people believed Muhammad and became his **disciples,** or followers. But most people ridiculed him. His preaching made him many enemies in Mecca. He was forced to flee to another town, **Medina.** Muhammad's flight from Mecca to Medina is called the **Hegira,** or flight. The Hegira is an important event in the Islamic religion. In fact, the

Islamic calendar begins with the Hegira (622 C.E.), just as the Christian calendar begins with the birth of Jesus.

In Medina, Muhammad was well received. He became the town's religious and political leader. But as the number of his followers grew, so did the hatred of his enemies in Mecca. In fact, the people of Mecca went to war against Muhammad and his followers in Medina. There were many battles, but Muhammad and his people were victorious. In 630, Muhammad reentered Mecca. This time, most of the people there accepted him as the prophet of God.

Two years later, Muhammad died. He was buried in Medina. Although his life had ended, the religion he founded, Islam, would live for centuries after his death.

■ PRACTICE 153: The Founding of Islam

Circle the letter of the correct answer to each of the following questions.

1. What religion was founded by Muhammad?
   a. Christianity
   b. Judaism
   c. Islam
   d. Catholicism

2. Where was Muhammad born?
   a. Mecca
   b. Medina
   c. Hegira
   d. Constantinople

3. To which city did Muhammad flee?
   a. Mecca
   b. Medina
   c. Hegira
   d. Constantinople

4. What is the term for Muhammad's flight?
   a. the Birth
   b. the Hegira
   c. the Flight
   d. the Passage

5. What event marks the beginning of the Islamic calendar?
   a. Muhammad's birth
   b. Muhammad's death
   c. the Hegira
   d. the day Muhammad reentered Mecca

Understanding Islam

The religion that Muhammad founded is called Islam. *Islam* is an Arabic word that means "submission." The religion is called that because followers of Islam "submit" to God. The people who follow this religion are called **Muslims.** *Muslim* is an Arabic word that means "one who submits to God." (Sometimes, people use the word *Moslem* instead of *Muslim.* Both words mean the same thing.)

Islam is a monotheistic religion. This means that Muslims, or followers of Islam, believe that there is only one god. During Muhammad's time, many people followed religions that worshiped more than one god. Muhammad urged people to give up these gods and embrace the one true god. In Islam, the word used for God is the Arabic word **Allah.**

Islam spread through many cultures in Asia, Africa, and parts of Europe. The term used for these areas is the **Islamic world.** Strong rulers came to control these areas. Under these rulers, the region is referred to as the **Islamic Empire,** or the **Muslim Empire.** At first, these rulers were Arabs. Later in history, though, they were not. In fact, there were several different empires over the centuries.

Remember, this area was very diverse. What united the people was the religion of Islam.

TIP

Islam, Muslim, and *Allah* are all Arabic words. This is because Muhammad and most of his early followers were Arabic people. However, it is important to remember that Arabs are not the same as Muslims. *Arab* refers to a culture. *Muslim* refers to a religion.

■ PRACTICE 154: Understanding Islam

Circle the letter of the correct answer to each of the following questions.

1. What is the Arabic word for God?
    a. Islam
    b. Allah
    c. Muslim
    d. monotheistic

2. What is a follower of Islam called?
    a. Islam
    b. Allah
    c. Muslim
    d. Arab

3. What religion was founded by Muhammad?
    a. Islam
    b. Muslim
    c. Arabic
    d. Hegira

4. What is the term for a religion in which people worship only one god?
    a. pantheistic
    b. atheistic
    c. monotheistic
    d. polytheistic

5. What term refers to the parts of the world to which Islam spread?
  a. the Islamic world
  b. Muhammad's Empire
  c. the Christian world
  d. the Kingdom of Islam

The Spread of Islam

To this day, the city of Mecca, where Muhammad was born, and the city of Medina, where he gained followers, are the sacred cities of Islam. It was from these two cities that the religion of Islam spread. Eventually, Islam spread throughout southwest Asia and north Africa. It also spread into parts of Europe.

Islam spread under the leadership of **caliphs,** or Muslim rulers. The first caliphs were members of Muhammad's family. Later, the position of caliph passed to friends of Muhammad's family, and then to others.

The first four caliphs after Muhammad are known as the **Rightly Guided Caliphs.** Perhaps more than anyone else, they are responsible for the rapid and widespread growth of Islam.

The first caliph to follow Muhammad was **Abu Bakr.** Abu Bakr was Muhammad's father-in-law. Abu Bakr was quite old. After only two years, he chose a man named **Umar** to be the next caliph. Umar led the Islamic people on conquests that would spread the religion over a great area.

The position of caliph was not only religious. It was also political and military. In fact, Umar was a great general. He led Arab Muslims on many wars of conquest. His armies invaded the Byzantine Empire. They captured Syria and Palestine and the cities of Jerusalem and Damascus. They also captured Egypt and much of the rest of North Africa. By the time Umar was finished, he had more than doubled the size of the Islamic world.

Uthman and Ali, the caliphs who followed Umar, continued to lead conquests. By the year 661, less than 30 years after Muhammad's death, Islam had spread over a huge region.

In 661, the caliphs began to come from a new family. This family was called the **Umayyads.** Caliphs from the Umayyad family ruled the Islamic world for nearly 100 years, from 623 to 750. Like the former caliphs, they worked to expand their rule and their religion.

The Umayyad caliphs won many victories. They expanded into central Asia, India, and even as far as the borders of China. They completed the conquest of North Africa and then conquered large islands in the Mediterranean Sea. Islam was spreading far and fast.

■ PRACTICE 155: The Spread of Islam

Circle the letter of the correct answer to each of the following questions.

1. What was a caliph?
   a. a relative of Muhammad
   b. a Christian leader
   c. a Muslim soldier
   d. a Muslim leader

2. What new family of caliphs expanded the Islamic world into Asia and India?
   a. the Muslims
   b. the Umars
   c. the Umayyads
   d. the Uthmans

THINK ABOUT IT

The Umayyads suffered one important defeat that would affect the history of the world. In 711, they invaded Europe through Spain. At the Battle of Tours, in 732, they were defeated by the king, Charles Martel. Charles Martel and the people he led were Christian. Why do you think this battle was so important? Write your answer on a separate sheet of paper.

The Islamic Empire

Despite their defeat at the Battle of Tours, the caliphs continued to spread Islam. The advance of Islam was remarkable. By 750, Islam had conquered a huge area: northern Africa, southern Europe, and western Asia.

As you recall, this area has very diverse geography. It also has a diverse population. But the religion of Islam united these people. Despite their differences, millions of people in Asia, Africa, and Europe became united in their beliefs.

Under Islam and its caliph rulers, Muslims built a remarkable empire and civilization. Many of the greatest advances in knowledge, art, and architecture came from Islamic civilization. You will read about life in the Islamic world in the next lesson.

The Spread of Islam, 623–750

■ PRACTICE 156: The Islamic Empire

Decide if each statement below is true (**T**) or false (**F**). Write the correct letter on the line before each statement.

_____ **1.** The Islamic world is the part of the world in which most people are Muslim.

_____ **2.** By 750, northern Europe and all of Asia were part of the Islamic world.

_____ **3.** Many great advances in learning and art came from Islamic civilization.

LESSON 22: Life in the Islamic World

GOAL: To understand basic ideas about the religion of Islam; to identify important contributions made by Islamic civilization

WORDS TO KNOW

Arabic numerals	hajj	minarets
astrolabe	Koran	mosque
caliphates		

NAMES TO KNOW

Rhazes	Uthman

The Koran

You may have heard of the **Koran.** It is the sacred book of the Islamic religion. It is as important to Muslims as the Bible is to Christians.

The word *Koran* means "something recited" or "recitation." This means that the words of the Koran are supposed to be recited, or spoken out loud, during worship.

Muslims believe that the Koran was revealed a little at a time by an angel who came to Muhammad in visions. Muhammad did not write the Koran himself. Rather, his followers memorized what Muhammad said and later wrote it down. Some historians think, however, that Muhammad did approve some of these writings himself.

The caliph **Uthman,** who was born shortly after Muhammad's death, ordered the Koran assembled from all that had been written down. He sent copies of the Koran throughout the Islamic world. Thus, the content of the Koran started to become widely known to Muslims over a great area. Muslims believe that the words of the Koran are the words of God, given to Muhammad by an angel.

The Koran consists of 114 chapters. Each chapter is filled with verses. The language of the Koran is widely recognized as beautiful, poetic, and powerful.

The Koran formed the basis of the great Islamic civilization. Thus, it is one of the most important and influential books in history.

IN REAL LIFE

Today, Islam is the second-largest religion in the world, just behind Christianity. Within your lifetime, it will probably become the largest.

■ PRACTICE 157: The Koran

Circle the letter of the correct answer to each of the following questions.

1. What is the Koran?
   a. a prophet of God
   b. the founder of Islam
   c. the sacred book of the Islamic religion
   d. the Islamic belief in God and family

2. What does the word *Koran* mean?
   a. something recited
   b. words of an angel
   c. written words
   d. sacred and holy

3. Who had copies of the Koran sent throughout the Islamic world?
   a. Muhammad
   b. Umar
   c. an angel
   d. Uthman

4. Where do Muslims believe the Koran came from?
   a. the caliph Uthman's writings
   b. an angel who came to Muhammad in visions
   c. Muhammad's own thoughts
   d. Muslim rulers

The Basic Beliefs of Islam

The Islamic religion, like any religion, is complex. But it is easy to remember some of its basic beliefs. First, Muslims believe that there is only one god, Allah. They believe that Allah created the universe and that He is a just and merciful god. Humans are Allah's highest creation, but they are imperfect. So, Allah sends prophets to guide humanity. The last and greatest of these prophets was Muhammad, who brought the Koran to be used as a guide. Muslims also believe in both Paradise and Hell.

These ideas, and many others, are found in the Koran. Also in the Koran is a list of the five duties that every Muslim must perform.

- The first duty is to profess complete faith in Islam. Muslims must say, "There is no God but Allah, and Muhammad is his prophet," and they must believe it.

- The second duty is to pray five times a day. In Islamic cities, the people are called to prayer from a tower on a **mosque.** A mosque is a Muslim house of worship.

- The third duty is almsgiving, or giving to charity.

- The fourth duty is fasting during the day in the Islamic month of Ramadan.

- The fifth duty is to make the **hajj,** or pilgrimage, to Mecca. Mecca is the holy city of Islam.

■ PRACTICE 158: The Basic Beliefs of Islam

Decide if each of the following statements is true (**T**) or false (**F**). Write the correct letter on the line before each statement.

_____ **1.** One of the five duties of Islam is to fight holy wars.

_____ **2.** One of the five duties of Islam is to give to charity.

_____ **3.** One of the five duties of Islam is to pray five times a day.

_____ **4.** One of the five duties of Islam is to make a pilgrimage to Mecca.

_____ **5.** One of the five duties of Islam is to fast for one week a year.

The Rule of the Caliphs

As you have read, the leaders of the Muslim Empire were called caliphs. Many caliphs ruled the Muslim Empire. All of them were very powerful.

The caliphs were in charge of the government. A caliph was both the religious leader of the empire and the leader of the military. As you have read, all the caliphs were strong generals. They ruled armies that spread their empire—and the Islamic religion—over a vast area.

Within the empire, the caliphs governed their land. Despite their strong religious beliefs, the caliphs did not expand their empire just to expand their religion. In fact, most caliphs practiced a policy of religious tolerance in the lands they conquered. This meant that they allowed people in the conquered lands to continue practicing their own religions. Over the centuries, however, most of the people in the conquered lands converted to Islam.

The caliphs also oversaw the economy of the empire. The Muslim Empire had an economy based largely on trade. As trade increased, so did manufacturing. The Islamic world produced a wide variety of products: silk, steel, textiles, pottery, glassware—the list goes on and on.

Because the Muslim Empire covered such a large area, it was impossible for one caliph to oversee everything that happened. In fact, the empire was eventually divided into three main areas, each ruled by a caliph. These areas were called **caliphates.**

Although the caliphs were the supreme rulers of the Muslim Empire, the Islamic world was divided. Traveling to different areas of the empire was like traveling to different countries. There were different languages, geography, cultures—even different religious customs. However, this area was united by the faith of Islam and the rule of the caliphs, who were some of the most powerful rulers in history.

Why do you think each division of the Muslim Empire was called a caliphate? Write your answer on a separate sheet of paper.

■ PRACTICE 159: The Rule of the Caliphs

Decide if each statement below is true (**T**) or false (**F**). Write the correct letter on the line before each statement.

_____ **1.** One caliph ruled the entire Muslim Empire.

_____ **2.** Caliphs were religious, military, and government leaders.

_____ **3.** Everyone who lived in the Muslim Empire had to become a Muslim.

_____ **4.** Everyone who lived in the Islamic world spoke the same language.

Advances in Learning

The Muslim Empire is famous for the advances its people made in learning. Science, math, philosophy, medicine—all of these fields, and many more, benefited from Muslim peoples.

One of the main reasons for these achievements was the people's willingness to learn from others. As the caliphs conquered new lands, scholars adopted the best ideas from the people there. Muslim scholars traveled throughout the empire to learn. In this way, the Muslims learned of Greek philosophy and science. They also learned of Persian literature. And they learned the history and science of all the places they traveled. For example, they learned how to make paper from the Chinese.

The Muslims honored learning and scholarship. They founded many universities and other centers of learning. Muslims also wrote encyclopedias, handbooks, and textbooks about many subjects.

One area in which the Muslims made important contributions was medicine. At this time, diseases were still a mystery to most people. However, the Muslims began to understand them. One Muslim doctor, Rhazes, wrote a medical encyclopedia. In it, he described how to perform surgery and discussed diseases, such as smallpox and measles. His work became a basic source of medical knowledge in Europe for hundreds of years.

IN REAL LIFE

The Muslims made so many advances that it would be almost impossible to list them all. If you did list them, though, you would be using another Muslim contribution: Arabic numerals. **Arabic numerals** are the ones with which you are familiar (1, 2, 3, and so on). Although these numerals were developed by the Hindus in India, it was the Muslims who refined them and expanded their use. The Muslims also developed and refined the concept of zero. The word *zero* comes from an Arabic word that means "empty."

The Muslims also became famous as geographers and navigators. They produced many beautiful maps. Muslim travelers, traders, and explorers contributed their observations to help make the maps accurate. Geography became a true science under Muslim attention.

The Muslims also developed advanced knowledge of astronomy. They could calculate the positions of the planets and the stars. This helped them to navigate, or find their way, while traveling. The Muslims perfected a device called the astrolabe. The **astrolabe** was used to help travelers, especially sailors, determine their location. The astrolabe was a vital piece of equipment that explorers relied on for centuries.

IN REAL LIFE

Many of the stars that people still use for navigation have Arabic names passed down by Muslim navigators. These include Vega, Aldebaran, and Betelgeuse.

■ PRACTICE 160: Advances in Learning

Circle the letter of the correct answer to each of the following questions.

1. Which of the following is NOT a contribution of the Muslim Empire?
   a. the concept of zero
   b. the astrolabe
   c. a medical encyclopedia
   d. the telescope

2. Why were the Muslims able to make so many advances?
   a. They were forced by the caliphs to learn.
   b. They were willing to learn from others.
   c. They believed in hard work and no play.
   d. They started school at a very young age.

3. Which fields benefited from Muslim learning?
   a. science
   b. mathematics
   c. philosophy
   d. all of the above

Art and Architecture

In addition to great works of scholarship, the Muslims created works of great beauty. Islamic art was a combination of art from the many countries in the Islamic world.

Islamic art was unique. The Koran forbids making images of living things. Therefore, the designs in Islamic art were more abstract. Images of people and animals appeared more as symbols than as likenesses. The result was a unique expression of beauty.

Islamic art was expressed in many ways. Elaborate rugs and textiles made by Muslims became world famous. Muslims were also excellent metalworkers. They made household items, such as trays and candlesticks, into works of art. They were skilled at making pottery and glassware, too.

One of the most wonderful ways in which Muslims expressed

beauty—and their faith—was by building lovely mosques. Throughout the Islamic world, the central feature of most towns was the mosque. Many of these mosques still stand today. From their towers, or **minarets,** Muslims are still called to prayer, just as they have been for more than 1,500 years.

Mosque

■ PRACTICE 161: Art and Architecture

Circle the letter(s) of the correct answer(s) to each of the following questions.

1. What made the art of the Islamic world unique?
    a. It was a combination of art from many different countries.
    b. The designs are abstract because the Koran does not allow Muslims to make images of animals or people.
    c. both *a* and *b*
    d. neither *a* nor *b*

2. Which of the following were ways in which Islamic art was expressed? (*Hint*: There is more than one correct answer.)
    a. elaborate rugs and textiles
    b. beautiful mosques
    c. famous paintings of people
    d. metals, such as trays and candlesticks

LESSON 23: Invasions

GOAL: To learn how control of the Islamic world went from the Arabs to the Seljuk Turks; to understand how this led to the Crusades

WORD TO KNOW
Seljuk Turks

PLACE TO KNOW
Jerusalem

EVENTS TO KNOW
Children's Crusade   **First Crusade**

The Seljuk Turks

As you have read, Muslim culture and civilization spread across large parts of Africa, Asia, and Europe. This culture began in the 600s, with the teachings of Muhammad. The Muslim culture and religion continue to this day. The greatest era of Muslim culture, however, lasted just about 300 years, from around 700 to 1000. During this time, Arab Muslims were a very powerful group of people. Soon, however, another group became even more powerful. These people were the Seljuk Turks. The Seljuk Turks were a people who lived in central Asia, in an area called Turkestan. Their first leader was a man named Seljuk.

Like many other peoples of the time, the **Seljuk Turks** converted to Islam. Over time, the Seljuk Turks grew powerful. During the 1000s, they captured a large amount of land from the Arab Muslims. The Seljuk Turks also invaded the Byzantine Empire. This was a great Christian empire that had developed from the Roman Empire. In the wars that followed, the Seljuk Turks were successful. At the Battle of Manzikert, they even captured the Byzantine emperor. For the next few centuries, the Seljuk Turks controlled the Islamic world.

The Seljuk Turks established an important kingdom near the Byzantine capital of Constantinople. Fearful of the future, the Byzantines turned to Europe for help. They turned to Europe because the Europeans, like the people of the Byzantine Empire, were Christians. Their common enemies, the Seljuk Turks, were Muslims. A great war between the two religions was about to begin.

TIP

Try to make connections between people, places, and events. These connections will help them to make sense. Then they will be easier to remember. For example, you just read that the Seljuk Turks lived in a country named Turkestan. This is why they were called Turks. You also read that their first leader was named Seljuk. So these particular Turks were called the Seljuk Turks. Look for logical connections like these whenever you read about history. They will help you to organize and remember names, dates, and places.

■ PRACTICE 162: The Seljuk Turks

Circle the letter of the correct answer to each of the following questions.

1. Which of the following statements is false?
   a. The Seljuk Turks came from central Asia.
   b. The Seljuk Turks converted to Christianity.
   c. The Seljuk Turks took over the Islamic world during the 1000s.
   d. The people of the Byzantine Empire asked Europe to help them fight the Seljuk Turks.

2. Why did the people of the Byzantine Empire turn to Europe for help against the Seljuk Turks?
   a. They followed the same religion.
   b. They thought the Europeans had strong armies.
   c. They had treaties with the European rulers.
   d. Europe was nearby.

3. What was the religion of the Seljuk Turks?
   a. Islam
   b. Christianity
   c. Judaism
   d. none

Capture of the Holy Land

For centuries, the land on the east coast of the Mediterranean Sea had been very important to the Christian peoples of Europe. This was the Holy Land. For Christians, the Holy Land is where the events told about in the Bible, including the life of Jesus, took place. This Holy Land is also called Palestine.

For centuries, the Holy Land had been controlled by the Byzantine Empire. The Byzantine Empire was a Christian empire. Pilgrims and others from Europe had little difficulty traveling to the Holy Land.

Palestine

As you have read, the Muslims expanded their control and their religion throughout this area in the 600s. These people were not Christians. But they still allowed Christians to come to the Holy Land.

This changed when the Seljuk Turks came to power. The Seljuk Turks were fierce warriors and devout Muslims. They refused to allow Christians to come to the Holy Land.

When the Seljuk Turks defeated the Byzantine Empire at the Battle of Manzikert, the Byzantines turned to the Europeans for help. The Europeans responded by gathering armies to try to recapture the Holy Land. These military expeditions became known as the Crusades.

People still talk about "going on a crusade" or "crusading for" something. This means they are working hard to achieve something they think is very important. These terms come from the Crusades against the Muslim Turks. The Christian Europeans wanted very much to regain access to their holy land.

■ PRACTICE 163: Capture of the Holy Land

Match each description with a term from below. Write the letter of the correct term on the line before each description.

> **a.** Crusades   **b.** Seljuk Turks   **c.** Palestine

_____ **1.** another name for the Holy Land

_____ **2.** the Muslims who refused to let Christians into the Holy Land

_____ **3.** military expeditions launched by Christians to try to capture the Holy Land from the Muslims

The Crusades

The Crusades lasted for about 200 years. All of the **crusaders** came from Europe, and they were all Christian. They came from many walks of life. Many were knights. Others were peasants. They all joined the Crusades for different reasons. Many joined in a real desire to capture the Holy Land for Christianity. Others, though, joined to gain more land for themselves or to begin trading with the people of Asia.

There were eight major Crusades. Some were more successful than others.

The **First Crusade** lasted from 1096 to 1099. The crusaders were mostly French. They traveled overland to Palestine, fighting many bloody battles along the way. In 1099, they reached **Jerusalem.** This is the holiest city of the Holy Land. After six weeks, the crusaders captured the city. Christians were once again in control of the Holy Land. The map below shows the land conquered by the Christians in the First Crusade.

Islamic rule   Christian rule

Crusader states established by the First Crusade

The Second Crusade lasted from 1147 to 1149. It was launched because the Christians in the Holy Land were becoming weak. The Seljuk Turks had continued to attack them, and they needed help. So, in the Second Crusade, more Europeans came to help. The Second Crusade was a failure. The Muslim forces easily defeated the crusaders.

The Third Crusade lasted from 1189 to 1192. By this time, the Christian forces in the Holy Land were extremely weak. The Muslims had recaptured Jerusalem, and the Christians held less and less of the area. The Third Crusade was launched in response to the loss of Jerusalem. Crusaders from Europe came to try and recapture Jerusalem. But these crusaders failed.

The Fourth Crusade lasted from 1202 to 1204. Like the Third Crusade, it was launched in an attempt to capture Jerusalem. However, the leaders of this Crusade never reached Jerusalem. Instead, they became involved in other political problems of the Byzantine Empire.

The **Children's Crusade** took place in 1212. It is one of the greatest tragedies in the history of the world. Led by adults, many young people between the ages of 10 and 18 became convinced that they could capture Palestine. They thought that because they were poor and faithful, God would grant them victory. Many of these children froze or starved on the long journey. Few made it as far as the Mediterranean. Those who did were sold into slavery.

Other crusades lasted until the 1200s. The Fifth and Sixth Crusades were failures. However, the leaders of the Sixth Crusade did manage to reach a truce with the Muslims. In exchange for peace, they were given the holy city of Jerusalem. However, this arrangement did not last.

The Seventh and Eighth Crusades also failed. By the 1300s, the Christians were losing interest in the Holy Land.

THINK ABOUT IT

You have just read about the Children's Crusade, in which many young people thought they could win against great odds. Is there any cause for which you would risk your life? Or if you were a parent, is there any cause that you would allow your child to risk his or her life for? Why or why not? Write your answers on a separate sheet of paper.

■ PRACTICE 164: The Crusades

Circle the letter of the correct answer to each of the following questions.

1. What was the main purpose of the Crusades?
    a. to capture Jerusalem from the Muslims
    b. to capture the Holy Land from the Muslims
    c. to drive the Muslims out of Europe
    d. to unite with the Muslims and rule the Holy Land together

2. Which of the following statements is false?
    a. The Christians gained control of the Holy Land during the Eighth Crusade.
    b. The Fifth and Sixth Crusades were failures.
    c. The Europeans were given Jerusalem at the end of the Sixth Crusade.
    d. all of the above

3. Which of the following statements is false?
   a. The Crusades lasted for about 200 years.
   b. There were eight Crusades in all.
   c. The First and Fifth Crusades succeeded.
   d. The First Crusade succeeded.

The Results of the Crusades

The Crusades failed. The main goal of the crusaders was to capture the Holy Land from the Muslims. For about 200 years, Christians did, in fact, control the area. This allowed many European pilgrims to visit the Holy Land. But the crusaders never managed to get firm control of the area.

However, this does not mean that the Crusades were not important. In fact, one of the most important results was that they stopped the expansion of the Muslim Seljuk Turks. Instead of further extending their territory, the Seljuk Turks had to concentrate on defending themselves from the crusaders.

The Crusades also enriched both European life and life in the Islamic world. Many new goods were exchanged between the two areas. Trade routes were developed, and the economy improved. The Crusades had a major impact on the history of Europe.

In the Islamic world, the Crusades helped people learn ways to grow more powerful. Among them were techniques of warfare, such as building good warships and cannons. They would use this knowledge to develop a powerful empire, soon to become the most powerful one on Earth.

■ PRACTICE 165: The Results of the Crusades

Decide if each statement below is true (**T**) or false (**F**). Write the correct letter on the line before each statement.

_____ 1. The crusaders succeeded in recapturing the Holy Land from the Muslims.

_____ 2. The Crusades had no effect on history.

_____ 3. Both the Islamic and European worlds learned from each other as a result of the Crusades.

LESSON 24: The Ottoman Turks

GOAL: To learn about the people, places, and events involved in the growth and achievements of the Ottoman Empire

WORDS TO KNOW

Grand Mufti	jihads	rayah
janissaries	Ottoman Turks	sultan

NAMES TO KNOW

Koca Sinan	Othman
Mohammed II	Suleiman I

PLACES TO KNOW

Anatolia	Palace School

The Ottoman Turks

As you have read, the Seljuk Turks grew to be a powerful force. Another powerful group of people also grew in the region. Like the Seljuk Turks, they were from central Asia. They were also a Muslim people who followed the Islamic religion. Also, like the Seljuk Turks, they grew from a small tribe into a large and powerful group of people. In fact, over hundreds of years, they created a large, rich, and powerful empire—the most powerful one on Earth during its time.

The people who came to be so powerful were called the Ottoman Turks. In the 1200s, they moved from central Asia to a region called Anatolia (today, the country of Turkey). The Ottoman Turks took their name from their first great leader, Othman. He lived from 1299 to 1326. Othman led his people in capturing the city of Bursa. They

Area of the Ottoman Turks

then attacked surrounding areas. By the time of Othman's death, the Ottomans had become a strong force, although they still only ruled a small area.

But the leaders who followed Othman worked to expand their territory. By the late 1400s, they had conquered a large region, including the Byzantine Empire. When they captured Constantinople, the capital of the empire, in 1453, the Byzantine Empire had ended.

The Ottoman Empire continued to expand for centuries. In fact, traces of the Ottoman Empire remained until the 1900s.

■ PRACTICE 166: The Ottoman Turks

Match each description with a term from below. Write the letter of the correct term on the line before each description.

a. Othman   **b.** Islam   **c.** Anatolia

_____ **1.** the region to which the Ottoman Turks moved and began to expand their empire

_____ **2.** the religion of the Ottoman Turks

_____ **3.** the first leader of the Ottoman Turks

The Sultans of the Ottoman Empire

The first ruler of the Ottoman Turks, Othman, was a sultan. The word *sultan* means "ruler." For hundreds of years, sultans ruled over the Ottoman Empire. Sultans were some of the most powerful people who ever lived.

The sultans of the Ottoman Empire were dictators. They made all of the important government decisions themselves. One of their most important tasks was to choose other government officials. They appointed officials to collect taxes, keep the peace, and other important functions. Sultans chose these people very carefully.

The sultans lived lives of great luxury. They were unbelievably rich. They lived in huge, lavish palaces. Millions of people revered the sultans as their leaders.

Although the sultans were very powerful, they could not do everything they wanted. An important official in the Ottoman Empire was the Grand Mufti. The Grand Mufti was a religious leader who worked in the government of the Ottoman Empire. The sultans and most of the people of the Ottoman Empire were devout Muslims. The Grand Mufti had to approve any law a sultan made to make sure it did not violate the religion of Islam.

The sultans passed their power down to their sons. In this way, control of the empire remained in the family.

■ PRACTICE 167: The Sultans of the Ottoman Empire

Decide if each statement below is true (**T**) or false (**F**). Write the correct letter on the line before each statement.

_____ **1.** A sultan was not allowed to pass a law unless the people of the Ottoman Empire voted in favor of it.

_____ **2.** The Grand Mufti would only approve laws that did not violate the religion of Islam.

_____ **3.** The sultans chose to live poorly so that the people they ruled would respect them.

_____ **4.** The sultans did not have absolute power.

Mohammed II

The first ruler of the Ottoman Turks was Othman. The next great sultan was **Mohammed II**. Mohammed II was the seventh ruler of the Ottoman Empire. He was called "the great" and "the conqueror," and for good reason. Under his rule, the Ottomans began a policy of growth and expansion that lasted for centuries.

Mohammed II captured Constantinople in 1453. (He had declared, "Give me Constantinople!" soon after becoming sultan.) The great city then became the capital of the Ottoman Empire. The city grew as Mohammed opened it to people of many nations and religions. Under the Ottomans, this city became known as Istanbul. But its name was not officially changed until 1930. Today, Istanbul is the largest city in Turkey.

Mohammed II also conquered many other lands. He led armies that captured all of the land around the Black Sea. Under his leadership, the army and the navy became increasingly powerful. By the time of his death, the Ottoman Empire stretched across a large area.

In addition to conquering other lands, Mohammed II made important contributions within the empire. He built palaces, mosques, and colleges. He also established the **Palace School,** where officials of the Ottoman Empire trained. This school, and the colleges he built, were centers of learning for many years.

Above all, Mohammed II will always be remembered as "the conqueror." At his death in 1481, the Ottoman Empire stretched over the largest area in its history. Mohammed II had started a conquest that would be continued by the sultans who followed him.

■ PRACTICE 168: Mohammed II

Match each description with a term from below. Write the letter of the term on the line before each description.

a. Constantinople   **b.** Mohammed II   **c.** Palace School

_____ **1.** a sultan of the Ottoman Empire who was a great conqueror

_____ **2.** an important city captured by the Ottoman Empire

_____ **3.** the place where leaders of the Ottoman Empire trained

The Ottoman Empire Reaches Its Peak

Sultan **Suleiman I** ruled the Ottoman Empire from 1520 to 1566. He was the tenth ruler of the empire. By that time, the Ottoman Empire was the largest and wealthiest empire in the world. Suleiman I set about making it even more powerful.

Suleiman I's armies conquered areas to the west and to the east. Suleiman I captured the kingdom of Hungary in 1526. Then he attacked Austria. He also conquered southern Arabia and North Africa. His navy attacked lands as far away as France and Spain.

The Ottoman Empire

Suleiman I brought the Ottoman Empire to its greatest height. During his reign, the navy controlled the entire Mediterranean Sea as well as the Black Sea and the Persian Gulf.

Europeans called Suleiman I "the Magnificent." This name recognized the fact that the arts and literature and social conditions advanced greatly during Suleiman's reign.

The people of the empire, though, called Suleiman I "the Lawgiver." This is because he changed the legal system of the empire to make it more efficient. But his greatest contribution was ably ruling over a great empire at the height of its power.

TIP

!

Historical maps, such as the one on page 265, can be hard to understand. This is because the borders are different from those you are familiar with today. To help make a historical map clearer, look for familiar cities, rivers, or bodies of water. These names tend to change less often, so they can help you orient yourself. For example, look for the Mediterranean Sea, the Black Sea, and the Caspian Sea in the map. These are the same bodies of water you will find on modern maps. They tell you that this region lies in what is today Europe, the Middle East, and North Africa.

■ PRACTICE 169: The Ottoman Empire Reaches Its Peak

Circle the letter of the correct answer to each of the following questions.

1. When did Suleiman I rule the Ottoman Empire?
    a. 1520–1566
    b. 1420–1456
    c. 1620–1626
    d. 1920–1926

2. What was Suleiman I's greatest accomplishment?
    a. changing the legal system of the Ottoman Empire
    b. ruling well over an empire at the height of its power
    c. capturing the kingdom of Hungary
    d. attacking lands as far away as Spain and France

Reasons for the Success of the Ottoman Empire

During the 1500s and 1600s, the Ottoman Empire was the most powerful empire in the world. From small tribes, the Ottoman Turks had grown into a massive power. This was accomplished by the boldness of the sultans and by growing military power.

But there were also other reasons for the growth of the Ottoman Empire. For one thing, the Ottoman rulers were Muslims. When they came to power, they could claim to be the defenders of the Muslim faith. This helped make the people of the Ottoman Empire—who were mostly Muslims—loyal.

The religion of Islam also helped the Ottoman rulers in another way. For centuries, Muslims had believed in holy wars, or jihads. These were wars of the faithful, the Muslims, against non-Muslim peoples. Thus, the leaders of the Ottoman Empire believed that they were spreading the word of Allah. (In this way, they were very much like earlier Muslim rulers.)

The Ottomans were also excellent rulers. When they conquered land, they did little to disturb the people there. The economy and society went on much as they always had. The Ottomans themselves worked only in the military and government.

A third factor was the janissaries. Most rulers of the time relied on hired soldiers or poorly trained soldiers. But the janissaries were a new breed: an elite group of highly trained fighting men. They were extremely loyal to the sultan. The janissaries were largely responsible for the Ottoman victories. (The word *janissary* means "new troops.")

IN REAL LIFE

Jihads still occur. You may have heard of the Persian Gulf War of 1991. In this war, armed forces led by the United States went to war against Iraq. The war started after Iraq invaded Kuwait, one of its neighboring countries. Both Iraq and Kuwait are Muslim countries in the Middle East. The president of Iraq, Saddam Hussein, declared a jihad, or holy war, against the United States-led forces. By doing so, Hussein framed the Persian Gulf War as a religious war—the Christian European and United States forces against the Muslim Iraqi forces. The Persian Gulf War is only one example. Much of the violence you read or hear about in the Middle East is related to a jihad.

■ PRACTICE 170: Reasons for the Success of the Ottoman Empire

Match each description with a term from below. Write the letter of the correct term on the line before each description.

 a. janissaries   **b.** jihads   **c.** Ottoman

_____ **1.** highly trained soldiers who led the Ottoman military

_____ **2.** people who held the most powerful empire in the world during the 1500s and the 1600s

_____ **3.** holy wars that are fought to spread the word of God

The Class System in the Ottoman Empire

It is important to remember that the peoples of the Ottoman Empire were very diverse. There were Turks, of course. But there were also Arabs, Slavs, Egyptians, and many other peoples. Two things united them: the rule of the Ottomans and the Muslim faith.

Throughout the empire, there were three main classes of people. At the top was the ruling class. This class was made up mostly of Ottoman Turks. They were the government, military, and religious leaders of the empire. The ruling class controlled the wealth. Many of them lived in fine stone houses and mansions. They led lives of relative ease.

However, most of the people of the Ottoman Empire were poor farmers. They belonged to a class called the **rayah,** or "protected flock." They were called this because the sultan was supposed to protect them. Most members of the rayah were Muslims. As such, their center of life was the mosque.

The third class of people were slaves. Usually, these were men, women, and children who were captured in battle or who were non-Muslim. But many slaves rose to great power. Under a special law, slaves and non-Muslim boys were taken by the government every five years. The most talented were trained and became janissaries or government officials. In fact, the grand vizier (a high officer) of the Ottoman Empire was usually a slave.

■ PRACTICE 171: The Class System in the Ottoman Empire

Match each description with a term from below. Write the letter of the correct term on the line before each description.

a. military and religious leaders   **b.** slaves   **c.** rayah

_____ **1.** members of the ruling class in the Ottoman Empire

_____ **2.** the class of poor farmers, the "protected flock," in the Ottoman Empire

_____ **3.** non-Muslims or people captured in battle in the Ottoman Empire

Ottoman Architecture

Every civilization in history has made important contributions to human life. The Ottoman Empire was no exception. Because the empire was so large and lasted so long, it is impossible to name all of its contributions. However, in Turkey, where the Ottoman Empire was centered, the period of Ottoman rule is often remembered as a period of great architecture.

Over the centuries, the Ottomans built many structures. Some of the larger structures remain today. They include libraries, government buildings, mosques, and shopping areas.

As you have read, Islamic mosques are beautiful pieces of architecture. Many of the most impressive mosques were built during the Ottoman Empire. They are famous for their large, beautiful domes.

One of the most beautiful—and famous—mosques is the Mosque of the Sultan Suleiman in Istanbul. It was designed by Koca Sinan. Even today, Koca Sinan is remembered as Turkey's greatest architect.

■ PRACTICE 172: Ottoman Architecture

Circle the letter of the correct answer to each of the following questions.

1. What are Ottoman mosques famous for?
   a. their brightly painted towers
   b. their carved wooden doors
   c. their large, beautiful domes
   d. their modern balconies

2. Who designed the Mosque of the Sultan Suleiman?
   a. Suleiman I
   b. Uthman
   c. Koca Sinan
   d. Rhazes

UNIT 6 REVIEW

Circle the letter of the correct answer to each of the following questions.

1. What are the followers of Islam called?
   a. Muslims
   b. Allahs
   c. Muhammads
   d. Arabs

2. What was a caliph?
   a. the founder of a religion
   b. a Muslim leader
   c. someone who knew Muhammad
   d. anyone who followed Islam

3. What happened to Islam in the years after Muhammad's death?
   a. It spread over a wide area.
   b. It had no strong leaders.
   c. It did not have many followers.
   d. It stopped existing as a religion.

4. What is the Koran?
   a. a holy city
   b. a Muslim holiday
   c. a Muslim prayer
   d. the sacred text of Islam

5. What were the main divisions of the Muslim Empire?
   a. caliphates
   b. caliphs
   c. hajjs
   d. minarets

6. How did the Seljuk Turks respond to Christians from Europe who wanted to visit the Holy Land?
   a. They welcomed them.
   b. They refused to let them visit.
   c. They let them visit only for short periods of time.
   d. They let them visit only if the Seljuk Turks could visit Europe.

7. What did the people of the Islamic world learn during the Crusades?
   a. how to be Christians
   b. ways to make better warships and cannons
   c. how to be Muslims
   d. how to avoid trading with Europe

8. What is a jihad?
   a. a war
   b. a city
   c. a place
   d. a person

9. Who were the janissaries?
   a. soldiers
   b. poor farmers
   c. sultans
   d. members of the ruling class

10. Why is Koca Sinan famous?
    a. It was a great city.
    b. He was a religious leader.
    c. He was a sultan.
    d. He was an architect.

UNIT 6 APPLICATION ACTIVITY
Two World Faiths

Today, Islam and Christianity are the two biggest religions in the world. About one third of the entire world population follows one of these two religions. In many ways, the religions are very different. But in some ways, they are also quite similar.

The chart below lists some ideas from the Koran (the sacred text of Islam) and the Bible (the sacred text of Christianity). Notice the similarities between meanings in the two texts.

The Koran says . . .	The Bible says . . .
Do unto all men as you would wish to have done unto you.	Do unto others as you would have them do unto you.
Serve and revere [respect] your parents.	Honor thy father and mother.
The poor, the orphan . . . feed them for the love of God alone, desiring no reward.	It is more blessed to give than to receive.
To honor an old man is to show respect for God.	Rebuke not an elder, but entreat him as a father.
On God's own nature has been molded man's.	God created man in His own image.

Now, look in newspapers or magazines for a story about a person or group of people who acted in a way that matches one of the ideas in the chart on page 272. For instance, you might find a story about a person who donated a large amount of money to a homeless shelter. This would be an example of giving of yourself, as taught in both the Koran and the Bible. Paste your article on another sheet of paper. Write a brief summary of it below. Then answer the questions.

■ Summary _____

_____

_____

_____

_____

■ Which idea does this article illustrate? _____

_____

_____

_____

■ Why? _____

_____

_____

_____

_____

UNIT 7
South and East Asia

LESSON 25: The Great Era of China

GOAL: To understand the people, places, and events that made the Tang and Sung dynasties important

WORDS TO KNOW

civil service system	movable type printing
climate	plateau
gunpowder	Sung dynasty
magnetic compass	Tang dynasty

NAMES TO KNOW

Empress Wu	Li Yuan
Li Po	Tang Taizong

PLACES TO KNOW

Chang'an	Himalayas	Tibetan Plateau
Gobi Desert	Huang He	Yangtze

The Geography of China

Before you start learning about the history of China, let us take a moment to discuss its geography. Geography is a description of land. In this case, it is the description of the land where historic events occur.

If you look at a globe, you can see that China is a very large country. Because China is so large, it has many different climates. A climate is a pattern of weather over a long period of time. In northern China, the climate is very cold. In western China, it is very dry. In southern China, it is warm and wet. In eastern China, the climate is mild.

The land of China is as varied as its climate. Northern China is rugged. It is covered with high mountains and huge deserts. The Gobi Desert stretches across much of this area. To the northeast, there are many hills. This part of China is also heavily forested.

Western China is also a rugged area. It consists of a large plateau and mountains. A **plateau** is a high, flat area. The **Tibetan Plateau** is surrounded by huge mountain ranges. The highest mountain in the world, Mount Everest, is located in this region. It is in the world's greatest mountain range: the **Himalayas.**

Like much of the rest of China, southern China is hilly. The land here is famous for its beautiful green hills and mountains.

Eastern China is the flattest part of China. Here, the vast plains and river valleys can be farmed. For thousands of years, many people have lived in this region.

China

Two great rivers cut through China, the **Huang He** and the **Yangtze.** Both begin in the mountains in the west and flow across all of China to the Pacific Ocean. The Huang He is also called the Yellow River. This is because the soil that it carries gives the water a yellowish color. The Huang He is also sometimes called "China's sorrow" because it has flooded many times and killed millions of people. The Yangtze, though, has helped the Chinese people for thousands of years. The Yangtze and the rivers that feed it have served as a highway through China's rugged land.

■ PRACTICE 173: The Geography of China

Circle the letter of the answer that correctly completes each of the following statements.

1. Mount Everest, the highest mountain in the world, is located in the _____ .

   a. Gobi Desert
   b. Huang He peninsula
   c. Himalayas
   d. Tibetan Plateau

2. The two great rivers of China are the _____ and the _____ .
   a. Himalaya, Gobi
   b. Yangtze, Huang He
   c. Yellow, Pacific
   d. none of the above

Chinese Dynasties

As you study the history of China, you will read the word *dynasty* many times. A dynasty is a series of rulers from the same family or group of people. For example, you will read about the **Tang dynasty.** The Tang dynasty consisted of a series of rulers that lasted for about 300 years. One man started the dynasty. He passed his rule down to his son, and so on. Often, though, the leadership did not pass directly from parent to child. Other family members and important people who were close to the ruling family also became rulers.

Chinese dynasties often lasted for centuries. And life in China was different under different dynasties. So, it is useful and convenient to break down the history of China into different dynasties. The name of each dynasty becomes the name used for that period of Chinese history. Remember this as you read about the history of China.

TIP

You have probably heard the word *dynasty* used to refer to a powerful family. In history, the word can refer either to the rulers themselves or to the period when the rulers were in power.

■ PRACTICE 174: Chinese Dynasties

Circle the letter of the correct answer to each of the following questions.

1. What is a dynasty?
   a. a series of rulers from the same family or group of people
   b. a term of office of about 300 years
   c. a Chinese ruler
   d. a system of sharing power

2. How long did dynasties in China often last?
- **a.** ten years
- **b.** three decades
- **c.** many centuries
- **d.** the lifetime of one person

Early Chinese History

People have been living in China for hundreds of thousands of years. The first people may have lived in China as long as 500,000 years ago. Chinese agriculture began about 10,000 years ago.

Chinese civilization gradually developed from the early peoples. The first kingdom, or dynasty, in China was the Shang dynasty. It developed between 1900 and 1700 B.C.E. The Shang dynasty was based in the rich valley of the Huang He.

THINK ABOUT IT

Chinese civilization, like many other civilizations, first developed in a river valley. Why do you think civilizations tend to start in river valleys? Can you name some other civilizations that began in river valleys? Write your answers on a separate sheet of paper.

The Shang dynasty was replaced by the Zhou dynasty. The great philosopher Confucius lived during this dynasty. The teachings of Confucius emphasize morality and responsibility. His work continues to influence life in China today.

The Zhou dynasty was replaced by the Qin (pronounced "chin") dynasty in 221 B.C.E. The Qin dynasty was the first empire in China. It had a strong central government. This strengthening of power by a single authority is still a major feature of Chinese civilization today. The famous Great Wall of China was built during this dynasty.

The Qin dynasty was followed by the Han dynasty. Han rulers greatly expanded the area they controlled. It was during this time that the Chinese invented paper, and the religion of Buddhism spread across the country.

After the Han dynasty fell, China split into many kingdoms. Invaders controlled much of the country. The Sui dynasty managed to unify China again for a short period. But the next dynasty, the Tang, became one of the greatest dynasties China has ever known.

■ PRACTICE 175: Early Chinese History

Circle the letter of the correct answer to each of the following questions.

1. During which dynasty was the Great Wall of China built?
    a. Shang dynasty
    b. Qin dynasty
    c. Tang dynasty
    d. Zhou dynasty

2. What was the first dynasty in China?
    a. Tang dynasty
    b. Shang dynasty
    c. Zhou dynasty
    d. Han dynasty

The Tang Dynasty

One of the greatest dynasties in China was the Tang dynasty. The Tang dynasty lasted from 618 to 907. So much was accomplished during the Tang dynasty that it is sometimes called the golden age of Chinese history.

The Tang dynasty began in 618 when **Li Yuan** overthrew the ruler of the Sui dynasty. However, Li Yuan was unable to control China. Many wars broke out. After a few years, he turned control over to his son, **Tang Taizong.**

Tang Taizong became one of the greatest emperors of China. He ended the civil warfare and expanded his empire. He also set up a very strong government. Under his leadership, armies conquered many areas.

Tang Taizong also encouraged the creation of trade routes that linked China to India and elsewhere. These trade routes brought great wealth to China. All of the Tang rulers who followed Tang Taizong continued to encourage trade. Chinese items, such as rice, jade, silks, spices, tea, and other goods, were sold in India, the Middle East, and even Europe. The wealth that this trade brought helped to keep the Tang dynasty in power.

TIP

Here is a tip to help you understand the names you will read in this book and in other books about China. In China, the family name comes before the person's given name. For example, in the name of the emperor Tang Taizong, the family name (Tang) comes first. This is the opposite of most Western names, in which a person's given name comes before his or her family name. (In the United States, however, most Chinese use the standard Western form.)

■ PRACTICE 176: The Tang Dynasty

Decide if each statement below is true (**T**) or false (**F**). Write the correct letter on the line before each statement.

_____ **1.** Li Yuan was one of China's greatest rulers.

_____ **2.** Tang Taizong set up an army to take over China.

_____ **3.** Tang Taizong helped to create trade routes between China and India.

Empress Wu

After Tang Taizong, Tang Gaozong became emperor. One of the members of his court was a woman named Wu. Slowly, Wu began to gain control over Gaozong and his family. She even had many members of the family killed. When Gaozong died, it was discovered he had named his son emperor. But Wu had grown so powerful that she had him thrown in jail and declared herself empress.

From 684 to 705, **Empress Wu** ruled China. She claimed to have started a new dynasty—the Chou. But historians think of her rule as part of the Tang dynasty. Regardless, Empress Wu was the only woman ever to have ruled China in her own name.

Empress Wu was an excellent leader. She was careful to appoint only intelligent and loyal people to important positions. She encouraged the creation of art and literature. She also promoted the religion of Buddhism.

Empress Wu also successfully worked with other countries. When armies to the west captured some of China's important trade routes, Empress Wu sent her own armies to reclaim them.

In 705, Empress Wu was overthrown. But during her 21-year reign, she protected and promoted the interests of the Chinese people.

IN REAL LIFE

Even today, the leaders of most countries are men. But several modern countries have had women leaders. These leaders included Margaret Thatcher in England, Indira Gandhi in India, and Golda Meir in Israel.

■ PRACTICE 177: Empress Wu

Circle the letter of the correct answer to each of the following questions.

1. Why does Empress Wu have a reputation as an excellent leader?
   a. She appointed intelligent people to important positions.
   b. She sent armies to reclaim China's captured trade routes.
   c. She encouraged the creation of art and literature in China.
   d. all of the above

2. What did Empress Wu accomplish that no one else in China ever has?
   a. She ruled for more than 20 years.
   b. She founded a dynasty.
   c. She was the only woman ever to rule China in her own name.
   d. She worked well with other countries.

The End of the Tang Dynasty

The next great emperor of the Tang dynasty was Tang Xuanzong. Xuanzong was Empress Wu's grandson. He ruled from 712 to 756. Under his leadership, China continued to be wealthy and peaceful. This period was the peak of the Tang dynasty.

Xuanzong's son, Suzong, was the next emperor. He was not as successful as his father. During his reign, many areas of China revolted against the emperor's rule. To make matters worse, armies from the west began invading China. Between revolts at home and invasions at the borders, the Tang dynasty grew weak. In 907, the last Tang emperor was removed from the throne. A golden age of Chinese history had ended.

■ PRACTICE 178: The End of the Tang Dynasty

Circle the letter of the correct answer to each of the following questions.

1. In what year did the golden age of Chinese history end?
   a. 712
   b. 756
   c. 907
   d. 1000

2. How did the Tang dynasty become weakened?
   a. Tang Xuanzong was unable to control China.
   b. Areas of China revolted against Tang Suzong.
   c. Armies from the west began invading China.
   d. both *b* and *c*

A Golden Age

As you have read, some historians call the Tang dynasty a golden age in Chinese history. There are many reasons for this.

First, the Tang period was a time of great wealth. The Tang rulers established trade routes to the west, reaching as far as Europe. They also sent armies to protect these routes. This trade made China rich.

Second, the Chinese used much of their wealth to support the arts and learning. All of the Tang rulers—from Li Yuan to Empress Wu and beyond—supported the arts and learning. The Tang capital city, Chang'an, housed many schools and communities of artists. Artists, writers, teachers, and other great thinkers settled in the Tang capital. Chang'an was a city of more than 2 million people—the largest city in the world at the time.

One of the greatest poets of all time, Li Po, lived during the Tang dynasty. He was just one of thousands of poets, scholars, and others who made important contributions to Chinese life during the Tang dynasty. The Chinese also took important steps toward the development of printing during this time.

During the Tang dynasty, Buddhism reached the peak of its popularity in China. There was also a renewed interest in Confucianism. Confucianism is a belief system based on the teachings of Confucius. Confucius was a Chinese philosopher who believed in justice, family loyalty, and fidelity. Confucianism continues to play a role in Chinese life today.

■ PRACTICE 179: A Golden Age

Circle the letter of the correct answer to each of the following questions.

1. Why is the Tang dynasty remembered as a golden age?
    a. It was a time of great wealth.
    b. Tang rulers established and protected trade routes to the west.
    c. Its capital was a great center of learning.
    d. all of the above

2. What brought wealth to the Tang dynasty?
    a. schools
    b. art
    c. trade
    d. literature

The Sung Dynasty

After the fall of the Tang dynasty, China was ruled by a series of dynasties that did not last very long. Then, in 960, Zhao Kuangyin came to power. He established the **Sung dynasty.** The Sung dynasty lasted from 960 to 1279.

Like the Tang, the Sung dynasty faced rebellions and warfare along its borders. But Zhao Kuangyin and the emperors who came after him managed to put down the revolts and secure China's borders. The Chinese economy expanded rapidly during the stable times of the Sung dynasty.

The leaders of the Sung dynasty made three important changes in Chinese life. These changes have shaped life in China for centuries, continuing to the present day.

First, the emperors improved the Chinese **civil service system.** Under the new system, people who wanted to work in the government had to take a series of tests. The tests were very difficult. Usually, only about one in ten people passed. The tests had two important effects. One was that only well-qualified people could serve in the government. This made the government stronger and more efficient. The other was that the civil service system promoted learning. As people throughout China studied for the tests, they became educated. This, too, helped to make China a strong country.

Second, the leaders of the Sung dynasty promoted Confucianism as the official way of thinking. So, people who were studying for the civil service examinations had to read the teachings of Confucius. In this way, the dynasty helped to shape Chinese life for hundreds of years to come.

A third important contribution of the Sung dynasty was improvements in agriculture. A new kind of rice was developed that produced a crop three times a year, rather than only once. As a result, rice became the basic food of the Chinese diet. More food also meant more people. During the Sung dynasty, the Chinese population increased to more than 100 million people for the first time. At least 10 cities were home to 1 million people each.

■ PRACTICE 180: The Sung Dynasty

Circle the letter of the correct answer to each of the following questions.

1. What were the great accomplishments of the leaders of the Sung dynasty?
   a. They improved the civil service system.
   b. They promoted the teachings of Confucius.
   c. They developed major improvements in agriculture.
   d. all of the above

2. How long did the Sung dynasty rule?
   a. 10 years
   b. 50 years
   c. more than 300 years
   d. none of the above

Inventions of the Sung Dynasty

The Chinese invented many important things during the Sung dynasty. These inventions are still with us today. In fact, many of them have changed the course of world history.

One of these inventions was printing. The Chinese had developed forms of printing earlier. But they made great advances in printing during the Sung dynasty. The most important was the invention of movable type. In **movable type printing,** different characters are first carved on blocks of wood. The characters are then arranged to form sentences. Ink, another Chinese invention, is applied to the blocks. Paper, which the Chinese also invented, is then pressed against the blocks to make a printed page.

A second important invention of the Sung dynasty was a way to use gunpowder in warfare. **Gunpowder,** which is used to make explosions and to shoot bullets and cannonballs, was invented during the Tang dynasty. At first, the Chinese used gunpowder just to make fireworks. During the Sung dynasty, however, they first used it as a weapon.

A third great invention of the Sung dynasty was the **magnetic compass.** A compass, whose needle always points north, helps travelers find their way. The magnetic compass made long sea journeys possible.

■ PRACTICE 181: Inventions of the Sung Dynasty

Circle the letter of the correct answer to each of the following questions.

1. Which of the following inventions was NOT made during the Sung dynasty?
   a. movable type printing
   b. gunpowder used for fireworks
   c. gunpowder used as a weapon
   d. magnetic compass

2. Which of the Sung dynasty inventions is still used today?
   a. gunpowder used as a weapon
   b. magnetic compass
   c. movable type printing
   d. all of the above

Invaders from the North

As you have read, the Chinese were frequently attacked by outsiders during both the Tang and Sung dynasties. Many of these attacks came from the north.

The northern peoples were nomads. This means that they did not lead a settled life. They traveled almost constantly, following their herds of animals to good grazing lands. They lived in tents.

There were many different nomadic tribes. During the early 1000s, these nomadic tribes became more powerful. They were increasingly successful in their attacks against the Chinese armies. By 1126, the Chinese had lost all of northern China to these northern invaders. The Sung were forced to move their capital to a city that was located farther south. The dynasty then became known as the Southern Sung.

The Southern Sung did not last long. As you will read in the next lesson, the invaders from the north became more and more powerful. In fact, they quickly conquered China completely.

■ PRACTICE 182: Invaders from the North

Decide if each statement below is true (**T**) or false (**F**). Write the correct letter on the line before each statement.

_____ **1.** The nomads formed a unified army to invade China during the Sung dynasty.

_____ **2.** The nomads followed their herds of animals toward the south.

_____ **3.** The Southern Sung gained power and became the Sung dynasty.

An Important Time in Chinese History

The Tang dynasty lasted from 618 to 907. The Sung dynasty lasted from 960 to 1279. These two dynasties ruled China for more than 600 years.

These dynasties are remembered as ruling during a golden age in Chinese history. During this time, art and literature flourished. Many important inventions, such as gunpowder and the magnetic compass, were made. Rice became the main food of the Chinese diet. And Confucianism was firmly established as an important influence on Chinese life. China was beginning to take shape as the country we know today.

■ PRACTICE 183: An Important Time in Chinese History

Circle the letter of the correct answer to each of the following questions.

1. Which of the following did NOT occur during the Tang and Sung dynasties?
   a. Art and literature flourished.
   b. Tea plantations made China self-sufficient.
   c. Rice became the main food of the Chinese diet.
   d. The ideas of Confucianism were firmly established.

2. How long did the Tang and Sung dynasties last?
   a. 25 years
   b. 600 years
   c. 100 years
   d. none of the above

LESSON 26: The Mongol Empire

GOAL: To understand the role played by Genghis Khan, Kublai Khan, and their armies in developing the Mongol Empire

WORDS TO KNOW

Ming dynasty	Mongols	Yuan dynasty

NAMES TO KNOW

Cheng Ho	Kublai Khan	Temujin
Genghis Khan	Marco Polo	

PLACE TO KNOW

Mongol Empire

The Mongols

You will remember that the Sung dynasty was under attack by nomadic peoples from the north. These people were called the **Mongols.** During the 1200s, the Mongols completely conquered China. They ruled China harshly for 100 years.

But the Mongols did not just conquer China. They also conquered almost all of Asia and even parts of Europe. In fact, the **Mongol Empire** became the largest land empire in the history of the world.

The Mongol Empire as of 1294

The Mongols came from central Asia. The peoples who lived in central Asia at this time were nomads. They herded horses and sheep. They lived in tents, which could be moved easily to better pastures. These nomads were not a single group of people. There were many different tribes of nomads in central Asia. They included the Huns, the Mongols, and others.

These peoples had many things in common. One of the most important was their horsemanship. Some historians call them the greatest horsemen in history. Their riders were so talented that they could shoot arrows while riding horses at full gallop. This horsemanship gave the nomads great advantages in warfare. Their cavalry, or horse soldiers, could easily defeat soldiers who were on foot.

These nomadic peoples often fought among themselves. In fact, war between these tribes was more common than war against China. Because there were so many different tribes, they needed a great leader to unite them. That leader, Genghis Khan, appeared in the late 1100s. To this day, he is remembered as being perhaps the fiercest conqueror in history.

THINK ABOUT IT

How do you think the Mongols' traditional life as nomads might have helped them as they set out to conquer other peoples? Write your answer on a separate sheet of paper.

■ PRACTICE 184: The Mongols

Decide if each statement below is true (**T**) or false (**F**). Write the correct letter on the line before each statement.

_____ **1.** The nomads had great advantages in warfare because they had advanced weapons.

_____ **2.** The nomadic tribes often fought amongst one another.

_____ **3.** Genghis Khan is famous for uniting the nomads.

Genghis Khan

Genghis Khan was born in 1162. He was the son of a nomadic tribal chief in central Asia. He was named Temujin. Mongol tradition says that the baby was born holding a blood clot. A Mongol holy man said this meant Temujin was destined to rule the world.

Like other boys of the tribe, Temujin grew up traveling the land. When he was 13, enemies from another tribe killed his father. Temujin and his mother were abandoned by the tribe. Fighting starvation, they somehow managed to survive in the rugged country.

When Temujin turned 17, he got married. But another tribe kidnapped his wife. Angered by the death of his father at the hands of one tribe and the kidnapping of his wife by another, Temujin swore revenge.

A powerful and resourceful man, Temujin gathered an army. He conquered the tribes that had harmed his family. He then set out to become an even greater conqueror. In 1206, he gathered together the leaders of many of the tribes. There, he proclaimed himself their "Universal Ruler," or Genghis Khan.

From that point on, the tribes of the region no longer fought one another. Under Genghis Khan's leadership, they became one Mongol people.

The Mongol people under Genghis Khan became great conquerors. They conquered most of Asia and parts of Europe. Genghis Khan rose from a hard early life and became the leader of the largest land empire in history.

■ PRACTICE 185: Genghis Khan

Circle the letter of the correct answer to each of the following questions.

1. What does the name Genghis Khan mean?
    a. Chief Warrior
    b. Young Leader
    c. Universal Ruler
    d. none of the above

2. Why did Temujin become a warrior?
  a. to take over China
  b. to stop nomadic tribes from invading China
  c. to punish the nomadic tribes that hurt his family
  d. to follow in his father's footsteps

The Mongol Empire Under Genghis Khan

After Genghis Khan became the Mongol ruler, he first conquered neighboring nomadic tribes. But he soon turned his attention to China. The Chinese had long been enemies of the nomadic peoples. And China was a rich and prosperous land.

It took Genghis Khan and his army just four years to conquer all of northern China. (The rest of China was later conquered by Genghis Khan's grandson.) He then turned his attention westward and conquered the rest of central Asia. By the time Genghis Khan died in 1227, the Mongol Empire he had founded stretched far and wide.

Genghis Khan's success as a leader stemmed from his ruthless and powerful rule. But his success as a conqueror was made possible by his fierce armies of horse soldiers. They were perhaps the most feared armies in history.

At times, the Mongol armies were huge: more than 100,000 fighting men. Almost all of them rode horseback. And every single one of them had been trained to be a fierce warrior from the time that he was very young. The Mongol culture valued fighting; it was the only way to acquire wealth and status.

The Mongols became experts in conquering cities. City after city fell to Genghis Khan's Mongol warriors. They used special techniques to fill moats and climb walls. No city could resist these huge, fierce, and well-trained armies.

The Mongol conquerors were also cruel. They often killed all the men, women, and children in the cities they captured. They burned cities and even the surrounding countryside to the ground. Often, all that was left after the Mongols passed through was wasteland.

Obviously, armies today do not ride on horseback. But other types of mobile units, such as tanks, still attack stationary targets, such as cities. And military officers still study the tactics that made Genghis Khan so successful.

■ PRACTICE 186: The Mongol Empire Under Genghis Khan

Decide if each statement below is true (**T**) or false (**F**). Write the correct letter on the line before each statement.

_____ **1.** Genghis Khan's largest army was more than 100,000 men.

_____ **2.** Soldiers in the Mongol armies were trained only to kill people who attacked them first.

_____ **3.** Most Mongol soldiers were poor peasants who were looked down upon by the rich.

_____ **4.** It took Genghis Khan more than four years to conquer all of Northern China.

Kublai Khan

The next great leader of the Mongols was **Kublai Khan.** He was the grandson of Genghis Khan.

Kublai Khan completed the conquest of China that his grandfather had begun. He established a new dynasty, the **Yuan dynasty.** The Yuan dynasty ruled China from 1279 to 1368. This marked the first time that China had ever been ruled by foreigners.

Kublai Khan also tried to invade Japan and lands to the south of China. He was unsuccessful. But he did bring the Mongol Empire to its height. It was the largest land empire in history. At no time before or since has a single person ruled so much land.

■ PRACTICE 187: Kublai Khan

Circle the letter of the correct answer to each of the following questions.

1. How was Kublai Khan related to Genghis Khan?
   a. He was his brother.
   b. He was his nephew.
   c. He was his son.
   d. none of the above

2. Why was the Yuan dynasty different from all the other dynasties that had ruled China in the past?
   a. Its rulers were foreigners.
   b. Its leader was a young boy.
   c. It ruled both China and Asia.
   d. none of the above

Marco Polo's Visit with Kublai Khan

You may have heard of **Marco Polo,** the famous traveler from Europe. Marco Polo's visit with Kublai Khan in China is one of the most famous events in history.

Marco Polo was an Italian trader. His brothers had visited Kublai Khan in China, and Kublai Khan had invited them to return. In 1271, they started to travel to China again—this time with their 17-year-old brother, Marco.

The journey was hard, dangerous, and long. It took the Polos three years to reach China. There, Kublai Khan welcomed them. He wanted to learn the languages that the Polos knew and to hear about the faraway lands that they had visited. The Polos stayed in China for 18 years.

Back in Italy, Marco Polo wrote about his adventures in a book called *Description of the World.* This book described the Mongol Empire and the riches in China to Europeans. In his book, Marco Polo told about paper money, burning coal for fuel, and other ideas that were new to Europeans. He described many aspects of Mongol and Chinese life and government.

Description of the World was read throughout Europe. It made many

Europeans interested in China for the first time. In fact, Christopher Columbus read it to help him plan his voyages.

■ PRACTICE 188: Marco Polo's Visit with Kublai Khan

Decide if each statement below is true (**T**) or false (**F**). Write the correct letter on the line before each statement.

_____ **1.** Marco Polo went to China alone.

_____ **2.** Marco Polo visited Kublai Khan.

_____ **3.** Marco Polo stayed in China for 18 years.

_____ **4.** Marco Polo wrote a book about his travels.

_____ **5.** Few people read Marco Polo's book.

The Decline of the Mongol Empire

Kublai Khan was the last great leader of the Mongol Empire. After he died in 1294, the empire broke up into smaller empires. Soon, even these empires ceased to exist. In China, the Chinese overthrew the Yuan dynasty that Kublai Khan had created.

By then, the Mongols had already started losing their empire. Why? Some historians believe that it was because the Mongols were excellent conquerors but poor administrators. In other words, they never managed to establish a strong government. And because their empire contained so many different peoples, there were many revolts and revolutions. Also, Mongol heirs and nobles competed for power within each section of the empire.

The Mongol Empire lasted just 200 years. It set a record for being the largest land empire in world history. The Mongol wars of conquest caused great destruction. But Mongol rule created a century of peace and stability over a vast region. Parts of the empire would continue, especially in India. But the period of great Mongol rule ended during the 1300s.

■ PRACTICE 189: The Decline of the Mongol Empire

Circle the letter of the correct answer to each of the following questions.

1. What record did the Mongol Empire set?
   a. It lasted longer than all preceding empires.
   b. It was the largest land empire in history.
   c. both *a* and *b*
   d. neither *a* nor *b*

2. Why did the Mongol Empire decline?
   a. The Mongols never set up a strong government.
   b. There were many revolts and revolutions.
   c. both *a* and *b*
   d. neither *a* nor *b*

The Ming Dynasty

Under Kublai Khan, the Mongols ruled China harshly. By the mid-1300s, rebels throughout China fought to push out the Mongols. The rebels eventually won. With the Mongols gone, the Chinese again established a Chinese dynasty. This was the **Ming dynasty.**

The Ming dynasty lasted from 1368 to 1644. Like the earlier Tang and Sung dynasties, the Ming dynasty ruled during a period of wealth and stability in China. In fact, the porcelain produced during this time is recognized as being among the greatest art in the history of the world.

During the Ming dynasty, the Chinese tried to return things to the way they were before the Mongols came. For example, the Mongols had done away with the Chinese civil service examinations. Under the Ming dynasty, these exams were put back in place.

But an important change had come to Chinese life. Before the Mongol Empire, Chinese rulers had been tolerant of foreigners. Now, affected by the harsh rule of the Mongols, they hated foreigners. In fact, they considered foreign people and ideas inferior to Chinese people and ideas. This attitude continues to influence Chinese life to the present day—a living legacy of the harsh Mongol rule of China.

■ PRACTICE 190: The Ming Dynasty

Circle the letter of the correct answer to each of the following questions.

1. What was the first Chinese dynasty after the Mongols left China?
   a. the Sung dynasty
   b. the Ming dynasty
   c. the Tang dynasty
   d. the Polo dynasty

2. What was produced during the Ming dynasty that is recognized as being among the greatest art in the history of the world?
   a. silk
   b. literature
   c. porcelain
   d. gold jewelry

Cheng Ho

During the Ming dynasty, the Chinese emperors wanted to demonstrate their wealth and power. They wanted to show the world that China, now free of foreign rule, was an important civilization.

One of the ways they did this was by sailing the seas. In 1405, a Chinese admiral named **Cheng Ho** set sail from China. Cheng Ho had a huge fleet under his command: 62 ships carrying nearly 30,000 men. The largest ships were more than 400 feet long. Cheng Ho led his ships from China south and west into the Indian Ocean. During this trip, he stopped at many ports and displayed the wealth and power of the Chinese emperor.

This voyage was the first of seven grand voyages that Cheng Ho would make. During his voyages, he traveled all along the coast of south Asia and India, southwest Asia, and the eastern coast of Africa. On one voyage, he brought 30 rulers from various kingdoms back to China to pay their respects to the emperor. On another voyage, he returned with a creature described in Chinese legend—a giraffe!

Cheng Ho's voyages lasted from 1405 to 1433. He died in 1435. Although his voyages did little to establish new trade routes, he successfully showed the power of China to many lands. His voyages are remembered as being some of the greatest in history.

■ PRACTICE 191: Cheng Ho

Circle the letter of the correct answer to each of the following questions.

1. Why did Cheng Ho make so many voyages?
   a. to recruit soldiers for the Chinese army
   b. to show the wealth and power of the Chinese emperor
   c. to expand trade routes
   d. to invade and conquer more land

2. In which direction(s) did Cheng Ho travel?
   a. north and east
   b. south and west
   c. due north
   d. none of the above

3. Which areas did Cheng Ho's voyages visit?
   a. Europe and south Asia
   b. India and Japan
   c. east Africa and India
   d. North America

4. In all, how many voyages did Cheng Ho make?
   a. 3
   b. 5
   c. 7
   d. 11

5. With what creature did Cheng Ho return to China, as described in Chinese legend?
   a. a giraffe
   b. a lion
   c. a monkey
   d. a tiger

LESSON 27: India Prospers

■ ■
■ ■ **GOAL:** To identify the people, places, and events involved in
■ ■   Indian history from about 300 to about 1500

WORDS TO KNOW

Age of Invasions   Kushan dynasty

Gupta dynasty   *Panchatantra*

PLACES TO KNOW

Brahmaputra River   Ganges River

Deccan Plateau   Gupta Empire

The Geography of India

A continent is a large body of land, such as Asia, Australia, or North
America. You learned in Lesson 9 that a subcontinent is a very large piece
of land that is attached to a continent. India is a subcontinent of Asia. It is
called the Indian subcontinent. As you can see from the map, it is a very
large piece of land. Shaped like a triangle, it is bordered by the Arabian Sea
to the west, the Bay of Bengal to the east, and the Indian Ocean to the
south. To the north, the rugged
Himalayas—the greatest mountain
range in the world—form a barrier
between India and the rest of Asia. To
the northwest, the Thar Desert and
rugged mountains make travel between
India and the rest of Asia difficult.

India

Most of India is one large plateau:
the Deccan Plateau. There are two
great rivers that cut through India. The
Ganges River is the sacred river of the
Hindu religion. The Brahmaputra
River joins the Ganges near its mouth.

■ PRACTICE 192: The Geography of India

Decide if each statement below is true (**T**) or false (**F**). Write the correct letter on the line before each statement.

_____ 1. Australia is a subcontinent.

_____ 2. India is a subcontinent of Asia.

_____ 3. The Himalayas form a barrier between northern India and the rest of Asia.

_____ 4. Most of India is covered by the Gobi Desert.

Early Indian History

During early Indian history, the area was divided into many separate groups of people. Generally, each village governed itself. This was true for hundreds of years. Although the people traded and spoke the same languages, they were not unified, or together, in the same country or empire.

You learned in Lesson 9 that the first great empire in India was the Mauryan Empire. It lasted from about 320 B.C.E. to 185 B.C.E. After this empire fell, a people called the Scythians invaded and ruled India. Their rule is called the Kushan dynasty. For two centuries, these foreigners ruled the people of India. Then, in about 320 C.E., the Gupta Empire emerged. The time of this empire is remembered as a golden age in Indian history.

■ PRACTICE 193: Early Indian History

Circle the letter of the correct answer to each of the following questions.

1. Which of the following statements about early Indian history is TRUE?
   a. One leader united all of the people.
   b. Each village ruled itself.
   c. Foreign rulers controlled most of India.
   d. India had a stable national government.

2. What was India's first great empire?
   a. the Kushan dynasty
   b. the Scythian Empire
   c. the Mauryan Empire
   d. the Gupta Empire

The Gupta Dynasty

The Gupta Empire was ruled by the Gupta dynasty. These rulers were all from the same family. They ruled India for more than 200 years, from 320 to 535.

The Gupta family was wealthy. In the 300s, the family began to control more and more land in northern India. In 320, one of the members of the family, Chandragupta I, began the Gupta dynasty. He ruled for 10 years, and he added to the family's land by marrying other landowners. His policy of expanding the area of the Guptas' control was followed by all of the Gupta rulers who came after him.

The Gupta Dynasty

The next two rulers of the Gupta dynasty added more and more land to the empire. By 400, the Guptas ruled all of northern India.

Some historians do not like the term *Gupta Empire*. This is because the Guptas never really ruled as emperors. Much of the land in the "empire" was controlled by local peoples. But these people had to pay tribute to the Guptas.

The Gupta Empire, or dynasty, lasted until invaders from the north overran it in 535.

■ PRACTICE 194: The Gupta Dynasty

Circle the letter of the correct answer to each of the following questions.

1. Where was the Gupta Empire?
   a. in northern India
   b. in southern India
   c. throughout all of India
   d. throughout all of India and China

2. When did the Guptas rule?
   a. from 320 to 400
   b. from 300 to 320
   c. from 200 to 535
   d. from 320 to 535

A Golden Age in Indian History

The Guptas were skilled at government, and the Gupta dynasty ruled during a period of peace for the people of northern India. Under these circumstances, the culture of India made important contributions to education, art, literature, medicine, and more. This is why the time of the Gupta dynasty is remembered as a golden age in Indian history.

The Guptas valued learning and education. They created many excellent schools, universities, and libraries. Indian mathematicians of this period invented the decimal system and developed the Arabic numerals that we use today. They also invented the concept of zero. Indian astronomers proved that the world was round.

Art also thrived under the Guptas. Indian artists painted beautiful murals. They also developed a style of sculpture that is still seen in India today. Many Indian sculptors carved large statues of Buddha.

Literature was another field of accomplishment. Southern India was the site of many writing schools. A number of writers collected and retold Indian folk tales and fables. One of the most important works of this time is the *Panchatantra,* a collection of fairy tales.

IN REAL LIFE

Have you ever heard the story of Sinbad the Sailor? How about Jack the Giant Killer? These familiar stories were first told in the *Panchatantra*. Even today, millions of copies of this book (and countless adaptations) are read and enjoyed throughout the world.

Styles of music and dance developed during the Gupta dynasty are still popular in India today. Playwrights were supported, and theater was popular.

Health and medicine were also supported by the Guptas. The Guptas built many free hospitals to care for the people of India. The doctors at these hospitals were among the most advanced in the world. For example, many knew of the importance of being especially clean before treating patients. This was an important medical idea that was not adopted in the West until much later.

The spread of the Hindu religion was another important result of the Gupta dynasty. Before the Gupta dynasty, most Indians were Buddhists. The Gupta rulers, however, followed the Hindu religion. Their belief in Hinduism helped make this religion the most popular one in India for centuries to come. (By about 800, Hinduism had all but replaced Buddhism in India.)

The Gupta dynasty lasted only about 200 years, but it continues to influence life in India today.

THINK ABOUT IT

India's golden age lasted about 200 years. You may have read about other golden ages in history, such as that of Greece. Do you think the United States has had a golden age? If so, when? And why do you consider this period a golden age? Write your answers on a separate sheet of paper.

■ PRACTICE 195: A Golden Age in Indian History

Circle the letter of the correct answer to each of the following questions.

1. Which of the following was NOT an accomplishment of the Gupta Empire?
   a. schools and libraries
   b. art and literature
   c. the spread of Buddhism
   d. hospitals

2. Why could a golden age flourish in the Gupta Empire?
   a. The Guptas owned all the gold in India.
   b. Indian painters made colorful murals.
   c. Theater and dance were popular.
   d. The Gupta dynasty ruled during a peaceful and stable time.

India's Age of Invasions

The Gupta dynasty ended around 535. For nearly a century before that, many peoples had begun to invade India. India suffered from these invasions for another 1,000 years. There were so many invasions by so many peoples that the period of Indian history from about 500 to about 1500 is sometimes called the Age of Invasions.

The first people to invade the Gupta Empire were the Huns. They came from the north and conquered all of northern India. Within a century, the Huns were defeated, but by then, northern India had been split into many smaller kingdoms. In 612, the leader of one of these kingdoms, Harsha, conquered the others and ruled what had once been the Gupta Empire. But, after his death, India once again was split into small kingdoms.

In the early 700s, the Muslims entered India. By about 1200, they had conquered the land. At this time, the Muslims ruled a great empire that stretched across much of Asia, Africa, and Europe. The Muslims treated the Hindu peoples of India harshly. They killed countless Hindus and took all that they had. Still, the Muslims brought many important ideas to India. They introduced such things as paper and gunpowder to the Indian peoples. They also took many Indian ideas, such as Arabic numerals, and spread them throughout the empire.

Eventually, though, the Muslims, too, were conquered. Then, an Indian named Babur the Tiger founded the Mogul Empire in India. The Mogul Empire lasted from 1526 to 1761.

Throughout this period, though, the Indians endured. Today, India is considered one of the great countries—and civilizations—of the world.

■ PRACTICE 196: India's Age of Invasions

Circle the letter of the correct answer to each of the following questions.

1. What years in Indian history make up the Age of Invasions?
   a. 1 to 500
   b. 100 to 650
   c. 700 to 1200
   d. 500 to 1500

2. Which were the first people to invade the Gupta Empire?
   a. Muslims
   b. Huns
   c. Mongols
   d. Arabs

3. What was a negative effect of the Muslim conquest of India?
   a. harsh treatment of the Hindus
   b. destruction of the economy
   c. introduction of paper and gunpowder
   d. the spread of Buddhism

4. What empire did Babur the Tiger found in India?
   a. the Muslim Empire
   b. the Gupta Empire
   c. the Mogul Empire
   d. the Hindu Empire

LESSON 28: Early Japan

> **GOAL:** To discuss the influence of China in the early history of Japan; to explain the Japanese system of clan and family rule

WORDS TO KNOW

daimyo

samurai

shogun

Tale of Genji

NAMES TO KNOW

Fujiwaras

Kotoku

Lady Murasaki Shikibu

Prince Shotoku

PLACES TO KNOW

Hokkaido

Honshu

Kyushu

Shikoku

The Geography of Japan

Geography is an important part of history. This is especially easy to see in the history of Japan. Because Japan is an island country, it has often been isolated from outside influences.

Japan consists of four main islands and thousands of smaller islands. The four main islands are Hokkaido, Honshu, Shikoku, and Kyushu.

All of the islands of Japan are rugged and mountainous. Most of them are nearly covered by forests. Most Japanese live on the coasts. So, for thousands of years, the Japanese people have made their living fishing from the ocean. There are also some rich, flatlands in Japan that have been farmed for thousands of years. Japan's most important crop is rice.

The islands of Japan stretch about 1,000 miles from north to south. Because Japan covers such a large area, it has many climates. In the south, the winters are mild and the summers are hot. As one travels north, the winters become longer and harder, and the summers become shorter and cooler. There is plenty of rain throughout the islands, which has always helped agriculture.

It was on this geographic stage that one of the greatest civilizations the world has ever seen developed. The history of Japan is as interesting as the land is beautiful.

■ PRACTICE 197: The Geography of Japan

Circle the letter of the correct answer to each of the following questions.

1. Which of the following is NOT one of Japan's main islands?
   a. Honshu
   b. Tokyo
   c. Shikoku
   d. Kyushu

2. What is Japan's most important crop?
   a. snow peas
   b. seaweed
   c. rice
   d. ginger

China's Influence on Early Japan

Today, we think of China and Japan as very different countries with very different people. But for an important part of Japanese history, the Japanese people tried hard to model themselves on Chinese culture.

This started during the late 400s and lasted for hundreds of years. The Japanese adopted many Chinese ideas. The Japanese began using Chinese writing around 405. They also began to use the Chinese calendar. Even Confucianism became important in Japan. By the late 500s, Buddhism, a religion brought over from China, was becoming popular in Japan.

During the 600s, the Japanese sent many representatives to China. They returned filled with ideas borrowed from China. In 702, the Japanese issued a new code of law based on the laws of the Chinese Tang dynasty.

Eventually, Chinese influence in Japan weakened. But it had an important influence during Japan's early stages.

The Japanese went on to create a unique civilization and culture. One important Japanese contribution was the invention of the novel. The world's first novel, *Tale of Genji,* was written by Lady Murasaki Shikibu in 1000. It is just one of the countless contributions the Japanese have made to world culture.

THINK ABOUT IT

Take a look at a map and note where Japan and China are located. What role do you think the location of China played in its influence on Japan? Write your answer on a separate sheet of paper.

■ PRACTICE 198: China's Influence on Early Japan

Decide if each statement below is true (**T**) or false (**F**). Write the correct letter on the line before each statement.

_____ **1.** Japan's earliest code of law was based on the laws of China's Ming dynasty.

_____ **2.** The Chinese invented the novel.

_____ **3.** Today, Chinese and Japanese cultures are very different.

Clans, Emperors, and Shoguns

By 200, the Japanese people had organized themselves into clans. Clans are groups of related families. Each clan was led by a chief. Different clans competed to become the most powerful. By about 400, the Yamato clan had become the most powerful clan in Japan.

Prince Shotoku was the most powerful clan leader in the early 600s. He sought out many Chinese ideas. The most important one he copied was the Chinese system of strong central government.

Japan had long had emperors, but these emperors did not really control the whole nation. Then, in 645, Kotoku became emperor. He led a more centralized government. Under his rule, Japan was divided into provinces. The leader of each province reported to the emperor. As a result, Japanese emperors controlled all of Japan for 200 years.

IN REAL LIFE

You are probably familiar with many Japanese brand names, such as Suzuki motorcycles, Fuji film, and Yamaha pianos. These are family names as well as brand names. Many Japanese businesses are family operated. This helps show how today's Japanese culture continues to place great importance on family ties and loyalty.

But then a powerful clan, the Fujiwaras, gained control of the government. This clan also gained control of much land. For 300 years, this powerful family ruled Japan. During this time, the emperors continued to lose power. More and more, Japan was controlled by the Fujiwaras and other wealthy, powerful families. These families ruled huge estates of land. The lord of each estate was called a daimyo. The warriors that worked for the daimyo were called samurai.

By the 1100s, two powerful families were fighting for control of Japan. The Taira family had overthrown the Fujiwaras. But they were defeated by the Minamoto family, headed by Yoritomo. The Minamoto family clan was now the strongest in all of Japan.

Throughout this period of ruling families, the Japanese always had an emperor. But he was emperor in name only. The families held the real power. The person who ruled when the Minamotos became powerful was Yoritomo. In 1192, the emperor gave Yoritomo the title of shogun, or supreme general, of Japan. The shogun ruled Japan like a military dictator. For the next 800 years, until 1868, the shoguns remained the real rulers of Japan. The shoguns ruled through the daimyos, who became military governors in charge of each province. Over time, these daimyos became very powerful.

■ PRACTICE 199: Clans, Emperors, and Shoguns

Match each description with a term from below. Write the letter of the correct term on the line before each description.

a. clan   **b.** shogun   **c.** daimyo   **d.** samurai

_____ **1.** a general of Japan

_____ **2.** the lord of a large estate

_____ **3.** warriors who worked for lords of large estates

_____ **4.** a group of related families

UNIT 7 REVIEW

Circle the letter of the correct answer to each of the following questions.

1. What is Tang Taizong famous for starting?
   a. trade routes
   b. the Chou dynasty
   c. the Tang dynasty
   d. many wars

2. Why is the rule of the Tang and Sung dynasties considered a golden age in Chinese history?
   a. because art and literature flourished
   b. because the ideas of Confucianism became firmly established
   c. because many important inventions were made
   d. all of the above

3. Which of the following statements about the Mongol Empire is TRUE?
   a. The Mongol Empire conquered China.
   b. The Mongol Empire was the largest land empire in history.
   c. The Mongol Empire grew by fiercely conquering other peoples.
   d. all of the above

4. Why did Cheng Ho go on his many long sea voyages?
   a. to explore unknown lands
   b. to capture and rob other ships
   c. to show the power of the Chinese emperor
   d. to capture new lands

5. What did Chandragupta I begin?
   a. civilization in India
   b. the Gupta dynasty
   c. the *Panchatantra*
   d. the Age of Invasions

6. What was the *Panchatantra*?
   a. a book of fairy tales
   b. a dynasty
   c. an empire
   d. a plateau

7. What was the religion of the people of the Gupta Empire?
   a. Buddhism
   b. Hinduism
   c. both Buddhism and Hinduism
   d. neither Buddhism nor Hinduism

8. Which foreign people most influenced the Japanese in the 400s?
   a. the Chinese
   b. the Fujiwaras
   c. the daimyos
   d. the samurai

9. For what is Lady Murasaki Shikibu remembered?
   a. ruling Japan as the chief of a clan
   b. becoming a powerful shogun
   c. becoming the first emperor of Japan
   d. writing the world's first novel

10. What was the lord of a powerful Japanese estate called?
   a. a daimyo
   b. a shogun
   c. a samurai
   d. an emperor

UNIT 7 APPLICATION ACTIVITY
Rivers of History

In Unit 7, you learned how important geography is to the history of a place. The land plays an important role in shaping both the culture and the people of a region.

The Yangtze and Huang He are two of the most important rivers in China. They have both had a significant impact on the history of the regions they flow through. You have already learned that the Huang He (also called the Yellow River) is sometimes called "China's sorrow," because it has flooded so often. You also know that the Yangtze River has acted as a highway through China for thousands of years. In this activity, you will research more reasons why one of these rivers is (and always has been) so important to China.

First, choose either the Yangtze or the Huang He River to research. Then, use library and Internet resources to find out more about either river. (*Hint*: If you cannot find any listings on the Internet or in an encyclopedia for the Huang He River, try looking it up as "Hwang Ho." This is another spelling used for the same river.) Finally, write a paragraph recording your findings. In your paragraph, try to answer at least two of the following questions.

- How does the river affect the livelihood of the Chinese people? (For instance, does the river provide fertile soil that creates rich farmlands?)

- Is the river used for transportation? Is it used for trade? In what ways?

- Have there been any significant changes in the landscape due to the river, such as floods that have washed out villages?

- Has the river always been used by the Chinese people in the same ways? If not, how have these uses changed over the years? Write your paragraph below.

_____

_____

_____

_____

_____

_____

_____

_____

_____

_____

_____

_____

_____

_____

_____

_____

_____

_____

_____

_____

_____

_____

UNIT 8

Africa and the Americas

LESSON 29: Early African Society

GOAL: To describe the continent of Africa and the different peoples who have lived there

WORDS TO KNOW

ancestor worship	continent	savannas
ancestral spirits	nation	traditional religions
animism	oral tradition	tribe
Bantu migrations	people	village

PLACES TO KNOW

Atlas Mountains	Namib Desert	Sahara Desert
Congo	Niger	Sahel
Mount Kilimanjaro	Ruwenzori Range	

The Geography of Africa

Geography is a description of an area of land. As you may already know, history is influenced by geography. So, before you start learning about the history of Africa, it is worthwhile to look at Africa's geography. Africa is a continent, or huge mass of land. Africa is the second-largest of the world's seven continents. Africa covers one fifth of all the land in the world. It is three times bigger than the United States. Africa has 23,000 miles of coastline—about the same distance that the equator travels around the world.

Africa is one enormous plateau. A plateau is a high, mostly flat region. But all of Africa does not look the same. In fact, Africa has a wide variety of landscapes. Each landscape is beautiful in its own way.

Near the equator, in central Africa, there is rain all year. This moisture gives rise to dense rain forests. To the north and south, the climate changes. These areas have wet seasons and dry seasons. Here, other forests and great grasslands—called savannas—grow. Savannas cover about half of Africa.

The climate grows drier as you move farther away from the equator. In the south, the **Namib Desert** stretches over a large area. In the north, the world's largest desert, the **Sahara Desert,** covers much of the land. The Sahara is bordered on the south by a region called the **Sahel.** This region is not as dry as the desert, but it still has few plants.

Africa

The world's longest river, the Nile, flows north from central Africa to the Mediterranean Sea. It is more than 4,000 miles long. Other major African rivers include the **Congo** and the **Niger,** both of which flow into the Atlantic Ocean.

Most of Africa's mountains are extinct volcanoes. The highest mountain in Africa is **Mount Kilimanjaro,** which rises 19,340 feet. Africa's major mountain ranges include the **Atlas Mountains** and the **Ruwenzori Range.**

Above all else, perhaps, Africa is a land of extremes. It has some of the driest, some of the wettest, some of the hottest, and some of the coldest places on Earth.

Africa is a wonderful land, filled with beauty and great variety. It was in this special place that some very special events in history took place, as you will learn in the next few lessons.

THINK ABOUT IT

Africa is very large. Africa also has a wide range of temperatures and amounts of rainfall. How do you think these two facts are related? Write your answer on a separate sheet of paper.

■ PRACTICE 200: The Geography of Africa

Circle the letter of the correct answer to each of the following questions.

1. How does Africa compare to the world's other continents?
    a. It is the smallest continent.
    b. It is the second-smallest continent.
    c. It is the largest continent.
    d. It is the second-largest continent.

2. What is the name of the world's largest desert?
    a. Sahara
    b. Namib
    c. Nile
    d. Congo

Africa's Earliest History

Today, most scientists agree that the earliest humans lived in Africa. Africa is therefore often called "the birthplace of humanity." Human beings lived in Africa at least 2 million years ago.

The earliest peoples in Africa lived by hunting and gathering in small bands. Eventually, some of these peoples developed agriculture. As people became farmers, they settled into communities. Over time, some of these communities grew in strength and power. Eventually, great ancient civilizations, such as the kingdom of Egypt, were born. South of Egypt, the great kingdom of Kush grew. It lasted more than 2,000 years.

About 2,000 years ago, certain African peoples began to migrate, or move. From a small area of central Africa, they moved throughout central, eastern, and southern Africa. These movements are called the **Bantu migrations** because the people spoke Bantu languages. These Bantu speakers were farmers and nomadic herders. The Bantu migrations were some of the greatest human movements in history. As the people moved, they spread their knowledge and their ways of life, including ironworking. They also adapted their farming and herding techniques to fit the new environments they moved into. They merged with the people they met and created vibrant new cultures. These cultures live on even today.

Do you enjoy a football game more if you know the records of the teams? How about if you know which players have been doing well and which are in a slump? Knowing some background helps you to enjoy the game. The same is true of history. By understanding what came before, you can better appreciate the new things you learn and hear about. That is just one reason to study history. It trains your mind to think about "the bigger picture."

■ PRACTICE 201: Africa's Earliest History

Circle the letter of the correct answer to each of the following questions.

1. For how long have people lived in Africa?
   a. 1,000 years
   b. 2 million years
   c. 5 million years
   d. none of the above

2. What are two important kingdoms of ancient Africa?
   a. the Bantu and Kush kingdoms
   b. the Sahara and Sahel kingdoms
   c. the Namib and Atlas kingdoms
   d. the Egypt and Kush kingdoms

3. What is the name of the great movement of black, Bantu-speaking peoples throughout Africa?
   a. the Bantu migrations
   b. the Kush explorations
   c. the savanna safaris
   d. none of the above

African Villages

It is important to remember that there really was, and is, no one "African" people. Over thousands of years, hundreds of different cultures developed in Africa. These people spoke different languages, had different traditions, and practiced different religions. Each culture was unique. The diversity, or variety, of the peoples of Africa makes African history among the most interesting on Earth.

Despite their differences, early African peoples did have many things in common. For example, most early people lived in villages. As you have read, the earliest Africans lived in small bands. Over time, these bands of peoples settled into villages. A **village** is a small settlement. For thousands of years, villages were the centers of African life. Some villages were tiny—home to just several families. Others were huge, with thousands of residents. In fact, the word *town* better describes these larger settlements.

Every African village was unique. This is because life in the village depended on the culture of the people who lived there. There are, however, certain general features that most African villages shared.

First, the buildings in an African village were made of local materials. Some were made of mud. Others were made of plant materials, such as wood and straw.

Second, the villages were planned. Buildings were arranged in special patterns to make village life efficient. Often, these patterns reflected the relationships of the families and the leaders of the village.

Third, villages were often made up of related families. Units of parents and children lived and worked together, alongside related parent-child units. Decisions at the village level were often made by consensus, or agreement of all residents.

Fourth, the villages were usually bordered by farm fields. Most early Africans were farmers. They left their villages during the day to tend their crops in the neighboring fields. Most people also kept some animals, such as goats. Back at home in the village, Africans attended to the important affairs of life: raising children, holding celebrations, trading, and so on. Often, religious ceremonies were held in special buildings in the village.

Fifth, the villages of Africa were connected by footpaths. Historians think that it was possible to cross the entire continent of Africa hundreds of years ago without ever leaving a footpath.

You read earlier that there were hundreds of cultures in Africa. Now you have read that there were thousands of villages in Africa, all connected to each other by footpaths. Think about these two facts. Why do you think there were thousands of villages, but only hundreds of different cultures? Why would each village not have its own culture? Write your answers on a separate sheet of paper.

■ PRACTICE 202: African Villages

Circle the letter of the correct answer to each of the following questions.

1. What did most early African villages have in common?
   a. Buildings were made of local materials.
   b. Villages were planned.
   c. Villages were homes to farmers and were bordered by farm fields.
   d. all of the above

2. What made it possible to cross the entire continent of Africa?
   a. villages
   b. farm fields
   c. footpaths
   d. planned roadways

Tribes, Cultures, Peoples, and Nations

You have read that hundreds of cultures developed in Africa. You have also read that there were many African peoples. You have probably heard people talk about the many tribes in Africa. In fact, the words *culture, people,* and *tribe* all mean pretty much the same thing.

Over the years, historians and other scholars have struggled with choosing the words to use to talk about history. A generation ago, people often used the word *tribe.* Then some people started to use the word in a negative way. To them, the word *tribe* implied a group that was "primitive" or "inferior."

In fact, a tribe is a group of semi-independent communities that share a language and culture. They live in the same area. And they cooperate on some level, such as banding together during an attack. There were many tribes in early African history. A tribe refers to the way a group of people organize themselves. It does not place any judgment on those people.

The term *culture* means "a set of rules and behaviors that the members of a group of people share." Any distinct group of people has its own culture. The rules of a culture cover a wide variety of things: marriage, language, religion, art, and so on. For example, American culture is very different from Chinese culture. In early Africa, the groups were smaller than in America or China, but their cultures were just as important and different.

When we say a **people,** we are usually referring to a group of people who share the same culture. We can use the word nation in the same way. A nation is not a country, such as France or South Africa. A **nation** is a group of people who share a culture.

■ PRACTICE 203: Tribes, Cultures, Peoples, and Nations

Circle the letter of the answer that correctly completes each of the following statements.

1. Hundreds of _____ developed in Africa.
    a. tribes
    b. cultures
    c. peoples
    d. all of the above

2. A tribe is _____ .
    a. a group that shares a language and culture
    b. a group that wages war
    c. a farming organization
    d. none of the above

The Oral Traditions of Early Africans

You have read that each of the hundreds of cultures in early African history was unique. You have also read that most had some things in common—for example, most peoples were farmers who lived in villages. Now you are going to learn about another important thing they had in common.

Illiterate means "unable to read or write." Today, people use the word *illiterate* as an insult. And it is true that in our culture it is important to know how to read and write. But the peoples of early Africa did not need to be able to read or write. They developed wonderful cultures without the written word.

Instead of reading and writing, most early African cultures had an oral tradition. An **oral tradition** simply means that information is passed down through the generations orally, or through the spoken word, instead of by the written word. Many African cultures appointed certain individuals to the task of remembering and telling the story of their people. (In West Africa, these storytellers were called *griots*.) But every adult was expected to know, remember, and pass down vital information about a people's history and culture.

The system worked very well. For centuries, peoples with an oral tradition thrived. The oral tradition had the advantage of promoting closer bonds among the people of a culture, the members of a family, and different generations.

IN REAL LIFE

Before children learn to read and write, they have a kind of oral tradition. For instance, most children know some nursery rhymes by heart. And many children can sing the ad jingles and other songs they hear on television. What nursery rhymes or childhood jingles do you remember from when you were very young? These are part of your own oral tradition. And whenever you hear a joke or a riddle and then tell it to a friend, you are taking part in an oral tradition.

■ PRACTICE 204: The Oral Traditions of Early Africans

Decide if each statement below is true (**T**) or false (**F**). Write the correct letter on the line before each statement.

_____ **1.** Cultures with oral traditions are not as good as cultures with written traditions.

_____ **2.** The oral traditions of early African cultures served their peoples well.

Early African Religious Traditions

Because each early African culture was unique, its religious practices were also unique. However, most early Africans practiced a type of religion called animism. Animism is the belief that spirit beings animate, or make alive, nature. To most early African peoples, the world was alive with spirits. Animals, plants, rivers, springs, mountains, and other natural features had spirits, just as people do. So did things people made, such as weapons and works of art. In addition, other spirits roamed throughout the land and sky, not attached to particular things. Boldly carved and decorated masks worn during religious ceremonies called up the presence of these spirits. Most African religions also held that there were many gods, including a single, superior god who made the universe.

Another common religious belief was a belief in ancestral spirits. This belief holds that the spirits of one's ancestors live on and play a vital role in the affairs of the living. Eventually, these spirits may be reborn in another person or animal. Many Africans worshiped ancestral spirits in a practice called ancestor worship.

Magic, too, was a feature common to most early African religions. Village religious leaders would use magic to cure and protect the people of the village. Individuals often wore charms, which they believed had magical powers, to protect themselves from harm.

There were countless variations of these ideas in early African religions. For example, not all religions believed in ancestral spirits, and those that did had different beliefs about them. Still, you can get a fair idea of early religion in Africa by keeping in mind the general points you just read. These religions are often called **traditional religions.**

■ PRACTICE 205: Early African Religious Traditions

Circle the letter of the correct answer to each of the following questions.

1. Which of the following features was NOT common to most early African religions?
   a. animism
   b. magic
   c. dynasties
   d. ancestor worship

2. What is animism?
   a. the belief that spirits can be reborn in another person or animal
   b. the belief that the spirits of one's ancestors live on
   c. the belief that spirit beings animate nature
   d. the belief that magical powers can cure people who are ill

3. What is the focus of ancestor worship?
   a. the spirits of nature
   b. the spirits of one's ancestors
   c. magical charms
   d. boldly carved masks

4. Which of the following statements is TRUE of most African religions?
   a. a belief in a single, superior god
   b. a worship of animals
   c. a fear of magic
   d. a belief in only one god

LESSON 30: The Influence of Christianity and Islam in Africa

 GOAL: To describe how two major religions influenced the people of Africa

WORD TO KNOW
Vandals

PLACES TO KNOW

Axum	Ethiopia	Nubia
Byzantine Empire	Islamic world	Roman Empire

Christianity in Northern Africa

In Lesson 29, you learned that many different religions developed among the peoples of early Africa. Although each traditional religion was unique, most had certain features in common. Animism, ancestor worship, and the power of magic were three such features. These early religions served the peoples of Africa well for thousands of years, and many still live on today, throughout the continent.

However, just a few centuries after Jesus Christ lived, the new religion of Christianity took hold in northern Africa. By this time, Egypt and the entire northern coast of Africa were part of the **Roman Empire.** During the 300s, Christianity became the official religion of the Roman Empire. Because so many Africans in the north were under Roman rule, many became Christians, either by choice or by force.

As the Roman Empire declined, it lost control of northern Africa. Invaders from central Europe called **Vandals** captured the region. The Vandals were also Christian, but they practiced a form of the religion that was outlawed in the Roman Empire. Still, the Vandals ruled northern Africa for a century, and throughout this period Christianity remained in northern Africa.

By the 500s, the Vandals had been pushed out by the forces of the Byzantine Empire. The **Byzantine Empire** had arisen from the eastern part of the old Roman Empire. The Byzantine Empire was Christian. So by the 500s, the people of northern Africa had been influenced by Christianity for a full 200 years.

Two great kingdoms of Africa were especially influenced by the Christian religion. The kingdom of **Axum** was located just south of Egypt, in what is today **Ethiopia**. Axum was a wealthy kingdom that thrived on trade. It was located along the busy trade routes between Egypt and India. Axum's close trading links with Rome helped spread Christianity in the kingdom. The strong king Ezana became a Christian after he took the throne around 325. He made Christianity the official state religion.

The kingdom of Axum survived only 200 years, but its Christian tradition lived on. Today, Ethiopia remains a largely Christian country. The Christian church of Ethiopia is a direct descendant of the Christian church of Axum.

In **Nubia**, near Axum, many small kingdoms developed after the fall of the great Kush civilization—around 350. These kingdoms grew wealthy on agriculture and trade. They traded their farm products with Egypt, which was at that time a part of the Christian Byzantine Empire. Missionaries from Egypt spread Christianity throughout Nubia. As in Axum, the influence of Christianity was felt in the region for centuries.

Christian Areas of Africa

As you study history, you will find certain "big ideas" that are repeated over and over again. For example, one "big idea" is that wars change the course of history. Another big idea is one you just read about—that trade changes history. When people trade, they always trade more than just goods and money. They also trade ideas. That is how Axum became a Christian kingdom. So, whenever you read about trade, think about the ideas—such as those of religion—that the traders might be "trading" along with their goods.

■ PRACTICE 206: Christianity in Northern Africa

Circle the letter of the correct answer to each of the following questions.

1. What two empires spread Christianity in northern Africa?
   a. the Axum and Byzantine Empires
   b. the Nubian and Roman Empires
   c. the Roman and Byzantine Empires
   d. the Ethiopian and Nubian Empires

2. What Christian country exists in northern Africa today?
   a. Ethiopia
   b. Nubia
   c. Axum
   d. Rome

Islam in Africa

From about 350 to the 500s, Christianity had a big impact on life in northern Africa. Hundreds of thousands of families who had previously followed traditional religions were now Christian. In what was to become Ethiopia, the religion has had a fundamental influence that continues to this day. Still, many people in northern Africa continued to practice traditional religions. And most of the African continent was not under Christian influence.

But in the 700s, another religion came to Africa. This religion was Islam. Islam was founded by the prophet Muhammad in the 600s, in what is now Saudi Arabia. Followers of Islam are called Muslims. Within a century after Muhammad's death, Arab Muslims had built an empire that stretched across southwestern Asia (the Middle East), parts of Europe, and northern Africa. By 710, all of northern Africa was under Arab Muslim control.

As a rule, the Arab Muslims allowed Africans to continue practicing Christianity and traditional religions. But over the centuries, more and more people in northern Africa accepted the teachings of Islam. Why? One reason was that Islam was not based on a particular culture or a particular nation. Conversion to Islam meant joining a great community. Another reason was that becoming a Muslim offered social and economic benefits in the empire.

Whatever the reasons, northern Africa eventually joined what has been called the **Islamic world.** This is the part of the world where Islamic religion and culture dominate. Even after the Arab Muslim Empire fell apart, Islam continued to play a central role in northern Africa. That influence continues to this day.

Unlike Christianity, Islam spread deep into the continent of Africa. Muslim merchants, religious leaders, and scholars traveled throughout northern Africa and into the lands that lay south of the Sahara Desert. Great caravans traveled between northern Africa and central and western Africa. Arab Muslims also traded along the coasts of Africa. As they traveled, they carried their ideas with them. Over time, Islam spread to all of these areas.

Muslim Areas of Africa

Muslims spread their culture as well as their religion. The Muslims honored learning. Wherever they went, they set up schools, which attracted students from throughout Africa. When the students left school, they carried their knowledge of Islam and other subjects back to their own peoples. In this way, Islam—along with many ideas about art, philosophy, science, and geography—spread. The Arabic language became widespread in Africa. For the first time, many African peoples learned to read and write.

As you can see, Islam had a major impact on African life. And as you will soon see, this religion—and the Arabs who brought it—continued to influence Africa for centuries.

TIP

You already know that geography influences history. Take a look at a map of the world. Note where Rome (a center of early Christianity) and Saudi Arabia (a center of early Islam) are located. This may help you to understand why certain parts of Africa were influenced by Christianity while other parts were influenced by Islam.

■ PRACTICE 207: Islam in Africa

Match each description with a term from the list below. Write the letter of the correct term on the line before each description.

a. Muslims   **b.** Muhammad   **c.** traders   **d.** northern

_____ **1.** the founder of the religion of Islam

_____ **2.** the followers of Islam

_____ **3.** the part of Africa first influenced by Islam

_____ **4.** people who helped to spread Islam in Africa

LESSON 31: The Great Kingdoms of West Africa

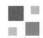

GOAL: To discuss three major trading kingdoms that rose and fell in West Africa

WORDS TO KNOW

caravan	Songhai
gold	Swahili
gold and salt trade	trade
salt	West African Kingdoms

NAMES TO KNOW

Askia the Great	Sundiata
Mansa Musa	Sunni Ali

PLACES TO KNOW

Gao	Kumbi Saleh	Mombasa
Ghana Empire	Mali	Songhai Empire
Kilwa	Mali Empire	Timbuktu

The Influence of Trade

In this lesson, you will learn about three great kingdoms that rose and fell in Africa during the course of about 1,000 years. These are called the West African Kingdoms because they existed in the area known as West Africa, just south of the Sahara Desert.

The great kingdoms of West Africa were all based on trade, which is the exchange of money and goods. Trade had always been important throughout Africa. But around the year 900, trade began to become more and more important in northern Africa.

This is largely because of the Arab Muslim influence there. The Arabs, like the Africans, had a long history and tradition of trade. It was natural, then, that trade between and among these people would begin to flourish.

The Muslim lands of northern Africa and the lands of central Africa are separated by the vast Sahara Desert. Incredibly, people had learned to cross the lonely desert thousands of years earlier. By 1000, trade by caravan, or convoy, was well established. Traders, Arab and African alike, led long caravans of camels across the desert, heading north and south. From seaports on the Mediterranean, the trade routes stretched to Europe, Asia, and beyond.

The two major goods that were traded in West Africa were gold and salt. Both were valued for the same reasons they are today. Gold was used for money and jewelry. Traders from the north wanted the gold to buy goods from Europe and Asia. Gold was found in mines in the forests of central Africa. Salt is a mineral that people need in their diet to sustain life, and salt was scarce in West Africa. Salt was mined in the Sahara Desert. In fact, it was so abundant in that barren region that people built their homes there out of salt blocks.

At the southern edge of the Sahara, where the West African kingdoms developed, gold was exchanged for salt, and vice versa. This was known as the gold and salt trade. In time, other things were also traded. Along with gold, traders from the south brought ivory and slaves. Along with salt, traders from the north brought horses, textiles, weapons, paper, and other manufactured goods.

At the sites where trading took place, important cities developed. These cities were located on trade routes between the gold mines to the south and the salt mines to the north. The people who controlled these areas controlled the trade and became wealthy. They did so by charging both import and export taxes that were paid in gold. Royal officials observed the trade, made sure it was conducted fairly, and collected the taxes. In return, royal guards protected the traders from robbers.

The trade in gold, salt, and other goods became the basis of the wealth of the great kingdoms of West Africa. You will read about three of these kingdoms on the following pages.

■ PRACTICE 208: The Influence of Trade

Circle the letter of the correct answer to each of the following questions.

1. What items were traded by the kingdoms of West Africa?
   a. horses and paper
   b. textiles and gold
   c. salt and weapons
   d. all of the above

2. Why did the kingdoms of West Africa arise where they did?
   a. They were surrounded by gold mines.
   b. They controlled the trade routes between the north and the south.
   c. They were surrounded by salt mines.
   d. They needed fertile farming lands.

The Ghana Empire

The **Ghana Empire** was the first great West African trading kingdom. It started as a small trading village called **Kumbi Saleh.** Kumbi Saleh was founded well before the increase in trade in the 900s. In fact, the city was founded in the 200s, a full 700 years before West African trade really began to surge. Today, this region is in the country of Mauritania.

The Ghana Empire lasted for more than 1,000 years. During this period, Ghana was a magnificent trading kingdom. Arab traders led long camel caravans loaded with salt from the Sahara and dried fruits from northern Africa to Ghana. There, these goods were traded for gold (and later ivory and slaves) from areas south of Ghana. As the great meeting place between north and south, Ghana grew rich on trade.

The Ghana Empire

The kings of Ghana charged both export and import taxes on goods that were traded there. They used their wealth to finance an efficient system of government. They also used it to finance a powerful army. The army kept the trade routes safe, protecting Ghana's income and source of wealth.

The village of Kumbi Saleh, from which the kingdom developed, grew in wealth, power, and population. By the 900s, it had a population of about 15,000. It was the largest city in the region.

Of course, the people of Ghana did more than trade. Many worked as farmers and craftspeople. The iron smiths of Ghana, who made weapons for the army, became famous for their work. Ghana was also known as a place where beautiful leather goods and fine jewelry were made.

For centuries, Ghana was a thriving, busy, wealthy kingdom. It reached its peak in the 900s and was attacked by rival tribes in the 1000s. These attacks were devastating. By 1235, the Ghana Empire was no more.

■ PRACTICE 209: The Ghana Empire
Circle the letter of the correct answer to each of the following questions.

1. From what trading city did the Ghana Empire grow?
   a. Mauritania
   b. Cairo
   c. Kumbi Saleh
   d. Axum

2. How did the kings of Ghana become rich?
   a. by controlling travel through the Sahara
   b. by selling slaves
   c. by selling gold
   d. by charging import and export taxes

The Mali Empire

In the early 1200s, the king of the Kangaba people, **Sundiata,** led a revolt against the Ghana Empire. In the Battle of Kirina in 1235, he defeated the last of the Ghana emperors. This battle was so famous that legends of it are still told by the people of the area.

Newly independent and powerful, Sundiata built a new city, Mali. Sundiata then conquered the neighboring Sasso people and the lands of other neighboring tribes, thus beginning the great Mali Empire. The Mali Empire replaced the Ghana Empire as the most powerful trading kingdom in West Africa. It was the supreme power in West Africa until the 1500s.

The Mali Empire

Like the Ghana Empire before it, the Mali Empire was built on trade. And, like Ghana, it owed its success largely to its location between the salt mines to the north and the gold mines to the south.

Sundiata ruled until 1240. After his death, other rulers rose to power and maintained the greatness of Mali. The most impressive of all was a man named Mansa Musa. You will read about him in the next section.

■ PRACTICE 210: The Mali Empire

Circle the letter of the correct answer to each of the following questions.

1. Which battle marked the end of the Ghana Empire and the beginning of the Mali Empire?
    a. the Battle of Kirina
    b. the Battle of Sundiata
    c. the Battle of Ghana
    d. the Battle of Kumbi Saleh

2. On what was the Mali Empire's economy based?
    a. slavery
    b. oppression
    c. taxes
    d. trade

Mansa Musa

Mansa Musa became king of the Mali Empire in 1312. He ruled Mali for 25 years. Few other leaders in history have been as effective as Mansa Musa. In fact, his reign is remembered as a golden age in West Africa.

Mansa Musa was a strong ruler. But he was wise enough to let the various peoples of the empire follow their own traditional ways of life. In this way, he kept the kingdom peaceful.

Mansa Musa's system of strong law, coupled with his tolerance of local practices, kept the peace in Mali. Mansa Musa worked hard at this. Historians believe that he settled many legal disputes himself. In addition, Mansa Musa worked to make Mali richer than ever before. He did this by expanding Mali's trade.

As you have read, Islam had become a powerful force in northern Africa a few centuries before the rise of the West African kingdoms. By Mansa Musa's time, the religion had spread to West Africa. Mansa Musa himself was a Muslim. In 1324–1325, Mansa Musa made a pilgrimage to Mecca, the holy city of Islam. His entrance to the city is remembered as being one of the most spectacular processions in history.

Mansa Musa led about 60,000 other Mali pilgrims into the city. Among them were 12,000 slaves—each carrying a 4-pound brick of gold. This display of wealth stunned the Arabs. News of the great, wealthy kingdom of Mali spread far and wide. This served to increase trade in Mali even further.

■ PRACTICE 211: Mansa Musa

Circle the letter of the correct answer to each of the following questions.

1. Which of the following contributions did Mansa Musa make to Mali?
   a. He kept the peace.
   b. He expanded Mali's trade.
   c. He helped make Mali famous through his memorable pilgrimage to Mecca.
   d. all of the above

2. How long did Mansa Musa rule Mali?
   a. a brief time
   b. 25 years
   c. many months
   d. a decade

Timbuktu

You may have heard of **Timbuktu.** It is one of the greatest cities in world history. Timbuktu still exists today, although it has lost its greatness. It was once one of the most remarkable places on Earth.

Timbuktu, which is now called Tombouctou, was founded around 1100. As a popular meeting place for traders, it rapidly grew in wealth and population. Mansa Musa made it the capital of the Mali Empire.

But Timbuktu was more than just a capital. And it was more than just a trade center. It was also a center of Muslim learning. During the Mali Empire, a great university at Timbuktu attracted scholars from throughout the Islamic world. More than 100 schools in Timbuktu taught Islam, geography, history, and other subjects. The university there educated 25,000 students at a time. Judges, doctors, and religious leaders also gathered in Timbuktu.

In Timbuktu, learning and education were just as highly respected as wealth. In fact, one scholar has said, "In Timbuktu, books were valued as much as salt, and salt as much as gold." Another African scholar in Timbuktu owned 700 books, a vast number for those times.

When he returned from Mecca, Mansa Musa ordered the building of many new, beautiful mosques in Timbuktu. Mosques are Muslim houses of worship. Mansa Musa also ordered that new buildings be made of long-lasting brick instead of mud.

Timbuktu thrived from the 1200s to the 1500s. During this 300-year period, it was recognized as one of the great cities of the world. Today, Tombouctou is a sleepy little town. Much of it lies in ruins. But even now, 500 years after its decline from greatness, it remains one of the most famous and fabled cities in history.

■ PRACTICE 212: Timbuktu

Decide if each statement below is true (**T**) or false (**F**). Write the correct letter on the line before each statement.

_____ **1.** Timbuktu grew rich because it was a center of learning.

_____ **2.** Timbuktu was a great trading city.

_____ **3.** Universities did not exist when Timbuktu was at its peak.

_____ **4.** The people of Timbuktu were Muslims.

The Songhai Empire

After Mansa Musa, the Mali Empire was ruled by a series of weaker kings. During this time, the city of **Gao** became a wealthy and powerful trading center in the empire. Gao soon decided to break away from the Mali Empire.

The rulers of Gao were of the **Songhai** people. By the late 1300s, they were strong enough to refuse to pay taxes to the rulers of Mali. By the mid-1400s, led by a fierce cavalryman, the Songhai began to conquer their neighbors. Their leader was **Sunni Ali,** who ruled from 1464 to 1492. Soon, Sunni Ali had conquered much of the Mali Empire, including the great city of Timbuktu.

Eventually, the **Songhai Empire** became the largest of the great trading kingdoms of West Africa. At its peak in the late 1400s and early 1500s, it covered an area the size of western Europe. Like the Ghana Empire and the Mali Empire before it, the Songhai Empire was based on trade.

The Songhai Empire

In 1493, Sunni Ali was succeeded by **Askia the Great.** Askia continued the tradition of strong government that Sunni Ali had established. He expanded trade and brought Songhai to its peak. But the Songhai Empire did not last. In 1591, a Moroccan army defeated the Songhai.

■ PRACTICE 213: The Songhai Empire

Circle the letter of the correct answer to each of the following questions.

1. Who was the first leader of the Songhai Empire?
    a. Gao
    b. Askia the Great
    c. Sunni Ali
    d. Muhammad

2. In which city was the Songhai Empire centered?
    a. Mali
    b. Timbuktu
    c. Gao
    d. Kirina

City-States in East Africa

You have read that, from about 900 to about 1500, three great trading kingdoms arose in West Africa: Ghana, Mali, and Songhai. During this same period, other great trading centers were growing on the opposite side of the continent, along the eastern coast of Africa. And, as in West Africa, Arab Muslim traders helped trade centers grow in the region known as East Africa.

By about 1100, Arab Muslim traders who traveled by ship were trading up and down the entire coast of East Africa. They traveled between Africa and China, India, and other nations along the Red Sea, the Persian Gulf, and the Indian and Pacific Oceans. The traders brought such goods as silk, cloth, and porcelain to Africa. From Africa, they took gold, ivory, artworks, and slaves.

Over time, many of these traders settled in Africa. As a result, city-states developed there. A city-state is a large, independent city that has its own ruler and laws. All of the East African city-states earned their wealth through trade. Two of the more powerful city-states were Kilwa and Mombasa.

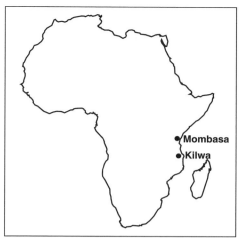

East African City-States

The people of these city-states developed a remarkable new culture. It was a unique mix of traditional black African and Arab cultures. This culture was called Swahili. Swahili is also the name of the unique language they spoke—a mix of African Bantu languages and Arabic.

The city-states of East Africa prospered from the early 700s through the 1300s. Like the kingdoms and cities of West Africa, the city-states of East Africa were thriving societies. Their contributions to culture, language, and trade became part of the proud tradition that is African history.

■ PRACTICE 214: City-States in East Africa

Circle the letter of the correct answer to each of the following questions.

1. Where did trading city-states emerge?
   a. along Africa's eastern coast
   b. along Africa's southern coast
   c. along Africa's northern coast
   d. along Africa's western coast

2. What were two important city-states in Africa?
   a. Ghana and Mali
   b. Songhai and Askia
   c. Kilwa and Mombasa
   d. Swahili and Mali

LESSON 32: Early American Society

WORDS TO KNOW

Aztecs	Indians	Quetzalcoatl
causeways	land bridge	Tenochas
culture areas	Maya Indians	Toltecs
human sacrifice	Olmec Indians	

PLACES TO KNOW

Amazon	Beringia	New World
the Americas	Central America	North America
Andes Mountains	Inca Empire	Pacific Ocean
Atlantic Ocean	Lake Texcoco	Rocky Mountains
Aztec Empire	Mesoamerica	South America
Bering Strait	Mississippi	Tenochtitlán

The Geography of the Americas

Most likely, you live in **North America.** Like Africa, North America is a continent. It is the third-largest of the seven continents on Earth.

South of North America is another continent. Not surprisingly, this continent is called **South America.** South America is the fourth-largest continent on Earth.

Even though they are separate continents, North America and South America are connected. The narrow strip of land that connects these two continents is usually called **Central America.** Central America is not a continent. In fact, it is part of North America. But it is convenient to refer to this area as Central America.

Why do you think people find it useful to talk about Central America, even though it is not a continent? Why not just call it part of North America? Write your answers on a separate sheet of paper.

The region comprising the continents of North and South America, together with Central America, has two other names that you should know about. One is the **New World.** It is called this because it was new to the Europeans, Africans, and Asians who originally came here. Since this book discusses this period in history, it is useful to learn this term. Another name people use to refer to North, South, and Central America is **the Americas.**

Look at the map below. You can see that the Americas cover a huge area. They stretch almost all the way from the North Pole, across the equator, to the South Pole. At their widest parts, they also stretch thousands of miles from east to west. Both continents lie between the Pacific Ocean and the Atlantic Ocean.

It should not surprise you that such a large area has many different landscapes. These range from polar ice to tropical rain forests, seacoasts, great plains, and tall mountain chains. One of the greatest mountain chains in the world stretches, almost unbroken, the full length of the two continents. In Canada and the United States, most of this chain is called the **Rocky Mountains.** The same mountain system runs almost all the way through Central America and

The Americas

into South America, where it joins the Andes Mountains. The major river of North America is the Mississippi. The major river of South America is the Amazon.

In the Americas, there are deserts and dense forests. In some places, it rains year-round. In others, it has not rained in years.

Today, we are used to thinking of North, Central, and South America as crisscrossed with highways that link some of the biggest cities on Earth. But for thousands of years, no one lived here—not even the Indian peoples that we often think of as natives. It might surprise you to learn that they, like everyone else on these two continents, are descended from immigrants.

■ PRACTICE 215: The Geography of the Americas

Decide if each of the following statements is true (**T**) or false (**F**). Write the correct letter on the line before each statement.

_____ **1.** The Atlantic and Pacific Oceans border the Americas.

_____ **2.** South America is the third-largest continent on Earth.

_____ **3.** North America is the fourth-largest continent on Earth.

_____ **4.** Central America is a narrow strip of land that connects North and South America.

_____ **5.** *New World* is another term for Africa.

_____ **6.** *The Americas* refers to North, Central, and South America.

The First Americans

The Ice Age was a time hundreds of thousands of years ago when the world was much colder than it is today. Actually, there was more than one ice age. But the one we are interested in started about 1 million years ago. At that time, huge sheets of ice more than a mile thick covered much of North America and other parts of the world.

During the Ice Age, the levels of the oceans were much lower than they are now. This is because so much of the world's water was frozen. With the water level lower, areas that had once been underwater became dry land. Many land areas that had been separated by water were now connected to one another.

One area that was exposed during this time was the land that separates North America from Asia, which now lies under a narrow strip of water (about 50 miles wide). Today, this strip of water is called the Bering Strait. As the water level decreased during the onset of the Ice Age, the land beneath the Bering Strait became exposed. Scientists call this area a land bridge between North America and Asia. The name given to this land bridge is Beringia.

Soon after Beringia was uncovered, plants began to grow on the dry land that had once been the seafloor. Next, animals wandered into the area, searching for food. Over time, hunters and gatherers from Asia followed the animals across Beringia. Although they did not know it, they were migrating, or moving, from one continent to another. This probably happened as far back as 50,000 years ago. Then, over thousands of years, the descendants of these people traveled south and settled throughout the Americas.

Beringia

Eventually, the Ice Age ended. The ice melted, and North America and Asia were again separated by water. Migration to North America stopped. But by then, the Americas, a part of the world where no one had lived before, was filled with people. These people developed many different cultures and built some of the most remarkable civilizations the world has ever known.

■ PRACTICE 216: The First Americans

Circle the letter of the correct answer to each of the following questions.

1. What was the name of the land bridge that once connected Asia
   and North America?
   a. Bering Strait
   b. Amazon
   c. Swahili
   d. Beringia

2. Who migrated across the land bridge between Asia and
   North America?
   a. animals
   b. hunters and gatherers
   c. Asian people
   d. all of the above

Early Indian Cultures

The first Americans, who came to be called **Indians** by later Europeans,
might have come to North America as far back as 50,000 years ago. There
were Indian settlements throughout the Americas by at least 6,000 years
ago, and probably much earlier than that.

Over thousands of years, these peoples developed many different
cultures. You read earlier that there is really no one African people. The
same is true of the American Indians. The key concept to remember is that
there was, and is, no single group of people called Indians. There were
hundreds of different American Indian cultures.

One of the reasons that so many different cultures developed was that
the peoples settled in different environments. Life in the cold north, for
example, was much different from life along the equator. Because the
environment was different, the peoples developed different styles of
clothing and housing. They grew to believe in different gods, and they
developed different cultures.

Because there were so many different groups of American Indians (most of whom were organized into tribes), it is impossible to describe them all. But the different American Indian tribes living in the same regions were similar in important ways. For example, they had similar languages, religions, and ways of building their homes. These areas where American Indian life was similar are called **culture areas.**

■ IN REAL LIFE

It might surprise you to learn that you frequently use words from the many American Indian languages. Over the years, these words have become part of the English language. Examples include *chipmunk, moose, canoe, squash, bayou,* and *raccoon.*

■ PRACTICE 217: Early Indian Cultures

Circle the letter of the correct answer to each of the following questions.

1. To what does the term *Indians* refer?
   a. people from Asia who settled in North America
   b. early Americans
   c. people who had hundreds of different cultures
   d. all of the above

2. To what does the term *culture areas* refer?
   a. areas where Indians had similar languages, religions, and ways of building their homes
   b. areas where immigrant tribes kept their own cultures separate
   c. areas where people spread art, music, and other cultural advances
   d. areas where Indians preserved their cultural heritage

The Olmec Indians

You have read that Central America is the narrow strip of land connecting North and South America. When we talk about human life there long ago, this area and some of the surrounding area is called **Mesoamerica** ("Middle America"). Some of the most impressive cultures of the Americas developed in Mesoamerica.

The first such group were the **Olmec Indians.** The Olmecs lived along the coast of the Gulf of Mexico, in what is today the country of Mexico. The Olmec civilization was perhaps the first great civilization in the Americas. It lasted from about 1200 B.C.E. to 400 B.C.E.

The Olmecs were farmers. They lived in small houses with thatched roofs. These small houses were part of large towns. There were many large Olmec communities. The communities were connected by paths and roads. The Olmecs probably engaged in a busy trading network through the region.

The Olmecs were an advanced people. They developed a number system, a calendar, and even a form of writing. But they are most famous for the giant stone heads they carved. These huge sculptures weighed as much as 30 tons and were transported over large distances. Scholars puzzle over how the Olmecs moved such massive objects so far, without draft animals or the wheel.

No one knows what became of the Olmecs. Some people think that they moved north and became the ancestors of the next great civilization in Mesoamerica, the Maya.

■ PRACTICE 218: The Olmec Indians

Circle the letter of the correct answer to each of the following questions.

1. What does *Mesoamerica* mean?
   a. early American culture
   b. Middle America
   c. Beringia
   d. a gathering place

2. For what are the Olmec Indians most famous?
   a. art and music
   b. establishing trade routes
   c. building giant stone heads
   d. continuing their civilization to the present

THINK ABOUT IT

You have just read that the Olmecs made huge, heavy sculptures and moved them long distances. Based on just this fact, what can you conclude about the Olmec civilization? Write your answer on a separate sheet of paper.

The Maya Indians

The Maya Indians lived in what is now Mexico, Belize, Guatemala, Honduras, and El Salvador. Like the Olmecs, the Mayas were an advanced people. They developed a system of writing, advanced mathematics, a calendar, and sophisticated artworks.

You may have seen a picture of a Mayan pyramid. But these pyramids are just one example of their many impressive stone structures. The Mayas also built observatories, palaces, baths, plazas, reservoirs, and almost any other kind of structure you would find in a modern city. In fact, the Mayas did build great cities. One such city included more than 600 major stone buildings and was home to more than 100,000 people. On the outskirts of Mayan cities, poor farmers lived in huts.

Mayan cities were actually city-states. They traded and sometimes warred with one another. The leaders of the city-states were considered to be gods. They led their people according to their religious beliefs. As in all of the early cultures you have read about, the religious beliefs of the Mayas were intertwined with their day-to-day lives. Priests had a lot of power, as they conducted the all-important religious ceremonies.

Mayan civilization thrived from about 250 B.C.E. to 900 C.E. Around 900, the Mayans suddenly abandoned their cities. No one knows exactly why. The reason could have been disease, or crop failure, or invasions, or revolts, or some other disaster. But the Mayas left a rich legacy of writing, science, art, and astronomy. Today, scientists are still learning about, and from, the Mayas. And millions of people in Central America and Mexico today are descended from the original Mayas and still speak Mayan languages.

■ PRACTICE 219: The Maya Indians

Match each description with a term from below. Write the letter of the correct term on the line before each description.

 a. about 250 B.C.E.   **c.** Mesoamerica

 b. about 900 C.E.   **d.** city-states

_____ **1.** where the Mayas lived

_____ **2.** when the Mayan civilization began

_____ **3.** a term for large, independent Mayan cities

_____ **4.** when the Mayan civilization ended

The Aztec Indians

By about 1000 C.E., the Indians known as the **Toltecs** had established their own society of city-states in what is today central Mexico. Like the Mayas, the Toltecs were great builders who left a rich legacy in stone. They made wonderful pottery and artwork, and they also had a system of writing. The Toltecs dominated the region for about 200 years.

A later people in the area revered the Toltecs. At first, these people were members of a wandering tribe—they had no homeland. Eventually, in the 1200s, they settled on some small islands in **Lake Texcoco,** a swampy lake in central Mexico. Their village was called **Tenochtitlán,** and they called themselves **Tenochas.** Today, Tenochtitlán is Mexico City.

Tenochtitlán quickly expanded. The Tenochas built many artificial islands in the lake that were connected by **causeways,** or raised bridges made of land. As the Tenochas grew in strength and power, they conquered neighboring city-states. They then took on a new name, calling themselves **Aztecs.** The **Aztec Empire** had begun.

In just a few centuries, the Aztec Empire grew to a magnificent size. The first and greatest empire builder of the Aztecs was Itzcoatl. Itzcoatl helped the Aztecs turn Tenochtitlán from a small city-state to the center of a huge empire. At its peak, the Aztec Empire may have had a population of 5 million people. Its capital, Tenochtitlán, grew as well. Hundreds of islands in the city were connected by a vast network of canals and causeways. This magnificent city became home to 300,000 people. It was larger than any capital city of Europe at the time.

The Aztec Empire reached its peak during the 1400s and 1500s. The empire included many cities and towns. Trade was important to the Aztec people, as was the making of handicrafts that were necessary for life: baskets, tools, and so on. But the most important part of Aztec civilization was religion. It affected every part of Aztec life.

Like other peoples in Mesoamerica, the Aztecs worshiped hundreds of gods. Because the Aztecs were farmers, it is not surprising that many of the gods had to do with farming and crops. But their major god was Quetzalcoatl. **Quetzalcoatl,** a winged serpent, had been worshiped by many peoples in Mesoamerica, including the Olmecs.

Many Aztec buildings were constructed for religious purposes and ceremonies. The most famous of these ceremonies involved **human sacrifice.** The Aztecs believed that their gods needed human hearts to remain powerful. So they ritually cut out the hearts of sacrificial victims.

No one knows how many people the Aztecs sacrificed. But the number is surely very high—the Aztecs remained powerful for centuries, and religion was central to their lives. In fact, the Aztecs often went to war for the sole purpose of capturing people to sacrifice. They also sacrificed their own people, including children and slaves.

The Aztecs were accomplished builders, mathematicians, astronomers, doctors, and farmers. Their culture was elaborate and impressive. They were "civilized" by any definition of the word. One thing that puzzles modern students of the Aztecs is how such a sophisticated people could engage in human sacrifice.

The Aztec Empire continued to flourish until 1521, when it was conquered by the Spanish.

■ PRACTICE 220: The Aztec Indians

Answer each question with a term from below. Write the letter of the correct term on the line before each question.

a. Texcoco   c. Itzcoatl   e. Tenochas

b. causeways   d. Quetzalcoatl

_____ 1. What was the winged serpent god called?

_____ 2. What did the Aztecs first call themselves?

_____ 3. What was the name of the lake where the Aztecs built their major city?

_____ 4. What connected the islands of the Aztecs' major city?

_____ 5. Who was the greatest empire builder of the Aztecs?

The Inca Indians

The Olmecs, the Mayas, and the Aztecs built great civilizations in Mesoamerica. Another great civilization was built in South America. This was the Inca Empire.

The Incas began building their empire around 1438. At its peak, the empire stretched through the Andes Mountains along the western coast of South America for more than 2,500 miles. The Incas linked their empire together with roads. Messengers ran along these roads carrying information and orders. A complicated system of government kept the empire together.

The Incas are known for many things. But their engineering skills easily top the list. They built roads and bridges to connect their mountainous empire. Many of these roads and bridges were so well built that they still survive today. The Incas' architecture was also outstanding. Inca buildings are known for their great size and careful construction. The Incas also built terraces, or flat areas, into hillsides so that they could farm. In flat areas, they built sophisticated irrigation systems. The Incas' skill in engineering was matched by their skill in handicrafts and weaving.

The Inca Empire lasted less than a century. In 1532, it was conquered by the Spanish.

■ PRACTICE 221: The Inca Indians

Decide if each statement below is true (**T**) or false (**F**). Write the correct answer on the line before each statement.

_____ **1.** The Incas built their empire in North America.

_____ **2.** The Inca Empire extended for 2,500 miles.

_____ **3.** Roads connected the parts of the Inca Empire.

_____ **4.** The Inca Empire lasted for 500 years.

UNIT 8 REVIEW

Circle the letter of the correct answer to each of the following questions.

1. What were most early Africans?
   a. farmers
   b. traders
   c. craftspeople
   d. builders

2. In early Africa, what were the centers of life for most people?
   a. huge cities
   b. footpaths
   c. villages
   d. deserts

3. What empire was the first to bring widespread Christianity to northern Africa?
   a. the Vandal Empire
   b. the Roman Empire
   c. the Byzantine Empire
   d. the Arab Muslim Empire

4. Who spread Islamic religion and culture throughout Africa?
   a. Arab Muslim traders
   b. Christian missionaries
   c. African farmers
   d. Muhammad

5. What were the two most important goods traded in West Africa?
   a. salt and gold
   b. slaves and salt
   c. ivory and slaves
   d. cloth and gold

6. What did the Battle of Kirina mark the beginning of?
   a. the Songhai Empire
   b. the Mali Empire
   c. the rule of Mansa Musa
   d. the rule of Sunni Ali

7. What is the culture of Kilwa and Mombasa called?
   a. Swahili
   b. Muslim
   c. Bantu
   d. Ghana

8. What was Beringia?
   a. a continent
   b. an island
   c. an ice age
   d. a land bridge

9. From where did the ancestors of the Indians come to North America?
   a. South America
   b. Africa
   c. Asia
   d. Central America

10. Which of the following came first?
    a. Olmec civilization
    b. Aztec civilization
    c. Mayan civilization
    d. Inca civilization

UNIT 8 APPLICATION ACTIVITY
Native Peoples

In Unit 8, you learned about the native peoples of Africa and North and South America. When a group of people is native to a place, we say that the group is indigenous. In this activity, you will research the indigenous group of your own area. (If you live in North America, the indigenous peoples of your area are probably American Indians.)

If you do not already know who the indigenous peoples of your area are, you might ask your local librarian or historical society director for some help. Then, use the Internet and library resources to find out as much as you can about the group. Try to find the answers to the following questions:

- During what era did the group live in your area?

- What kind of lifestyle did this group have before European settlers arrived? (For instance, were these people hunters, farmers, or fishermen? How much interaction did these people have with other groups of people?)

- What is special about this group's culture?

- How many members of this group still live in the area?

Write a paragraph reporting your findings on the lines below. Use another sheet of paper, if necessary.

_____

_____

_____

_____

_____

_____

_____

_____

_____

_____

_____

_____

_____

_____

_____

_____

_____

_____

_____

_____

APPENDIXES
A. Dates to Know

c. 2,000,000–1,000,000 B.C.E.—Humanlike creatures appear; Old Stone Age begins.

c. 350,000 years ago—Early humans exist in China.

c. 100,000 B.C.E.—The first modern human beings appear.

c. 13,000–11,000 B.C.E.—The earliest people settle in Greece, near the Aegean Sea.

c. 8000 B.C.E.—Old Stone Age ends; New Stone Age begins.

c. 7500–6500 B.C.E.—Cities such as Jericho and Çatal Huyuk first appear.

c. 7000–6000 B.C.E.—Aegean people begin farming.

c. 5000 B.C.E.—Sumerians settle in southern Mesopotamia.

c. 3500 B.C.E.—Sumerian civilization begins.

c. 3100 B.C.E.—Menes unites Upper and Lower Egypt; Upper and Lower Nubia are united.

c. 3000 B.C.E.—Aegean Bronze Age begins.

c. 2800 B.C.E.—Nubia and Egypt go to war.

c. 2700–2200 B.C.E.—Old Kingdom in Egypt

c. 2600 B.C.E.—The Great Pyramid is built for Pharaoh Khufu.

c. 2600–1700 B.C.E.—Indus Valley civilization

c. 2400 B.C.E.—Earliest evidence of Shang people in China

c. 2350 B.C.E.—Sargon of Akkad creates the world's first empire.

c. 2150 B.C.E.—End of Sargon's empire; Sumerian city-states regain power.

c. 2050–1850 B.C.E.—Middle Kingdom in Egypt

c. 2000–1700 B.C.E.—Beginning of the Minoan civilization on Crete

c. 2000–1400 B.C.E.—Waves of Aryans invade India from the north.

c. 2000 B.C.E.—Mesopotamia is invaded by Amorites, who build the city of Babylon.

c. 2000 B.C.E.—Hebrews leave Ur and end up in Canaan.

c. 2000 B.C.E.—Latins begin migrating into Italy from central Europe.

c. 1900–1700 B.C.E.—Beginning of the Shang dynasty in China

c. 1790 B.C.E.—The Babylonian Empire of Hammurabi begins.

c. 1600 B.C.E.—Nubia comes under Egyptian rule.

c. 1600 B.C.E.—Beginning of the Mycenaean civilization

c. 1570–1090 B.C.E.—New Kingdom in Egypt

c. 1500 B.C.E.—Phoenicians invent the alphabet.

c. 1500 B.C.E.—Latins have a cluster of towns on seven hills overlooking the Tiber River.

c. 1450 B.C.E.—Minoan civilization fades; Mycenaean civilization rises.

c. 1400–1200 B.C.E.—Hittite Empire

c. 1361–1352 B.C.E.—Tutankhamen in Egypt

c. 1200 B.C.E.—Believed to be the beginning of the Trojan War

c. 1200–499 B.C.E.—Olmec civilization in the Americas

c. 1111–770 B.C.E.—Western Zhou dynasty in China

c. 1100 B.C.E.—Dorians conquer the Mycenaeans.

c. 1100–800 B.C.E.—Greece's Dark Age; little is known about it.

c. 1000 B.C.E.—David becomes king of Israel.

c. 900–605 B.C.E.—Assyrian Empire

c. 800–500 B.C.E.—Greece's Archaic (very old) period

776 B.C.E.—The first Olympic Games are held in the city-state of Olympia.

c. 770–221 B.C.E.—Eastern Zhou dynasty in China

c. 750 B.C.E.—The city-state of Rome is created.

c. 750–660 B.C.E.—Nubian kings rule Egypt as pharaohs.

c. 700 B.C.E.—Actual historical record of Italy and Rome begins.

621 B.C.E.—Draco creates the first code of law for Athens.

c. 605–539 B.C.E.—Chaldean Empire

c. 600 B.C.E.—Hinduism spreads throughout India.

c. 600–509 B.C.E.—Etruscan kings rule Rome.

594 B.C.E.—Solon's new laws prevent civil war in Athens.

c. 563 B.C.E.—Siddhartha Gautama (Buddha) is born.

c. 551 B.C.E.—Confucius is born.

c. 539 – 486 B.C.E.—Persian Empire

c. 509 – 280 B.C.E.—Early Republic of Rome

500 – 479 B.C.E.—Wars between Greece and Persia

c. 500 B.C.E.–1500 C.E.—Bantu migrations in Africa

c. 460 – 408 B.C.E.—Peloponnesian Wars between Sparta and Athens

c. 450 B.C.E.—The first Roman code of law—Twelve Tables—is created.

390 B.C.E.—Gauls sack Rome.

359 B.C.E.—Philip II becomes king of Macedonia.

348 B.C.E.—Rome and Carthage sign treaty.

338 – 336 B.C.E.—Philip rules Greece, is murdered.

336 B.C.E.—Philip's son Alexander takes the throne.

334 – 323 B.C.E.—Alexander establishes a huge empire by military conquest; he dies in 323.

c. 320 – 185 B.C.E.—Mauryan Empire, begun by Chandragupta Maurya

c. 290 B.C.E.—Romans gain control over northern and southern Italy.

c. 280 – 275 B.C.E.—Pyrrhic War; Rome wins and gains control over most of the Italian peninsula.

c. 272 – 232 B.C.E.—Asoka's reign; Buddhism is made the official Indian religion.

c. 270 B.C.E.– c. 300 C.E.—Meroë is the center of Nubia.

264 – 133 B.C.E.—Middle Republic of Rome

264 – 241 B.C.E.—First Punic War, won by Rome

c. 250 B.C.E.– 900 C.E.—Mayan civilization

221 B.C.E.—Qin Dynasty begins in China; Shih Huang-ti is the first emperor.

218 – 201 B.C.E.—Second Punic War, won by Rome

c. 214 B.C.E.—Building of the Great Wall of China begins.

202 B.C.E.–220 C.E.—Han dynasty in China

c. 185 B.C.E.–300 C.E.—Hinduism gradually replaces Buddhism as the major religion in India.

149 B.C.E.–146 B.C.E.—Third Punic War, won by Rome, which burns down the city of Carthage.

133 B.C.E.–31 B.C.E.—Late Republic of Rome

133–121 B.C.E.—Gracchus reform movement in Rome

c. 100 B.C.E.—Silk Road trade routes are set up.

73 B.C.E.—Spartacus leads a slave revolt in Rome that fails.

49–44 B.C.E.—Julius Caesar rules Rome, dies by assassination.

31 B.C.E.–14 C.E.—Octavian rules Rome; becomes Augustus, in effect an emperor.

27 B.C.E.–476 C.E.—Roman Empire

1—Common Era begins (approximate birth of Jesus Christ)

30 C.E.—Christ is crucified, but his apostles spread his teachings.

64 C.E.—Great Fire of Rome; Nero blames Christians and begins their persecution.

98–117 C.E.—Rule of Trajan; the Roman Empire is at its peak.

c. 100 C.E.—The first Chinese dictionary is assembled.

c. 105 C.E.—Paper is first manufactured in China.

Second and fourth centuries C.E.—Largely a period of confusion and unrest in China

c. 265–317 C.E.—Western Qin dynasty unites China.

284 C.E.—Diocletian divides the Roman Empire into two parts.

c. 300 C.E.—Buddhist Age begins in China.

312 C.E.—Emperor Constantine makes Christianity the official religion of Rome.

c. 320–467 C.E.—Gupta dynasty, founded by Chandragupta I, becomes a golden age of India.

c. 325 C.E.—Axum adopts Christianity as the official state religion.

330 C.E.—Constantine moves capital of the Roman Empire east to Byzantium, renamed Constantinople.

395 C.E.—Roman Empire officially splits in two, East and West.

395–1453 C.E.—Byzantine Empire

400s–700s C.E.—Japan models itself on Chinese culture.

472 C.E.—Franks defeat Muslim Moors at Battle of Tours.

476 C.E.—Roman Empire in the west collapses after hundreds of years of invasions.

500–1500 C.E.—Middle Ages (medieval period) in Europe

500–1500 C.E.—India's Age of Invasions

527–565 C.E.—Justinian rules the Byzantine Empire.

570 C.E.—Muhammad is born.

early 600s C.E.—Muhammad founds the religion of Islam.

618–907 C.E.—Tang dynasty, a golden age of China

645 C.E.—Kotuku begins era of strong rule by emperor in Japan.

661–750 C.E.—Umayyad caliphs lead Muslim Empire.

684–705 C.E.—Empress Wu rules China.

700s C.E.—Islam spreads to North Africa.

700s–1000s C.E.—Vikings raid and invade.

771–814 C.E.—Charlemagne rules an empire in Europe.

800s C.E.—Vikings sail to Iceland.

800s–1000s C.E.—Ghana Empire in Africa

900s–1100s C.E.—Fujiwara clan rules Japan.

960–1279 C.E.—Sung dynasty in China

962 C.E.—Holy Roman Empire begins.

982 C.E.—Erik the Red sails to Greenland.

1000 C.E.—Feudalism is established throughout western Europe.

c. 1000 C.E.—Leif Eriksson sails to North America.

1000s C.E.—Seljuk Turks take control of much of the Islamic world.

1066 C.E.—William the Conqueror of France takes control of England.

1096–1270 C.E.—Crusades occur in Palestine.

1126 C.E.—Sung lose control of northern China.

1162 C.E.—Genghis Khan is born, as Temujin.

1192 C.E.—Rule by shoguns begins in Japan.

c. 1200–1521 C.E.—Aztec Empire in the Americas

1200s–1300s C.E.—Mongol Empire

1200s–1500s C.E.—Mali Empire in Africa, founded by Sundiata

1206 C.E.—Genghis Khan unites all Mongols under his rule.

1215 C.E.—King John of England signs the Magna Carta.

1279–1368 C.E.—Yuan dynasty in China, founded by Kublai Khan

1300–1326 C.E.—Rule of Sultan Othman of the Ottoman Turks

1300s–1400s C.E.—Ottoman Turks establish a Muslim empire.

1312–1337 C.E.—Mansa Musa rules the Mali Empire.

1337–1453 C.E.—Hundred Years' Wars between England and France

1368–1644 C.E.—Ming dynasty in China

1405–1433 C.E.—Voyages of Cheng Ho

c. 1438–1532 C.E.—Inca Empire in South America

1453 C.E.—Byzantine Empire falls to the Ottoman Turks, who capture Constantinople.

1464–1591 C.E.—Songhai Empire in Africa, founded by Sunni Ali

1500s–1600s C.E.—Ottoman Empire is the most powerful in the world.

1520–1566 C.E.—Rule of Suleiman I in the Ottoman Empire

1526–1761 C.E.—Mogul Empire in India, founded by Babur the Tiger

B. Names to Know

Abraham—a man who lived as a nomad and finally settled in Canaan and made an agreement with Yahweh; patriarch (father figure) of Jews and Muslims

Abu Bakr—the first caliph to follow Muhammad

Aeneas—a Trojan prince who was a mighty warrior during the Trojan War and who fled to Italy

Aeschylus—a dramatist who wrote tragedies

Aesop—a slave who is believed to have put together a collection of fables

Akkadians—people of Akkad who came from the deserts at the edge of the Fertile Crescent

Alexander the Great—a king of Macedonia who created a large empire

Antipater—a Macedonian general whom Alexander made governor of Greece

Aristophanes—a dramatist who wrote comedies

Aristotle—a philosopher who taught Alexander the Great

Aryans—people who invaded the Indus Valley

Askia the Great—the leader of the Songhai Empire at its peak

Asoka—a Mauryan emperor for almost 40 years

Assyrians—conquerors of Egypt who drove out the Nubians and took over Israel

Augustus—the name given to Octavian by the Senate

Babylonians—people of Babylon

Buddha—a follower of Siddhartha Gautama who attracted many other followers and started Buddhism

Cato—a Roman speech maker

Chaldeans—people who conquered Judah

Chandragupta I—the founder of the Gupta dynasty

Chandragupta II—the best known Gupta king; he ruled during India's golden age

Chandragupta Maurya—an emperor of Magadha who began the Mauryan dynasty in India

Charlemagne—a Frankish king who united much of Europe in an empire

Charles Martel—a Frankish king who won the Battle of Tours

Charles V—a strong emperor who came close to uniting the Holy Roman Empire

Cheng Ho—a Chinese admiral who made several voyages to show the power of the Ming dynasty

Cicero—a Roman speech maker

Cleopatra—a woman who became queen of Egypt with Julius Caesar's help

Confucius—one of the great thinkers of ancient China

Constantine—a Roman emperor who protected Christians and built the city of Constantinople

Cyrus—a king of Persia

Darius I—Persia's greatest leader

Darius II—a king of Persia who began a war with Greece but was defeated at the Battle of Marathon

Darius III—a king of Persia who was conquered by Alexander the Great

David—the boy who killed the giant Philistine warrior Goliath; he eventually became king

Democritus—a thinker who believed that everything is made up of atoms

Diocletian—a Roman emperor who reorganized Rome's government

Dorians—people who may have ruled Greece during the Dark Age

Empress Wu—the only woman ever to rule China in her own name; she ruled from 684 to 705

Erik the Red—a Viking who discovered Greenland

Etruscans—the most powerful pre-Roman group in ancient Italy

Euripides—a Greek dramatist who wrote tragedies

Fujiwaras—a powerful clan that ruled Japan for 300 years

Gauls—a tribe of Celts who conquered Rome

Genghis Khan—"Universal Ruler"; the first great leader of the Mongol Empire

Gracchi brothers—brothers who led reform movements in Rome

Great Wall of China—a wall built to protect the Qin dynasty from northern invaders; it stretched more than 1,000 miles westward from the Yellow Sea to the edge of Tibet

Gupta dynasty—a dynasty in India

Hamilcar Barca—a Carthaginian leader who began to create a rich empire in Spain

Hammurabi—the greatest ruler of Babylon

Han dynasty—the dynasty in China that began in 202 B.C.E.

Hannibal—a hater of Rome who began the Second Punic War

Hatshepsut—one of the only female rulers of ancient Egypt

Hebrews—followers of Abraham who were the first to practice monotheism

Herodotus—a historian who recorded the Greek-Persian Wars

Hippocrates—a thinker who showed how illness results from natural causes

Hittites—the civilization that ruled most of the Fertile Crescent between 1400 B.C.E. and 1200 B.C.E.

Homer—a Greek poet who is believed to have created two epic poems, the *Iliad* and the *Odyssey*

Horace—a Roman poet

Howard Carter—British archaeologist who discovered the tomb of the pharaoh Tutankhamen

Hugh Capet—the first king of the Capetian dynasty

Indus Valley people—people who lived in the Indus Valley

Jesus Christ—a man who lived in Palestine; Christianity developed around his life and teachings

Joan of Arc—a woman who led the French against the English, who later burned her as a witch

Julius Caesar—a Roman general who gained control of Rome

Justinian I—the greatest emperor of the Byzantine Empire

Kalidasa—a writer of poetry and plays during India's golden age

King John—an English king who signed the Magna Carta

King Piye—Nubian king who invaded Egypt, took over the government, and became pharaoh

King Pyrrhus—the ruler of the Greek region of Epirus

Koca Sinan—an Ottoman architect who designed the Mosque of the Sultan Suleiman

Kotoku—a Japanese emperor who managed to control all of Japan

Kublai Khan—Genghis Khan's grandson; he ruled the Mongol Empire at its peak

Lady Murasaki Shikibu—the author of the world's first novel

Latins—ancient people who migrated to Italy from Central Europe

Leif Eriksson—a Viking who discovered Vinland

Li Po—a great poet who lived during the Tang dynasty

Li Yuan—the founder of the Tang dynasty

Mandate of Heaven—a command given to the kings of Zhou by the gods to rule the country

Mansa Musa—the greatest leader of the Mali Empire

Marco Polo—a traveler from Europe who visited Kublai Khan and then wrote about his travels

Marcus Aurelius—a ruler of Rome who continued the persecution of Christians

Marius—a Roman army general who found needed soldiers

Mark Anthony—Julius Caesar's second-in-command who took over for him when he was assassinated

Menes—a king of Lower Egypt who eventually gained control of Upper Egypt and united them into one kingdom

Minoans—people who lived on the island of Crete from about 2000 to 1700 B.C.E.

Minos—the legendary king of the Minoans

Minotaur—the legendary monster that lived in the Labyrinth

Mohammed II—a sultan of the Ottoman Empire who expanded the empire

Moses—the man who led the Hebrews out of Egypt and back to Canaan

Muhammad—the founder of the religion known as Islam

Mycenaeans—people who lived in south and central Greece from about 1600 to 1100 B.C.E.

Nebuchadnezzar—the most famous Chaldean king; he ruled from 605 to 562 B.C.E.

Nero—a ruler of Rome who persecuted Christians

Octavian—Julius Caesar's adopted son; he challenged Mark Anthony

Othman—the first great leader of the Ottoman Turks

Otto I—the first king to be crowned emperor of the Holy Roman Empire

Pepin the Short—a Frankish king who made an alliance with the pope

Pericles—the leader of Athens during the Golden Age

Persians—people of Persia who were originally nomads from Central Asia

Philip II—a king of Macedonia; Alexander's father

Philistines—a group of Sea People living in Canaan

Phoenicians—people who were known for their sailing, exploring, and trading abilities

Plato—a Greek philosopher who was a student of Socrates

Pompey—a Roman general

Pope Urban II—the pope who organized the First Crusade

Prince Shotoku—a powerful Japanese clan leader of the early 600s who copied the Chinese system of strong central government

Qin dynasty—the dynasty that defeated the Zhou and took over China

Rhazes—a Muslim doctor who wrote a medical encyclopedia

Rightly Guided Caliphs—the first four caliphs after Muhammad

Romulus and Remus—twin brothers who are said to have founded the city of Rome

Rosetta Stone—a large, black stone covered found near the Egyptian city of Rosetta that led to the deciphering of hieroglyphics

Sallust—a Roman historian

Sappho—a woman who was a great lyric poet

Sargon the Great—the king of Akkad who wanted to rule all the cities and people of the Fertile Crescent

Saul—a king chosen by the Hebrews

Sea People—a culture of people who settled around the Mediterranean Sea and were fierce in battle

Shang dynasty—the earliest dynasty in China; it ended in the twelfth century B.C.E.

Shih Huang-ti—the first king of the Qin dynasty

Socrates—a Greek philosopher and teacher who developed the question-answer method

Solomon—the son of David who became king when David died

Solon—an Athenian who created a more democratic set of laws

Sophocles—a Greek dramatist who wrote tragedies

Spartacus—a gladiator who started a small slave revolt in ancient Rome

Suleiman I—a sultan who ruled the Ottoman Empire at its peak

Sulla—a Roman who trained under Marius and later made himself dictator

Sumerians—people who settled in an area of Mesopotamia called Sumer

Sundiata—the king of the Kangaba people who led a revolt against the Ghana Empire and founded Mali

Sunni Ali—the leader of the Songhai people and founder of the Songhai Empire

Tang Taizong—a great Tang emperor who set up a strong government and encouraged the creation of trade routes

Tarquin dynasty—three kings who ruled Rome

Temujin—the name of Genghis Khan before he ruled the Mongols

Themistocles—a Greek commander who defeated the Persians at Salamis

Theodora—the wife of, and adviser to, Justinian I

Theodosius—the last emperor to lead a single Roman Empire

Tutankhamen—an Egyptian king who died when he was only a teenager

Twelve Tables—the first Roman code of law, which was written on bronze tablets

Umar—a caliph who greatly expanded the Islamic world

Umayyads—the family from whom caliphs came for 100 years

Uthman—a caliph who ordered the Koran assembled as one book

Virgil—the Roman poet who wrote the epic *Aeneid*

William the Conqueror—a king who unified England under his strong rule

Xerxes—a Persian king who tried to conquer Greece

Zhou dynasty—the dynasty that defeated the Shang and took over China

C. Places to Know

Aegean Sea—the sea between Greece and Asia Minor

Akkad—a city to the north of Sumer

Alexandria, Egypt—a Hellenistic city that was a center of learning

Alps—the mountain range that separates Italy from the rest of Europe

Amazon—the major river of South America

Americas, the—North, South, and Central America

Anatolia—the region where Ottoman Turks came to power, now known as Turkey

Andes Mountains—the major mountain chain of South America

Asia Minor—the area that today is known as Turkey

Athens—a Greek city-state known for its relatively democratic laws

Atlantic Ocean—the ocean that borders the Americas to the east

Atlas Mountains—a major African mountain chain

Axum—an African kingdom that became Christian

Aztec Empire—a Mesoamerican empire built by the Aztec Indians

Babylon—a city beside the Euphrates River

Bering Strait—a narrow strip of water separating North America and Asia

Beringia—the land bridge that once connected North America and Asia

Brahmaputra River—an important river in India that joins the Ganges River near its mouth

Byzantine Empire—the domain that arose from the East Roman Empire and that controlled Northern Africa for a time

Carthage—the Phoenicians' most famous trading city, located on the North African shore of the Mediterranean Sea

Central America—a narrow strip of land connecting North and South America

Chang'an—the capital city of the Tang dynasty

Coliseum—a gigantic arena in Rome that was used for public entertainment

Congo—a major African river

Constantinople—the new capital of the Roman Empire established by Constantine

Crete—an island south of Greece

Deccan Plateau—a large plateau that covers most of India

Ethiopia—a modern Christian African country

Fertile Crescent—rich farmland that reached from the eastern shore of the Mediterranean Sea north to the Syrian Desert and south to the Persian Gulf

Forum—the center of Rome from which all roads began and were measured

Ganges River—an important river in India; the sacred river of the Hindu religion

Gao—a great trading city from which the Songhai Empire grew

Ghana Empire—the first of the great trading kingdoms of West Africa

Gobi Desert—a great desert in northern China

Greenland—a large island in the North Atlantic Ocean

Gupta Empire—a great empire in India; lasted from the 300s to the 500s

Hagia Sophia—a great church built by Constantine in Constantinople

Hanging Gardens of Babylon—a garden in Nebuchadnezzar's palace that contained plants from all over the ancient world

Harappa—a city in the Indus Valley that was uncovered in the 1920s

Himalayas—a great mountain range in western China

Hokkaido—one of the main islands of Japan

Holy Land—land on the coast of the eastern Mediterranean; now known as Israel

Holy Roman Empire—a kingdom that united much of central Europe toward the end of the Middle Ages

Honshu—one of the main islands of Japan

Huang He—a river in China that is important for transportation

Iceland—a large island in the North Atlantic Ocean

Inca Empire—a great American Indian empire of South America

Indian subcontinent—a large landmass attached to Asia

Islamic Empire—a term for empires in the Islamic world

Islamic world—a region of the world, including northern Africa, where Muslim religion and culture are dominant

Jerusalem—the holiest city of the Holy Land

Kerma—a city in southern Nubia that became the center of the kingdom

Kilwa—a great East African city-state

Knossos—an ancient Minoan city on Crete

Kumbi Saleh—a small trading village from which the Ghana Empire developed

Kyushu—one of the main islands of Japan

Lake Texcoco—the lake where the Aztecs built Tenochtitlán

Macedonia—a country north of Greece from which Alexander came

Magadha—a kingdom located just south of the Ganges River in India

Mali—a city built by Sundiata that became the center of the Mali Empire

Mali Empire—a powerful trading kingdom of West Africa

Marathon—a plain where the Greeks defeated the Persians

Mauryan Empire—the empire created by Chandragupta Maurya that covered most of the Indian subcontinent; it lasted from 320 to 185 B.C.E.

Mecca—the holy city of Islam and the birthplace of Muhammad

Medina—the city to which Muhammad fled from Mecca

Meroë—a large city in Nubia

Mesoamerica—"Middle America"; Central America and some of the surrounding area

Mesopotamia—the location of the oldest of the early civilizations located in the valley of the Tigris and Euphrates rivers (it means "the land between the rivers")

Mississippi—the major river of North America

Mohenjo-Daro—a city in the Indus Valley that was uncovered in the 1920s

Mombasa—a great East African city-state

Mongol Empire—the largest land empire in history

Mount Kilimanjaro—the highest mountain in Africa

Mount Olympus—the highest point in Greece; Greeks believed it was the home of the gods on Earth

Muslim Empire—a term for empires in the Islamic world

Namib Desert—a desert that covers a large area of southern Africa

New World—another term for the Americas

Niger—a major African river

Nile—the longest river in the world; it flows north through Africa to the Mediterranean Sea for more than 4,000 miles

Nineveh—the capital of Assyria

North America—the third-largest continent on Earth

Nubia—African kingdoms south of Egypt that became Christian

Pacific Ocean—the ocean that borders the Americas to the west

Palace School—the school where officials of the Ottoman Empire trained

Palestine—another name for the Holy Land

Parthenon—a temple built on the Acropolis in Athens

Peloponnesus—the southern half of Greece

Persepolis—a city in Persia; the site of Darius's palace

Pharos—a lighthouse that was one of the Seven Wonders of the Ancient World

Plataea—a Greek city-state that was an ally of Athens

Rocky Mountains—the major mountain chain of North America

Roman Empire—an empire that controlled most of the Mediterranean region and much of western Europe

Rome—a city in Italy that was founded on the Tiber River

Rubicon River—a river in Italy

Ruwenzori Range—a major African mountain chain

Sahara Desert—the world's largest desert; it covers much of northern Africa

Sahel—a dry region in Africa that borders the Sahara Desert

Salamis—the northeast coast of Greece, where the Greek navy defeated the Persians

Shikoku—one of the main islands of Japan

Silk Road—trade routes set up in the desert of ancient China

Songhai Empire—the largest of the great trading kingdoms of West Africa

South America—the fourth-largest continent on Earth

Sparta—a Greek city-state known for its strict military laws

Sumer—an area in southern Mesopotamia settled by the Sumerians

Tenochtitlán—the major city of the Aztecs; Mexico City today

Thermopylae—a mountain pass where the Greeks lost a battle against the Persians

Tiber River—a river in Italy that runs through Rome

Tibetan Plateau—a great plateau in western China

Tigris and Euphrates rivers—the two rivers that border the region of Mesopotamia

Timbuktu—a great center of trade and learning in the Mali and Songhai empires

Tours—the site of the battle where the Christian Franks defeated the Muslim Moors

Ur—a major trading city-state in Sumer

Vinland—the Viking name for North America

Yangtze—a river in China; it is also called the Yellow River

D. Events to Know

Battle of Agincourt—an important English victory in the Hundred Years' War

Battle of Hastings—a battle at which William the Conqueror defeated the English nobles and declared himself king of England

Battle of Tours—the battle that stopped the Muslim advance into Europe

Children's Crusade—a tragic Crusade of children; it took place in 1212

Crusades—military expeditions made by Christian Europeans against Muslim Turks to try to recapture the Holy Land

First Crusade—the Crusade that captured Jerusalem; lasted from 1096 to 1099

Hegira—Muhammad's flight from Mecca to Medina

Hundred Years' War—a series of wars between England and France that lasted from 1337 to 1453

GLOSSARY

abolished (uh-BO-lishd) got rid of; put an end to

acropolis (uh-KRO-puh-lus) a hilltop fortress in an ancient Greek city; when spelled with a capital *A*, it refers to the fortress in the ancient city-state of Athens

Age of Invasions (AYJ UV in-VAY-zhunz) the period of Indian history from about 500 to about 1500

agora (A-guh-ruh) the marketplace of an ancient Greek city-state

agriculture (A-gri-kul-chur) the raising of crops and the keeping of domesticated animals; farming

Allah (A-luh) the Arabic word for God

ally (A-ly) a person or country that joins with another for a special purpose

amphitheaters (AM-fuh-thee-uh-turz) outdoor theaters arranged in a half circle, with rows of seats rising outward from an open space or arena at the center

ancestor worship (AN-ses-tur WUR-ship) the practice of worshiping ancestral spirits

ancestral spirits (AN-ses-trul SPIR-uts) according to one belief, the spirits of one's ancestors that live on and play a vital role in the affairs of the living

animism (A-nuh-mi-zum) the belief that spirit beings animate, or make alive, nature

aqueducts (A-kwuh-dukts) structures like bridges that contain pipes or channels to carry water and that stretch over low ground or a river

Arabic numerals (AR-uh-bik NOO-mur-ulz) numerals (1, 2, 3, and so on) developed by the Arab Muslims

archaeologist (AR-kee-o-luh-jist) a scientist who studies the remains of the past to figure out how ancient people lived

archbishops (arch-BI-shups) church officials in charge of archdioceses

artifacts (AR-ti-fakts) objects made by humans, especially humans from earlier societies

assassinated (uh-SAS-in-ay-ted) attacked and killed an important person

assembly (uh-SEM-blee) a group of lawmakers

Assyrians (uh-SIR-ee-unz) warlike people who conquered Egypt

astrolabe (AS-truh-layb) a device used to help sailors determine their location

Augustine Age (OH-gus-teen   AYJ) a period of improvement and excellence in Rome

authority (uh-THOR-uh-tee) the right or power to control people or things

Aztecs (AZ-teks) advanced Mesoamerican Indian people who built an empire

Bantu migrations (BAN-too   MY-gray-shunz) major movements of black African peoples who spoke Bantu languages and who came from central Africa throughout central, western, and southern Africa

bishops (BI-shups) church officials in charge of dioceses

Black Death (BLAK   DETH) another term for the bubonic plague

bronze (BRONZ) a yellow-brown metal that is a mixture of copper and tin

bronze casting (BRONZ   KAS-ting) the act of making bronze objects by pouring bronze that has been heated to the melting point into molds

---

PRONUNCIATION KEY

CAPITAL LETTERS show the stressed syllables.

a	as in mat	f	as in fit
ay	as in day, say	g	as in go
ch	as in chew	i	as in sit
e	as in bed	j	as in job, gem
ee	as in even, easy, need	k	as in cool, key

bubonic plague (BOO-bo-nik PLAYG) a disease that killed many people in Europe during the Middle Ages

Buddhism (BOO-di-zum) a religion of eastern and central Asia founded by Siddhartha Gautama

caliphs (KA-lufs) Muslim rulers

caliphates (KA-luf-ayts) three main areas of the Muslim Empire ruled by caliphs

candake (KAN-dayk) a female ruler of the Kingdom of Meroë

Capetian dynasty (kuh-PAY-shun DY-nuh-stee) a series of kings in France who helped make the country a single kingdom

caravan (KAR-uh-van) a convoy, especially of camels

castes (KASTS) in India, the Hindu social classes into which a person is born

cathedrals (kuh-THEE-drulz) large, beautiful churches

causeways (KOZ-wayz) raised bridges made of land

cavalry (KA-vul-ree) soldiers who fight on horseback

chivalry (SHI-vul-ree) the code of conduct by which knights were supposed to live

Christianity (kris-chee-A-nuh-tee) a religion founded by the followers of Jesus of Nazareth

---

PRONUNCIATION KEY

CAPITAL LETTERS show the stressed syllables.

ng	as in runni**ng**	u	as in b**u**t, s**o**me
o	as in c**o**t, f**a**ther	uh	as in **a**bout, tak**e**n, lem**o**n, penc**i**l
oh	as in g**o**, n**o**te	ur	as in t**er**m
oo	as in t**oo**	y	as in l**i**ne, fl**y**
sh	as in **sh**y	zh	as in vi**s**ion, mea**s**ure
th	as in **th**in		

citizen (SI-tuh-zun) a person who is an official member of a political body, such as a country

city-state (SI-tee   STAYT) a city and surrounding land that make up an independent state, with its own ruler, army, and laws

civil service (SI-vul   SUR-vis) those branches of the government that are not legislative (lawmakers), judicial (courts of law), or military (armed forces)

civil service system (SI-vul   SUR-vis   SIS-tum) a system of tests used to choose government officials, such as used by the Chinese

civilian (suh-VIL-yun) a person who is not in the armed forces

civilization (si-vuh-luh-ZAY-shun) a highly organized society

clan (KLAN) group of related families, ruled by a chief

classes (KLAS-ez) groups to which certain people in society belong

climate (KLY-mut) a pattern of weather over a long period of time

Code of Hammurabi (KOHD   UV   HAM-ur-ah-bee) a single set of laws that everyone in Hammurabi's empire had to follow

colonies (KO-luh-neez) groups of people who make homes in a new land but who are ruled by the nation from which they came

commoners (KO-muh-nurz) the class that included merchants, scribes, farmers, and skilled workers

---

PRONUNCIATION KEY

CAPITAL LETTERS show the stressed syllables.

a	as in m**a**t		f	as in f**i**t
ay	as in d**ay**, s**ay**		g	as in **g**o
ch	as in **ch**ew		i	as in s**i**t
e	as in b**e**d		j	as in **j**ob, **g**em
ee	as in **e**ven, **ea**sy, n**ee**d		k	as in **c**ool, **k**ey

concrete (kon-KREET) a building material made of cement (clay and limestone powders), sand, pebbles, and water

Confucianism (kun-FYOO-shu-ni-zum) a belief system based on the teachings of Confucius, a Chinese philosopher

conquerors (KON-kur-urz) those who overcome by force

consuls (KON-sulz) two heads of the government in the Roman Republic, elected for one year

continent (KON-tun-unt) a huge mass of land

convents (KON-vents) religious communities formed by nuns

crucified (KROO-suh-fyd) having put a person to death by nailing or tying to a cross

crusaders (KROO-sayd-urz) people who joined the Crusades

cultivate (KUL-tuh-vayt) to raise crops by preparing the land, planting seeds, and growing plants

culture (KUL-chur) a way of life, set of beliefs and customs, and language shared by a group of people

culture areas (KUL-chur   AYR-ee-uhs) areas where the lives of different Indian peoples were similar

cuneiform (KYOO-nee-uh-form) the wedge-shaped characters used in Sumerian writing

daimyo (DY-mee-oh) the lord of a large family estate in Japan

---

PRONUNCIATION KEY

CAPITAL LETTERS show the stressed syllables.

ng	as in running	u	as in but, some
o	as in cot, father	uh	as in about, taken, lemon, pencil
oh	as in go, note	ur	as in term
oo	as in too	y	as in line, fly
sh	as in shy	zh	as in vision, measure
th	as in thin		

dark age (DARK AYJ) a time when learning is not valued and knowledge is kept hidden

Dark Ages (DARK AYJ-uz) another term for the Middle Ages

debt (DET) something that is owed to another

democracy (di-MO-kruh-see) a form of government in which power is held by the people

descent (di-SENT) having certain people as ancestors; coming from a certain line of people

dialect (DY-uh-lekt) a variety of a language that is spoken by a particular group or in a particular part of a country

dictator (DIK-tay-tur) a ruler who has complete power

diocese (DY-uh-sees) a group of parishes

disciples (di-SY-pulz) followers of a religious leader

discipline (DI-suh-plun) a branch of knowledge or teaching

diverse (DY-vurs) varied

domesticate (duh-MES-tuh-kayt) to tame animals and get them used to living with human beings

drama (DRO-muh) a story that is meant to be presented by actors reciting lines to an audience

---

PRONUNCIATION KEY

CAPITAL LETTERS show the stressed syllables.

a	as in mat	f	as in fit
ay	as in day, say	g	as in go
ch	as in chew	i	as in sit
e	as in bed	j	as in job, gem
ee	as in even, easy, need	k	as in cool, key

due process of law (DOO   PRO-ses   UV   LO) the idea that people must be treated fairly under the law

dynasties (DY-nuh-steez) ruling families in which one ruler passes along the control of a kingdom to a son or a daughter

edicts (EE-dikts) formal statements or commands from someone in power

emperor (EM-pur-ur) the male ruler of an empire

empire (EM-pyr) a group of different people and places under a single ruler

empress dowager (EM-prus   DOW-uh-jur) the favorite wife or widow of an emperor

epic (E-pik) a long poem that tells the story of a legendary hero or heroes

excommunicate (ek-skuh-MYOO-nuh-kayt) to cut someone off entirely from the Church

expansionism (ik-SPAN-shuh-ni-zum) a nation's practice of expanding, or adding to, its wealth or size, thus gaining more power

exports (EK-sports) goods sent to another country for sale or trade

fable (FAY-bul) a brief story with a lesson to teach, often using animal characters that speak and act like human beings

famine (FA-mun) a period when there is little or no food

PRONUNCIATION KEY

CAPITAL LETTERS show the stressed syllables.

ng	as in running	u	as in but, some
o	as in cot, father	uh	as in about, taken, lemon, pencil
oh	as in go, note	ur	as in term
oo	as in too	y	as in line, fly
sh	as in shy	zh	as in vision, measure
th	as in thin		

feudal system (FYOO-dul   SIS-tum) a system of states, each given by a king to a noble, who has power over the state and over the people who live in it

feudalism (FYOO dul-is-um) a system of government based on the feudal system, above

fief (FEEF) an estate of land

First and Second Peloponnesian Wars (FURST   AND   SEK-und pe-luh-puh-NEE-zhun   WORZ) a long series of wars between Athens (with its allies) and Sparta (with its allies) between 460 B.C.E. and 404 B.C.E.

founded (FOWND-ed) set up; Rome was founded on the Tiber River.

Franks (FRANKS) peoples who took over the West Roman Empire

frontier (frun-TEER) a boundary between countries or the land along such a boundary

geography (jee-O-gruh-fee) the natural features of an area

glaciers (GLAY-shurs) huge sheets of ice that slowly flow over the land or into a valley

gladiator (GLA-dee-ay-tur) a man in ancient Rome who fought to the death in an arena to entertain the public

gold (GOHLD) a metal traded in West Africa

gold and salt trade (GOHLD   AND   SOLT   TRAYD) the exchange of gold and salt that was the basis of wealth for the West African kingdoms

---

PRONUNCIATION KEY

CAPITAL LETTERS show the stressed syllables.

a	as in m**a**t	f	as in **f**it
ay	as in d**ay**, s**ay**	g	as in **g**o
ch	as in **ch**ew	i	as in s**i**t
e	as in b**e**d	j	as in **j**ob, **g**em
ee	as in **e**ven, **ea**sy, n**ee**d	k	as in **c**ool, **k**ey

Golden Age (GOHL-dun AYJ) a period of great peace, prosperity, and happiness

goods (GUHDZ) things that can be bought, sold, or traded, such as food items, clothing, tools, and crafts

Gordian knot (GOR-dee-un NOT) a complicated knot cut by Alexander the Great (also, a very difficult problem)

Grand Mufti (GRAND MUF-tee) the religious leader of the Ottoman Empire

Greco-Roman (GRE-ko-ROH-mun) of or relating to something that is both Greek and Roman, such as Greco-Roman mythology

Greek-Persian Wars (GREEK-PER-shun WORZ) a series of wars that began in 490 B.C.E.

guilds (GILDZ) organizations of traders and other businesspeople

gunpowder (GUN-pow-dur) a substance invented by the Chinese to create explosions and to be used as a weapon

Gupta dynasty (GOOP-ta DY-nuh-stee) the family who ruled the Gupta Empire

hajj (HAJ) the pilgrimage to Mecca, the holy city of Islam, dictated by the Koran

Hellenistic (he-luh-NIS-tik) the period after the Classical Greek period and before the Roman rule of Augustus; also used to describe the period's culture and architecture

---

PRONUNCIATION KEY

CAPITAL LETTERS show the stressed syllables.

ng	as in running	u	as in but, some
o	as in cot, father	uh	as in about, taken, lemon, pencil
oh	as in go, note	ur	as in term
oo	as in too	y	as in line, fly
sh	as in shy	zh	as in vision, measure
th	as in thin		

herbs (URBS) plants whose leaves, roots, or other parts are used to flavor food or used for medicine

hieroglyphics (hy-ruh-GLI-fiks) the ancient Egyptian writing system of pictures and symbols

Hinduism (HIN-doo-i-zum) a major religion of India that emphasizes good behavior and reincarnation

historical narrative (hi-STOR-i-kul   NAR-uh-tiv) a true account of an event or a time in history that is told as a sequence of events

human sacrifice (HYOO-mun   SA-kruh-fys) a ritual practice of the Aztecs involving the killing of selected victims

Ice Age (YS   AYJ) a period of time that began hundreds of thousands of years ago when much of the world was covered in ice

imperial (im-PIR-ee-ul) relating to an empire

imports (IM-ports) goods brought in from another country for sale, trade, or use

Indians (IN-dee-uns) a term used by Europeans to describe the original peoples of the Americas

influence (IN-floo-uns) the power to cause changes or to have an effect without using direct force

irrigated (IR-uh-gayt-ud) to have used streams, ditches, canals, and other means to water crops

---

PRONUNCIATION KEY

CAPITAL LETTERS show the stressed syllables.

a	as in mat	f	as in fit
ay	as in day, say	g	as in go
ch	as in chew	i	as in sit
e	as in bed	j	as in job, gem
ee	as in even, easy, need	k	as in cool, key

Islam (is-LAM) a major religion founded by Muhammad that influenced areas of the Mediterranean region, especially northern Africa

isthmus (IS-mus) a narrow strip of land that runs between two bodies of water and joins two bodies of land

janissaries (JA-nuh-ser-eez) members of an elite group of fighting men of the Ottoman Empire

jihads (ji-HADZ) holy wars of the Muslims against nonbelievers

just (JUST) right and fair

Justinian Code (just-IN-ee-un   KOHD) an organized collection of laws created by order of Justinian I

knights (NYTS) fighting men who rode horses and led others into battle

Koran (kuh-RAN) the sacred text of the Islamic religion

Kushan dynasty (KOO-shan   DY-nuh-stee) the rule of the Scythians in India from 185 B.C.E. to 320 C.E.

land bridge (LAND   BRIJ) an area of dry land that connects two continents

legends (LE-jundz) stories handed down from earlier times that many people believe to be true but that cannot be proved as true

lord (LORD) a king or noble with vassals

lyric poem (LIR-ik   PO-um) a short poem expressing the personal mood or feeling of the poet

---

PRONUNCIATION KEY

CAPITAL LETTERS show the stressed syllables.

ng	as in running	u	as in but, some
o	as in cot, father	uh	as in about, taken, lemon, pencil
oh	as in go, note	ur	as in term
oo	as in too	y	as in line, fly
sh	as in shy	zh	as in vision, measure
th	as in thin		

Magna Carta (MAG-nuh   KAR-tuh) a document signed by King John that limited the power of the king and set forth important ideas about law

magnetic compass (mag-NE-tik   KUM-pus) a device invented by the Chinese to help people find their way

mandarins (MAN-du-runz) public officials in the Chinese Empire

manor (MA-nur) a large farm or estate

manorialism (ma-NOR-ee-uh-li-zum) the economic system of the Middle Ages

Maya Indians (MY-uh   IN-dee-unz) advanced Indian people of Mesoamerica

medieval period (mee-DEE-vul   PIR-ee-ud) another term for the Middle Ages

Middle Ages (MI-dul   AYJ-us) a period in western Europe, from 500 C.E. to 1500 C.E.

military dictatorship (MI-luh-ter-ee   dik-TAY-tur-ship) a form of government in which the army has complete power and control

minarets (mi-nuh-RETS) towers of mosques

Ming dynasty (MING   DY-nuh-stee) the Chinese dynasty that replaced the foreign Mongol Yuan dynasty and lasted from 1368 to 1644

missionaries (MI-shuh-ner-eez) persons who spread a religion and do good works, often in a foreign land

---

PRONUNCIATION KEY

CAPITAL LETTERS show the stressed syllables.

a	as in mat	f	as in fit
ay	as in day, say	g	as in go
ch	as in chew	i	as in sit
e	as in bed	j	as in job, gem
ee	as in even, easy, need	k	as in cool, key

moderation (mo-duh-RAY-shun) a state that is not extreme but that is within reasonable limits

monarchy (MO-nur-kee) a government or country ruled by a monarch, such as a king or a queen

monasteries (MO-nuh-ster-eez) religious communities formed by monks

monasticism (muh-NAS-tuh-si-zum) the way of life followed by monks and nuns

Mongols (MON-gulz) nomadic peoples of central Asia who built an empire

monotheism (MO-nuh-thee-i-zum) belief in only one god

mosque (MOSK) a Muslim house of worship

movable type printing (MOOV-a-bul   TYP   PRIN-ting) a kind of printing invented by the Chinese in which characters can be moved and arranged

multiple causes (MUL-tuh-pul   CO-zez) when more than one condition triggers an event

mummy (MUH-mee) the body of a person that has been preserved, or kept intact after death

Muslims (MUZ-lumz) followers of Islam

mythology (mi-THO-luh-jee) a collection of related tales that are shared by a group of people and that tell about their culture and beliefs

nation (NAY-shun) another term for a group of people who share the same culture

PRONUNCIATION KEY

CAPITAL LETTERS show the stressed syllables.

ng	as in runni**ng**	u	as in b**u**t, s**o**me
o	as in c**o**t, f**a**ther	uh	as in **a**bout, tak**e**n, lem**o**n, penc**i**l
oh	as in g**o**, n**o**te	ur	as in t**er**m
oo	as in t**oo**	y	as in l**i**ne, fl**y**
sh	as in **sh**y	zh	as in vi**s**ion, mea**s**ure
th	as in **th**in		

New Stone Age (NOO   STOHN   AYJ) a period of time that began 10,000 years ago when the Ice Age ended and people came together to live in settlements, where they cultivated crops and domesticated animals

noble class (NOH-bul   CLAS) the highest class—kings and priests and their families

nobles (NOH-bulz) people of high social rank

nomads (NOH-mads) people who do not live a settled life but who travel constantly, usually with herds of animals

Old Stone Age (OLD   STOHN   AYJ) a period of time when early people existed, living as nomads in caves and making simple stone tools

Olmec Indians (OL-mek   IN-dee-uns) people of Mesoamerica who created the first great civilization in the Americas

Olympic Games (uh-LIM-pik   GAYMZ) games that were held every four years between Greek city-states

opponents (uh-POH-nunts) people who are against one another in a fight or contest

oracle bones (OR-uh-kul   BOHNZ) bones (usually shoulder blades) of animals or the shells of turtles used by ancient Chinese fortune-tellers to predict the future; the source of the earliest known Chinese writing

oral tradition (OR-ul   truh-DI-shun) the communication of important ideas passed down through the generations by use of the spoken word

---

PRONUNCIATION KEY

CAPITAL LETTERS show the stressed syllables.

a	as in mat	f	as in fit
ay	as in day, say	g	as in go
ch	as in chew	i	as in sit
e	as in bed	j	as in job, gem
ee	as in even, easy, need	k	as in cool, key

Ottoman Turks (O-tuh-mun TURKS) a central Asian tribe of Muslim people that grew in power and formed an empire

page (PAYJ) the first rank of a boy who is training to become a knight

Panchatantra (PAN-chuh-tan-truh) an Indian literary work that is a collection of famous fairy tales

papyrus (puh-PY-rus) writing material made from the stems and insides of papyrus, a tall water plant of northern Africa

parishes (PAR-ish-ez) areas served by village priests

Pax Romana (PAX roh-MA-nuh) a time of peace in Rome

peasants (PE-zunts) poor, working people

peninsula (puh-NIN-suh-luh) a piece of land that sticks out from a larger landmass into a body of water

people (PEE-pul) a group of persons who share the same culture

persecuted (PUR-si-kyoot-ud) caused suffering to a person because of that person's beliefs

pharaohs (FER-ohz) kings of ancient Egypt

philosophy (fuh-LO-suh-fee) a system of ideas and principles developed by a philosopher that presents a model to people for living their lives

plateau (pla-TOH) a high, mostly flat region

polis (POH-lus) a city-state of ancient Greece

PRONUNCIATION KEY

CAPITAL LETTERS show the stressed syllables.

ng	as in running	u	as in but, some
o	as in cot, father	uh	as in about, taken, lemon, pencil
oh	as in go, note	ur	as in term
oo	as in too	y	as in line, fly
sh	as in shy	zh	as in vision, measure
th	as in thin		

pope (POHP) the leader of the Church

population (poh-pyuh-LAY-shun) the total number of people living in a particular place

propaganda (pro-puh-GAN-duh) information that is spread to help a government or special group

provinces (PRO-vunts-ez) political divisions in a nation, such as states in the United States

pyramid (PIR-uh-mid) a huge stone structure built in ancient Egypt with three or more sides shaped like triangles that meet in a point at the top

Quetzalcoatl (kwet-sul-kuh-WA-tul) the winged serpent god of Mesoamerican Indians

rayah (RY-uh) the poor class of people of the Ottoman Empire; also called the "protected flock"

reform (ri-FORM) to make or become better by getting rid of faults

reincarnation (ree-in-kar-NAY-shun) the belief that when a person dies, the soul is reborn in another body

representative government (re-pri-ZEN-tuh-tiv   GUH-vur-munt) a form of government in which the people elect officials to represent them in the running of the government

republic (ri-PUH-blik) a form of government by the people, who elect representatives to run the government for them

---

PRONUNCIATION KEY

CAPITAL LETTERS show the stressed syllables.

a	as in mat	f	as in fit
ay	as in day, say	g	as in go
ch	as in chew	i	as in sit
e	as in bed	j	as in job, gem
ee	as in even, easy, need	k	as in cool, key

revolt (ri-VOHLT) a rebellion, or act of rising up, against a ruler, government, or state

rival (RY-vul) someone who tries to do as well as or better than another

Romance languages (roh-MANTS LANG-gwij-ez) languages that developed from Latin, such as French, Italian, and Spanish

sacraments (SA-kruh-munts) special church ceremonies

salt (SOLT) an important mineral in the ancient world; traded in West Africa

samurai (SA-muh-ry) a warrior who served the daimyo in Japan

savannas (suh-VA-nuhz) great grasslands that cover about half of Africa

scribe (SKRYB) official writer or recorder of information

scroll (SKROHL) a long roll of paper or other writing material

Seljuk Turks (SEL-juk TURKS) a people from central Asia who rose in power and came to control the Islamic world

Senate (SE-nut) the most important state council in ancient Rome

serf (SURF) peasant who is bound to a manor

sharecroppers (SHAYR-kro-purz) farmers who rent farmland to grow food on and, in return, give a share of what they grow to the owner

shogun (SHOH-gun) a general who ruled Japan through the daimyos

---

skin graft (SKIN GRAFT) a process in which healthy skin is attached to an area where skin is damaged or missing

Songhai (SONG-HY) a people who ruled Gao and later built an empire

squire (SKWYR) the second rank of a boy who is training to become a knight

standardization (stan-dur-duh-ZAY-shun) the act of making something an accepted standard (model), so that everyone follows this standard

status (STA-tus) a person's social standing

subcontinent (sub-KON-tun-unt) a large landmass, such as India, that is part of a continent but is separated from it in some way

sultan (SUL-tun) the ruler of the Ottoman Turks

Sung dynasty (SUNG DY-nuh-stee) one of the greatest dynasties in Chinese history; lasted from 960 to 1279

Swahili (swa-HEE-lee) the culture and language of the East African city-states

Tale of Genji (TAYL UV GEN-jee) the world's first novel, written by Lady Murasaki Shikibu in 1000

Tang dynasty (TANG DY-nuh-stee) one of the greatest dynasties in Chinese history; lasted from 618 to 907

Taoism (Dow-i-zum) a Chinese philosophy that focuses on the individual

Tenochas (TAY-nohch-us) the original name of the Aztecs

PRONUNCIATION KEY

CAPITAL LETTERS show the stressed syllables.

a	as in mat	f	as in fit
ay	as in day, say	g	as in go
ch	as in chew	i	as in sit
e	as in bed	j	as in job, gem
ee	as in even, easy, need	k	as in cool, key

tolerated (TO-luh-rayt-ed) allowed without interference

Toltecs (TOHL-teks) early Indian people of Mesoamerica

trade (TRAYD) the exchange of money and goods

traditional religions (truh-DI-shuh-nul ruh-LIJ-unz) the ancient, common, widely practiced religions of Africa

treaty (TREE-tee) an official agreement between two or more countries, governments, or rulers

tribe (TRYB) a group of semi-independent communities that all share a language and culture

tribune (TRI-byoon) an officer of ancient Rome who was elected by the plebeians to protect their interests

triumvirate (try-UM-vuh-rut) a government in ancient Rome made up of three men who shared the responsibility for running the state

Trojan War (TROH-jun WOR) a legendary war between Greeks and Trojans that was fought around 1200 B.C.E.

tyrant (TY-runt) a person, especially a ruler, who uses power unfairly or in a cruel way

vaccination (vak-suh-NAY-shun) a special mixture containing weak or dead germs that is used to protect a person against the disease that is caused by those germs

---

PRONUNCIATION KEY

CAPITAL LETTERS show the stressed syllables.

ng	as in running	u	as in but, some
o	as in cot, father	uh	as in about, taken, lemon, pencil
oh	as in go, note	ur	as in term
oo	as in too	y	as in line, fly
sh	as in shy	zh	as in vision, measure
th	as in thin		

Vandals (VAN-dulz) Christian invaders from central Europe who ruled northern Africa from 429 to 534

vassals (VA-sulz) nobles who were loyal to a king in exchange for a fief

Vedas (VAY-duhz) the ancient sacred writings of the Hindu religion, which include poems and hymns of the Aryan people

veto (VEE-toh) the right or power of a government officer to vote down a law and keep it from being passed

Vikings (VY-kingz) fierce peoples from the north who invaded much of Europe

village (VI-lij) a small settlement

village priest (VI-lij   PREEST) the Christian religious leader of a village

weights and measures (WAYTS   AND   ME-zhurz) a system or systems that set up units of weight (such as ounce and pound) and units of measure (such as inch and foot)

West African Kingdoms (WEST   A-fri-kun   KING-dumz) great trading kingdoms that arose in West Africa, south of the Sahara Desert

Yuan dynasty (yoo-ON   DY-nuh-stee) a dynasty started in China by Kublai Khan

ziggurat (ZI-guh-rat) a temple of ancient Mesopotamia; the house of the god of the city

INDEX

Abraham, 35
Abu Bakr, 243
Acropolis, 70
acropolis
    Etruscan, 145
    meaning of Greek, 59
acupuncture, 117
Aegean Sea, 50
    earliest Greeks along, 51
Aeneas, 142
Aeneid (Virgil), 142, 169
Aeschylus, 75, 79
Aesop, 76, 79
Africa, 318. *See also* East Africa; West
  African kingdoms
    as birthplace of humanity, 3, 319
    Christian areas of, 328
    Christianity in northern, 327–328
    earliest history of, 319
    early religious traditions in, 325–326
    footpaths covering, 321
    geography of, 317–318
    Islam in, 329–331
    Muslim areas of, 330
    oral traditions of early, 324
    villages in, 320–321
Age of Invasions, 305–306
Agincourt, Battle of, 227
agora, 59
agriculture, 6. *See also* farming
    in Africa, 319
    Chinese
        beginning of, 280
        improvements in, 286
    in early Rome, 143
    Japanese, 307–308
Akkad, 17
Akkadians, 17
Alexander the Great, 41
    death of, 87
    empire of, 86
    marches into northwestern
        India, 105–106
    as student of Aristotle, 79
    takes Egypt, 84–85

takes over Greece, 83–84
takes Persia and India, 85–86
Alexandria, 85
    special features of, 88
Ali, 243
Allah, 241, 248
    use of jihads to spread word of, 267
alphabet
    Etruscan, 146
    Greek, 58
    Nubian, 32
    Phoenician, 42
    pinyin, 116
    Roman, 147
Alps, 141–142
    Hannibal crosses, 153–154
Amazon River, 344
the Americas, 343
    components of, 343
    culture of Indians in, 346–347. *See also*
        Indians (of the Americas)
    geography of, 342–344
    Indian settlements throughout, 346
    Mesoamerican cultures of, 347
Amorites, 18
amphitheaters, 75
Analects, 136
Anatolia, 261
ancestor worship, 325, 327
ancestral spirits, 325
Andes Mountains, 344, 352
animism, 325, 327
Antipater, 83
Antoninus Pius, 176
Apennine Mountains, 141–142
apostles, 178
Appian Way, 158
application activities
    democracy in action, 91–92
    native peoples, 355–356
    rivers of history, 313–314
    sayings of Confucius, 136–137
    Seven Wonders of the Ancient
        World, 45–46
    social satire, 185

two world faiths, 272–273
women's rights in Byzantine
Empire, 234
aqueducts, 158, 181
Arabic numerals, 111, 112, 251, 303, 306
Arab Muslims, 254
in Africa, tolerance of other religions
by, 330
control of northern Africa by, 330
help growth of trade centers in East
Africa, 340
influence on West African kingdoms
of, 332–333
trade of, 330
Arabs, 242
archaeologists
dig up skeleton of Peking (Beijing)
Man, 113
discovery of Knossos by, 51–52
discovery of Mohenjo-Daro by, 96–97
finds in Egypt by, 25
objects from Zhou dynasty recovered
by, 121
Archaic Greek period, 57–58
archbishops, 216
architecture
of ancient Greece, 70
Greek, 64
Greek Revival, 71
Hagia Sophia, 195
of Hellenistic Age, 88
Inca, 352
Islamic, 253
mosques, 269. *See also* mosques
in Ottoman Empire, 269
Roman, 181
Aristophanes, 75, 79
Aristotle, 78–79
and Alexander the Great, 83
art
classical Indian, 112
Etruscan, 146
Greek, 80
under Guptas, 303
Islamic, 252
Mycenaean, 54

Old Stone Age cave paintings, 4–5
Olmec, 348
porcelain from Ming dynasty, 297
during Tang dynasty, 285
Toltec, 350
artifacts, 52
Aryans, 98
from classes to castes in society
of, 100–101
invade Indian subcontinent, 99
Asia
bubonic plague brought to Europe
by traders from, 228
land bridge between North America
and, 345
separation of North America and, 345
trade between Europe and, 218,
220–221
decline of feudalism and manorialism
with increase of, 231
tribes of nomads in central, 291
Asia Minor, 7–8, 50
Greek colonies in, 64
Askia the Great, 339–340
Asoka
edicts of, 108–109
rule of, 106–107
turns against violence, 107
assembly, 61
Assyrians
conquer Egypt, 31
rule of Fertile Crescent by, 39
take over Israel, 37
astrolabe, 251
astronomy, Muslim knowledge of, 251
Athens, 59
alliance with Plataea of, 65
creation of Delian League by, 67
Persian destruction of, 67
rise of, 62
under Solon's laws, 63
Atlantic Ocean, 343
Atlas Mountains, 318
Attica, 62, 67
Augustine Age, 174

Augustus, 172
    accomplishments under, 173–174
    rule of Roman world by, 172–173
Axum, 328
Aztec Empire, 350
    at its peak, 351
Aztec Indians, 350–351

Babur the Tiger, 306
Babylon, 18–19
    as greatest city in Fertile Crescent, 40
Babylonians, 18–19
Balkan Peninsula, 49
Bantu migrations, 319
barbarians, 160
    invasion of Roman Empire by, 190
Baths of Caracalla, 181
B.C.E. (before the common era), *vii*
Beringia, 345
Bering Strait, 345
Bible, 36, 218, 256
    similarities between Koran and, 272
Bindusara, 106
bishops, 216
Black Death, 228
Blackstone, Sir William, 224
Brahmaputra River, 96, 300
bronze, 38, 51. *See also* bronze casting
Bronze Age, 51
bronze casting, 118, 119. *See also* bronze
bubonic plague, 228
Buddha, 103–104
Buddhism, 103–104
    Asoka turns to, 107
    in China
        arrival of, 131
        at peak of popularity, 285
        promoted by Empress Wu, 283
        spread of, 280
    fading in India of, 109
    in Japan, 308
Burgundians, 200
Byzantine Empire
    asks Europe for help against Seljuk
        Turks, 255
    Christian Church of, 195

end of, 198–199
falls to Muslim Turks, 218
height of, 196
importance of, 194–195
invasion of, by Seljuk Turks, 254
under Justinian and Theodora,
    196–197
Pope Urban II tries to help, 218
size of, 195
Umar leads invasion of, 243
Vandals pushed out of northern
    Africa by, 328
women's rights in: application
    activity, 234

c. (circa), *vii*
Caesar, Julius, 164
    assassination of, 167
    crosses Rubicon and invades Italy, 165
    in Egypt, 166
    rise to power of, 165
calendar
    Chinese, 131, 308
    Christian, 240
    Islamic, 240
    lunar, developed by Sumerians, 14
    Olmec, 348
    similarity of our calendar to Julian, 166
Caligula, 175
caliphates, 249
caliphs, 243
    conquests of Umayyad, 243–244
    rule of, 249
camels, 333, 334
Canaan, 34–35
    becomes known as Israel, 36
    famine in, 35–36
canals, 14, 351
candake, 32
Capetian dynasty, 225–226
caravans, 330, 333, 334
Carter, Howard, 25, 29, 30
Carthage, 42, 150
    crushing of, 154–155
    and Rome go to war, 152–153.
    See also Punic Wars

kingdoms of Africa influenced by, 328
in northern Africa, 327–328
practice of, under Arab Muslims, 330
rise of, 178
spreads throughout Nubia, 328
Christians, persecution of, 177, 179
Cicero, 169
cities
built by Mayas, 349
earliest, 7–8
layout of Etruscan, 146
sacred, of Islam, 243
Sumerian, 13
towns grow into, 221
citizens, Roman, 148
city-states. *See also* Athens; Sparta
in Archaic Greece, 57
in East Africa, 340–341
in Egypt, 22
Greek
appearance of, 56
fighting weakens, 68
growth of, 59–60
organization of, 59
unite to fight Persia, 66–67
war among, 82
Mayan, 349
Phoenician, 42
Roman, 144. *See also* Rome
Sumerian, 15–16
warring of, 17
Toltec, 350
civilization(s)
of ancient Egypt, span of, 28
beginning of, 8
Chinese, 280
start of, 113–114
in the desert, 21–22
earliest, 11
Etruscan, 145
first four, 10–11
first great, in the Americas, 348
Harappan, 97
Hittites, 38
Inca, 352
Islamic, 245

Koran as basis of, 247
Japanese, 309
map of early, 10
Mayan, 349
Minoan, 52–53
of Mohenjo-Daro and Harappa, 97
most important part of Aztec, 351
Nubian, 30–31
Olmec, 348
originating near river valleys, 11, 50
of people in Indus Valley, 97, 98
civil service, 128–129. *See also* civil
service system
examinations restored under Ming
dynasty, 297
civil service system, 286. *See also* civil
service
clans, 59
fighting among Japanese, 309, 310
Classical Greek period, 58, 64–65
architecture of, 64
class system
of Aryans, 100–101
beginning of, 9
in Egypt, 23
in India. *See* castes
in Ottoman Empire, 268–269
in Rome, 148–149
under Solon's laws, 63
in Sumer, 16
Claudius I, 175
Cleopatra, 166
death of, 171
climate
in Africa, 317–318
defined, 277
of Islamic world, 238
during New Stone Age, 5
variation in Japan, 307–308
varied, of China, 277
Code of Hammurabi
physical aspects of, 18–19
provisions of, 19–20
Coliseum, 181
colonies
Greek, in Asia Minor, 64

map of, 13
other cultures of, 34–35
role of Babylon in, 40
ruled by Assyrians, 39
Sargon the Great's desire to rule, 17
settlement of Persians in, 41
feudalism, 231
Chinese, 119
breakup of, 121–122
complicated relationships under, 211
in decline, 220–221
in England established by William the
Conqueror, 222–223
in Europe established by
Charlemagne, 203
as system of government in
Europe, 210–212
fiefs, 211, 217, 220
under William the Conqueror, 223
First Crusade, 257–258
land conquered by Christians in, 258
First Peloponnesian War, 68
First Punic War, 153
fishing reel, invention of, 131
Flaccus, Quintus Horatius. *See* Horace
flood control
development of, 14
used in Zhou dynasty, 120
fortresses, 59
fortune-tellers, Chinese, 114–115
Forum, 181
Fourth Crusade, 258
"The Fox and the Goat" (Aesop), 76
France
becomes country, 226
during Middle Ages, 225
war between England and, 226–227
Franks, 200–201
Charlemagne becomes king of, 202
Fujiwara clan, 310

Gandhi, Indira, 283
Ganges River, 96, 300
Gao, 339
Gauls, 149
conquered by Caesar, 165

Genghis Khan, 291
background of, 292
Mongol Empire under, 293
success of, as leader and
conqueror, 293
geography
of Africa, 317–318
of the Americas, 342–344
becomes true science under Muslim
attention, 251
of China, 277–278
defined, 238
of Greece, 49–50, 59
of India, 300
of Indian subcontinent, 95–96
of Islamic world, 237–239
of Italy, 141–142
of Japan, 307–308
of Roman Empire, 189
Ghana Empire, 334–335
glaciers, 3. *See also* Ice Age
shrinking of, 5
gladiators, 164
Christians killed by, 179
Gobi Desert, 277
gold, 333, 334, 336
gold and salt trade, 333
Goliath, 36
goods
from Asia reach Europe, 220–221
brought back by crusaders, 218
early trade of, 6
exchanged between Europe and Islamic
world resulting from Crusades, 260
Gordian knot, 84, 85
Goths, 196
government. *See also* democracy
Athenian, 62
under Augustus, 173
beginning of, 8
caliphs in charge of, in Muslim
Empire, 249
efficient system of, in Ghana, 335
feudalism as form of, 211. *See also*
feudalism
Han contributions to, 128–129

pilgrimage, 248
  of Mansa Musa, 337
King Piye, 31
Plataea, 65, 67
plateaus, 278
  defined, 317
Plato, 78, 80
Platonic ideals, 78
plebeians, 149
plow, invention of, 14
Plutarch, 151
polis, 57, 63
Polo, Marco
  Description of the World, 295–296
  visits with Kublai Khan, 295
Pompey, 163
  Caesar defeats, 165
  and Crassus share power, 164
  sons of, put together army, 166
pope, 216
  crowning of emperors by, 229, 230
  as leader of Christian Church, 201, 216
population
  increase in Chinese, 286
  increase in Rome, 158
  of Kumbi Saleh, 335
porcelain, 297
Po River, 142
propaganda, 84
prophets, 248
Protestant Reformation, 230
provinces
  division of Japan into, 310
  in Persian Empire, 41
  Roman, 155
Ptolemy, 166
Punic Wars, 152, 153–155
  effect on Rome of, 159
  Roman Empire after, 156
pyramids
  Egyptian, 25
  Mayan, 349
Pyrenees Mountains, 153
Pyrrhic War, 151
King Pyrrhus, 151

qen, 123
Qin dynasty, 125–126, 280
  end of, 126–127
Quetzalcoatl, 351

rajas, 105
Ramadan, 248
Ramayana, 99
ravens, 205
rayah, 268
record-keeping system, beginning of, 8–9
reincarnation, 102
religion. *See also specific religions*
  of ancient Greece, 71–74
  of Assyrians, 39
  Aztec, 351
  birth of Christianity as new, 177. *See also* Christianity
  Buddhism, 103–104
  in early Africa, 325–326
  Egyptian, 23–24
  of Hebrews, 35
  Hinduism, 102–103
  Islam, 239–240
  Mayan, 349
  Minoan, 54
  of Muslims. *See* Islam
  spread of Hindu, 304
  in Sumer, 15–16
  two world faiths: application activity, 272–273
  of Vikings, 207
Remus, 142–143
The Republic (Plato), 80
Republic of Rome
  Carthage surrenders its empire to, 154
  controls most of Italian Peninsula, 151, 152
  influence of Greek culture on, 156–157
  Mediterranean world controlled by, 155–156
republics, 147
Rhazes, 251
rice
  becomes main food of Chinese diet, 289

Chinese develop new kind of, 286
in Japan, 307
Rightly Guided Caliphs, 243
Robin Hood, 211
Rocky Mountains, 343–344
Romance languages, 182
Roman Empire. *See also* Rome
under Augustus, 173–174
Christianity becomes official religion
of, 327
Christianity in, 178
civil war in, 192
dividing, 191–193
division and reunification of, 180
Egypt becomes part of, 171
emperors after Augustus, 175–177
growth of, 158
loses control of northern Africa, 327
major opponents of, 159–160
multiple causes for fall of, 189–191
northern coast of Africa as part of, 327
peak of, 177
revolutions in, 190
triumvirate takes over, 167–168
on verge of collapse, 192
weakening of, 179
Rome, 141. *See also* Roman Empire
becomes a republic, 147. *See also*
Republic of Rome
birth as city-state of, 144
Caesar takes control of, 165
and Carthage go to war, 152–153. *See
also* Punic Wars
controls most of Italian Peninsula, 152
early, 143–144
Early Republic, 148–149
economic problems of, 190
enemies overrun, 191
expansionism leads to war, 149–150
first emperor of, 171–172
generals fight for control of, 163
gods of, 146
immensity of, 189
imperialism and "just wars" of,
154–155
invasions of, 190

Late Republic, 160
accomplishments of, 169
culture of, 168–169
legacy of, 181–182
legendary founding of, 142–143
Marius reforms the army of, 161–162
Middle Republic, 152
economic and social change in,
157–158
Greco-Roman culture of, 156–157
military dictatorship in, 180
multicultural nature of, 144
Pax Romana, 173
reforms of Gracchi brothers, 160–161
roads of, 158, 181
slaves in, 190
social problems in, 190
Sulla becomes dictator of, 162–163
war inside, 159–160
weak government of, 190
Romulus, 142–143
Rosetta Stone, 27
Rubicon River, 165
rudder, invention of, 131
Ruwenzori Range, 318

sacraments, 216
Sahara Desert, 318
caravan trade across, 333
mining of salt in, 333
Sahel, 318
sail, invention of, 14
Salamis, 67
Sallust, 169
salt, 333, 334, 336
Samnites, 150, 151
Samudragupta, 110
samurai, 310
Sanskrit, 99
Sappho, 76, 80
Sargon the Great, 17
Sasso people, 336
Satires **(Horace),** 185
Saudi Arabia, 330, 331
Saul, 36–37
savannas, 317

science
Greek, 77
in Han dynasty, 131
Muslim, 251
Scipio, 154
scribes
Egyptian, 23, 26
Sumerian, 14, 26
scrolls, 26
Scythians, 301
seafarers, 204
Phoenicians, 42
skill of Vikings as, 205
Sea People, 36
Second Crusade, 258
Second Peloponnesian War, 68
Second Punic War, 153
Seljuk Turks, 254–255
Crusades stop expansion of, 260
refusal to allow Christians into holy
land by, 256
Senate, Roman, 148, 149
Gracchi brothers' reforms abolished
by, 161
orders Caesar to return to Rome, 165
under Pompey and Crassus, 164
pronounces Augustus a god, 174
serfs, 214–215, 220, 231
Seven Wonders of the Ancient World
application activity, 45–46
Hanging Gardens of Babylon, 40
Pharos (lighthouse at Alexandria), 88
sewer systems, Roman, 181
Shang dynasty, 114, 280
achievements of, 118
sharecroppers, in ancient India, 102
Shih Ching, 131
Shih Huang-ti
builds Great Wall of China, 126
death of, 126
reforms of, 125
standardization under, 125–126
Shikoku, 307
shoguns, 310
Prince Shotoku, 309
Sicily, 153

Siddhartha Gautama, 103–104. *See also*
Buddha; Buddhism
signal words
for cause-effect relationships, 108
to help figure out sequence, 115
to indicate opinions, 98
silk, 118
Silk Road, 130
silkworms, 118
Koca Sinan, 269
Sixteen Kingdoms, 132
skin grafts, used in early India, 111, 112
slaves
in early Greece, 61
Egyptian, 23
in Etruscan society, 146
freeing of Roman, 158
human sacrifice of Aztec, 351
on Mansa Musa's pilgrimage, 337
in Ottoman Empire, 268–269
problems caused by, in Roman
Empire, 190
revolt of Roman, 163–164
Romans turn people of Carthage
into, 155
trading of, in Africa, 333, 334
in villages of ancient India, 102
Socrates, 78, 80
Socratic method, 78
Solomon, 37
destruction of temple of King, 40
Solon, 62
reforms of, 63
Songhai Empire, 339–340
Songhai people, 339
Sophocles, 75, 80
South America, 342
Inca civilization built in, 352
Southern Sung, 288
South Pole, 343
Sparta, 59
alliance between Persia and, 68
creation of Peloponnesian League
by, 67–68
rise of, 61
Spartacus, 164

earliest, 6
of East African city-states, 340
between Egypt and Meroë, 32
expansion of Mali's, 337
flourishing, in Byzantine Empire, 196
of goods during early village life, 6
between Greek city-states and other
    countries, 59
during Han dynasty, 129–130
influence of, in kingdoms of West
    Africa, 332–333
influence on history of, 329
leads to new kind of economy, 221
on Mediterranean Sea, 150
in Minoa, 53
promoted by Crusades, 218
routes
    bringing wealth to China, 281–282
    developed after Crusades, 220–221
sea, of Phoenicians, 42
in Zhou China, 121
traditional religions, 326, 329
practice of, under Arab Muslims, 330
Trajan, 176
treaties, 150
tribes, 322–323
defined, 323
Indian, in Americas, 346–347
of nomads in central Asia, 291
tribunes, 148–149
triumvirate, 167–168
Trojan War, 54–55, 142
Troy, 54
Turkestan, 255
Turkey, 7–8. *See also* Seljuk Turks
Turks, 218
King Tut. *See* Tutankhamen
Tutankhamen, 25, 29
Twelve Tables, 149
tyrants, 174

Umar, 243
Umayyads, 243–244
defeat of, 245
Upper Egypt, 22
Ur, 13, 15, 35

Urban II, 218
U.S. Constitution, 224
Uthman, 243
orders assembly of Koran, 246

vaccination
principle of, in early China, 117
used in early India, 111, 112
Vandals, 196, 200
capture northern Africa, 327
vassals, 211
Vedas, 99
Vespasian, 176
Vesuvius, Mount, 141
veto, 149
Vikings
cruelty of warfare of, 204
exploration by, 206
home life of, 207
settling in Iceland of, 206
shipbuilding and navigation skills
    of, 205
village priests, 216
villages
in Africa, 320–321
    unique qualities of, 321
defined, 321
life in early, 6
in Middle Ages, 221
Vinland, 206
Virgil, 142, 169
Visigoths, 200
volcanoes, extinct, 318
Voltaire, 230

Wang Mang, 127
warfare
Aztec, 351
change in Roman, 160
conducted by Assyrians, 39
costs of, takes toll on Byzantine
    Empire, 199
cruelty of Viking, 204
Crusades bring new techniques of, 260
elephants used in, 86, 153
Hittite innovations in, 38